Huntingdon Paint.ʳ C.E. Wagstaff & J. Andrews Eng.ˢ

John Codman

MEMOIR

OF

JOHN CODMAN, D. D.

BY

WILLIAM ALLEN, D. D.

LATE PRESIDENT OF BOWDOIN COLLEGE:

WITH

REMINISCENCES,

BY

JOSHUA BATES, D. D.

LATE PRESIDENT OF MIDDLEBURY COLLEGE.

BOSTON:

T. R. MARVIN AND S. K. WHIPPLE & CO.

1853.

MEMOIR

OF

JOHN CODMAN, D.D.

BY

WILLIAM ALLEN, D. D.

MEMOIR.

CHAPTER I.

INTRODUCTORY REMARKS.—DR. CODMAN'S ANCESTRY.

The annals of the American pulpit are yet very imperfect; but it may well be doubted, whether any nation, in the same period, has ever produced a greater number of able and eminent ministers. Certainly no country, of equal extent, can rival New England in this respect. In its earliest settlement, and amidst its privations and hardships, the establishment of Harvard College attested the wisdom of our ancestors and their fidelity to the interests of education and religion. They knew that, without a clergy of piety and intelligence, there was little hope of a safe and flourishing Commonwealth; hence it was their earliest care to provide the best means of education, and to send forth to their churches a well-instructed and faithful ministry. How well they succeeded, and how extensive and salutary was their influence, is seen in the high tone of morals which pervades New England; in the strength and beauty of its social and civil compact; in its far-reaching enterprise, its institutions of philanthropy, and its many visible tokens of primitive and intelligent piety.

To give to the world a record of the virtues and labors of the New England clergy, is one of the best methods of perpetuating the blessings with which they have enriched us. Whenever a minister has been eminent in the cause of Christ, it becomes an imperative duty to hold his character and services in grateful remembrance. If, after his death, his worth is commemorated, and his life and character are presented to the world, he is still a preacher of righteousness on the earth, while he mingles in the worship above, and praises his Redeemer in the upper temple, "not made with hands, eternal in the heavens."

The important relations which the late Rev. Dr. CODMAN sustained to our churches, the eminent services rendered by him to the evangelical faith, the unsullied purity of his character, and the warm and grateful love of his church and people, demand that a life, thus devoted to the service of Christ, should be fully and faithfully delineated. Such a biography belongs to the ministry, of which he was an ornament and a model, and to the community, who honored him while living and deeply lamented him in death.

We shall give some account of Dr. Codman's ancestry, because men, who have done worthily in their generation, ought not to be forgotten in subsequent ages. They were among the laity of New England, always remarkable for integrity, and enjoying a large and valuable influence, both in social and civil relations.

The earliest of the paternal ancestry of Dr. Codman, in America, was Stephen Codman, of Charlestown, Massachusetts, in the year 1680. His youngest son, John Codman, (the only one of eight children, who survived him,) married, in 1718, Parnel Foster, daughter of Richard Foster, a man of eminence in the Colony, whose wife was the daughter of Isaac and Mary Winslow. And it may here be mentioned, that the mother of Isaac Winslow was the first female who landed from the Mayflower, December 21, 1620. Capt. John Codman held a commission under the king, and was an officer in the Ancient and Honorable Artillery

Company in 1745. He was a highly respectable and useful citizen, and an active military officer. The circumstances attending his death were most afflictive. He had three negro slaves, named Mark, Phillis, and Phœbe, who poisoned him with arsenic. The two former were convicted and executed. The place of Mark's execution was on the northerly side of Cambridge road, about a quarter of a mile above the peninsula, and the gibbet remained until a short time before the Revolution. Phillis was burned at the stake, about ten yards from the gallows. It has been said that, in the history of the country, this is the only instance of that method of punishment under the authority of the law. It is well for New England, that her records can furnish no other example.

John Codman, son of Capt. John Codman, was born in Charlestown, in the year 1719, and died at his residence in Boston, January 17, 1792. Early in life he was deeply impressed with the importance of religion, under the eloquent preaching of Whitefield and of Gilbert Tennent, during the first visit of the former to New England. He was admitted to the church in Charlestown, at the age of twenty. About the year 1754, he married Abigail Asbury, widow of John Asbury and daughter of

John Soley, of Charlestown, an excellent woman, of strong mind and ardent piety. Mr. Codman was a decided whig, and a warm friend to his country. In February, 1770, he was one of the committee of inspection in Charlestown as to the non-importation agreement. In November, 1773, he, with many other whigs, petitioned for a meeting on the subject of the tea, which was soon to be imported, and he was one of a committee to recommend measures that should be adopted.

Hon. John Codman, the third of the name, and father of the Rev. Dr. Codman, was born in Charlestown, January 17, 1755. He was married at Lincoln, July 15, 1781, to Margaret Russell, youngest daughter of Hon. James Russell, by whom he had two children; John, the subject of this Memoir, and Charles Russell Codman of Boston, recently deceased. The father of Dr. Codman received his early education at Dummer Academy, in Byfield, and subsequently entered the counting house of Isaac Smith, Esq. in Boston. He died at the early age of forty-eight, leaving a large estate; and at the time of his decease was a member of the Senate of Massachusetts. The following tribute to his memory was penned by the late John Lowell, Esq. "Amidst the awful and sudden dispensations of Providence, which we are occasionally called upon to witness, few have ever produced more public regret or private calamity, than the death of this truly excellent and respectable citizen. Of manners gentle, of affections warm and glowing, of habits industrious and enterprising, with an understanding clear and masculine, with an eloquence impressive and energetic, with a heart expanded and generous, he was excellently qualified to fill and honorably to discharge the various important public and private relations in which he stood to society. As a husband, father, friend, he yielded to no one in the tender, affectionate, constant performance of all those interesting attentions which these endearing relations require. As a merchant, his assiduity, honor, fidelity, enterprise and discernment, rendered him an object of sincere respect to the old, and an excellent model to the young. As a citizen, he was generous, affable, kind, compassionate and patriotic. In public life, he exhibited capacity, information, eloquence and an ardent love for his country. In the meridian of life, in the full career of usefulness and reputation, just entering into the higher councils of the State, and while his fellow citizens were presaging his future eminence, the destroying angel aimed the silent but fatal blow, and left nothing to his affectionate survivors but unavailing regret. Regret? No. When we recollect the brightest and hitherto unnoticed trait in the character of this admirable man, we ought not to *express*, scarcely to *feel* regret. Mr. Codman died, as he had lived, a warm, sincere, pious believer in the Christian religion, its hopes, and future rewards. His death was even more honorable and distinguished, certainly more extraordinary, than his life. After a very short sickness, he yielded up his spirit into the hands of his Maker, without a sigh or a murmur, with calmness, resignation, and heroic fortitude. In the full possession of all his faculties, he died a hero, patriot, and Christian."

In the year 1791, Mr. Codman married his second wife, Catharine Amory, daughter of John Amory, Esq., a lady of singular intelligence, enlarged benevolence, and devoted piety, by whom he had six children. She died in Boston, December 22, 1831.

It seems proper to add to this account some notice of the maternal ancestry of Dr. Codman, as they occupied important stations in society, and were highly influential and useful in the civil and ecclesiastical affairs of New England.

Margaret Russell, the mother of Dr. Codman,

was a descendant of Richard Russell of Hereford, in the County of Hereford, in England, who came to America and settled in Charlestown in the year 1640. He was elected a Representative and was Speaker of the House for several years, and for a long time was Treasurer of the Colony. He purchased a part of the Pemaquid Patent, and most of the town of Medford once belonged to him. He died in the year 1676. To the church in Charlestown, with which he had been in Christian fellowship for many years, he bequeathed a portion of his property, the annual proceeds of which have been dispensed to the poor of that church down to the present day. He also gave one hundred pounds to Harvard College.

James Russell, son of Richard Russell, was born in Charlestown in 1640, and was elected a Councillor for the Colony in the year 1680, from which time until his death he was annually chosen, excepting during the few years of the reign of King James, when the people were deprived of the privilege of that office. He served God and his country also as Treasurer, Judge, and in other offices of the highest influence and trust. His mortal career was closed, April 28, 1709, in the full hope of a happy immortality.

Daniel Russell, son of James Russell, was born in Charlestown, November 30, 1685, and died December 6, 1763. He was for more than twenty years a member of His Majesty's Council and Commissioner of Imports, and also for about fifty years was Treasurer of the County of Middlesex. It is observable that, in the several offices which he sustained he succeeded his worthy father and grandfather. Chambers Russell, his eldest son, was Judge of the Court of Vice-Admiralty for the Province of Massachusetts Bay, New Hampshire, and the Colony of Rhode Island; and, in the year 1752, he was appointed one of the Justices of the Superior Court of Judicature. He was heir to Charles Chambers, Esq., who came from Lincoln, in England; and when a separation of the town of Lincoln from Concord took place, it was called Lincoln, in honor of him.

James Russell, second son of Daniel Russell, succeeded to the public honòrs of his ancestors as Representative, Councillor and Judge. His youngest daughter, Margaret Russell, was the mother of Dr. Codman.

Judge Russell, in a letter to his son, remarks as follows: "Our family has great reason to bless God, that its reputation has been preserved. You are of the fifth generation. In the year 1646, Richard Russell entered upon public life; and from that time to the present, I may say that the family have had every office of profit and honor, which the public could give them in the town of Charlestown, in the County of Middlesex, and State of Massachusetts; and I do not find, that any one was left out of office for misbehavior. Let our hearts be filled with gratitude to Him who has thus distinguished us, and let us evince this our gratitude to our Maker, by a good improvement of our talents."

Such was the ancestry, and such the honorable descent of the Rev. Dr. Codman.

CHAPTER II.

HIS EARLY CHARACTER AND EDUCATION — INCIDENTS OF COLLEGE LIFE — RELIGIOUS IMPRESSIONS — COMMENCEMENT OF THEOLOGICAL STUDIES — JOURNEYS IN NEW ENGLAND.

Dr. Codman was born August 3, 1782, and was baptized in Brattle Street Church by Rev. Dr. Cooper. "His parents," says the Rev. Dr. Storrs in his funeral sermon, "educated their children faithfully in the principles of scriptural morality and strict regard to the institutions of revealed religion." At this time there was no visible departure from an evangelical faith. It was undoubtedly true, that many circumstances had lowered the standard of religious practice; and, among these, the war of the Revolution had contributed its fatal influence. But, whatever were the causes which in twenty-five years from Dr. Codman's birth had nearly subverted the ancient faith of the churches, there was no marked distinction of doctrine, during his childhood and youth, which might prevent the appropriate influence of divine truth on his mind. It does not however appear, that he experienced any strong religious impressions in very early life.

"Of his early youth," continues Dr. Storrs, "the prominent characteristics were a marked buoyancy of spirits, gaiety of manners, sociality of feeling, sprightliness of mind, facility of intellectual acquisition, frankness of disposition, and ardent attachment." His youthful studies were prosecuted at Andover Academy, and under the care of the Rev. Henry Ware of Hingham. He entered Harvard College in 1798, and was graduated with honor in 1802, in a class of sixty—the largest class which had been connected with the college.

His amiable deportment, his exemplary discharge of moral and social duties, greatly endeared him to his classmates and friends; but we have no important records of his college life, and he appears to have given no remarkable indication of that firmness and fortitude, and of those rare attainments in prudence and wisdom, which, in after life, no emergency could baffle, and of which neither persecution nor flattery could disarm him.

In so large a class, it was necessary that a considerable number should be excluded from the opportunity of a public performance at commencement. In the first arrangement of the exercises,

Mr. Codman's name was omitted. The class, however, elected him to deliver a poem on the occasion of their departure from college; and this was so creditable to him, that it induced the college government immediately to repair the injustice, as the President expressed himself, which had been done to Mr. Codman, and to assign him a commencement exercise. This affair was always a matter of pleasant reminiscence.

President Willard, who had just recovered from sickness, was present at the delivery of the poem, the following lines of which, containing an affectionate address to himself, drew tears from his eyes:

"Pause! ye who aim the sacred desk to fill,
Look, ere you strive to climb the holy hill;
Supremely blest, if with magnetic charm
You lure the giddy multitude from harm,
Stoop not to pluck the flowerets by the way,
That bloom for seizure, but when pluck'd decay;
Receive and give to thousands of the fruit,
And water with your tears Religion's root.
Those who have claimed their blest abodes on high,
To form new planets, risen to the sky,
Belknap and *Clarke*, as second stars, shall guide
To show, how Jesus lived, and how he died;
But, when a saint, almost expiring, strove
To join the kindred spirits gone above,
Thanks to Almighty power, which from the dead
Raised to new life the reverend Clergy's head.—

Kind father of our literary days!
Permit thy children to express their praise
To Him, who stretched his ready hand to save
The guide to truth from a too early grave.

"Indulgent Heaven, with wisest motives fraught,
Our greatest good, by contrast, oft hath taught,—
So, from the sky, sickness commissioned came
To blast the hopes of literature and fame;
Round our horizon clouds of sorrow hung,
Prayer filled each heart and trembled on each tongue,
Till health unveiled her rainbow to the sight,
Dispersed the clouds, and bade the sun delight."

In bidding farewell to his companions, he described, with prophetic truth, his own satisfaction in after years, in recalling the scenes of his college life.

"Harvard! thy walls now lessen from my view,
Friends of my youth, classmates, a long adieu.
Old time hath brought our journey to a close,
Who heeds no feeling, and no friendship knows;
Relentless tyrant! cruel were thy sway,
Hard to acknowledge, harder to obey,
Had not sweet memory said and promised true,
That times, so pleasant, ever should be new,
And penciled on the canvass of the mind
In brightest colors all we've left behind."

While pursuing the study of the law in the office of his kinsman, John Lowell, Esq., the sudden death of his father was the means of changing his destined profession. In his last sickness, his father intimated a wish that his son should become a minister of the gospel. This circumstance, and the subsequent deep affliction, working on a most affectionate heart, were doubtless instrumental, through the mercy of God, in giving him religious impressions which he had never before experienced. He commenced the study of theology, in 1803, with his early instructor, Rev. Henry Ware of Hingham, with whom he remained about a year; and then removed to Cambridge, there to continue his theological pursuits.

Dr. Tappan, the Professor of Theology, was now deceased, and he was not succeeded by Dr. Ware until June of the next year. But at Cambridge, Mr. Codman found congenial society, associates engaged in the same pursuits. He formed a particular intimacy with several students and preachers of evangelical sentiments, with one of whom, the writer of this Memoir, he entered into a peculiar and strong friendship, which lasted during his subsequent life.

At this period the preachers and students in theology, resident at Cambridge, united in a society called the Kappa Delta, from the initials of two Greek words denoting the School of Preachers. Of this society, Mr. Codman was the secretary. At the meetings, which were held in a retired room, prayers were offered and a sermon was delivered, which was subject to the criticisms of the members present. Sometimes the discourses assumed a polemical form, and important doctrines were discussed. This institution was not without its advantages. Of its members, at this period, five or six were subsequently honored with the title of Doctors in Theology.

There existed, at the same time, at Cambridge, a society designed to promote practical religion, consisting of the members of the college, but which was often attended and encouraged by the resident theological students. It was called the Saturday Evening Religious Society, and was useful in keeping alive, in a time of degeneracy, a spirit of piety. Of this society Mr. Codman was an active friend.

At this period, either at Hingham or at Cambridge, William Cooper's "Four Sermons on Predestination" were put into his hands, with a request that he would write a review of them for the Monthly Anthology. This journal was the organ of the liberal party, which had just begun to present somewhat distinctly the features of Unitarianism. It was, of course, expected that the review would be in accordance with the liberal opinions of that periodical. Mr. Codman read the book, undoubtedly under the influence of the general prejudice against the doctrines which it advocated. But "its perusal opened his eyes, for the first time, on the beautiful consistency of the doctrines there defended, with the Scriptures of truth, and on their excellency as revealing God on the throne of the universe, controlling at his pleasure the movements of rebellious man."* The review which was written did not appear in the polished though frigid pages of the Anthology, but met the public eye in the first number of the Panoplist for June, 1805.

Of the kind, sympathizing and benevolent spirit, which ever marked the character of Mr. Codman, the following instance may here be mentioned :—A young student, of Londonderry, N. H., was dangerously sick at Cambridge, and his father came to remove him to his home. Mr. Codman proposed to the writer to accompany with him, in his own sleigh, the sick man in his slow and melancholy journey. At the end of three days, the son and brother reached the bosom of an interesting family, whose gratitude to Mr. Codman was without bounds. The young student died on the fourth of March

* Rev. Dr. Storrs's Sermon.

following, crying out in his delirium, "Mr. Codman! my friend, Mr. Codman!" A brief account of the religious experience of this young man was given by Mr. Codman, at the next meeting of the Saturday Evening Society. He stated that, after suffering the deepest anxiety from a sense of ill-desert, and his exposure to the just punishment of sin, on one morning the light broke in upon his mind, and from that moment, as he was persuaded, he loved God and relied upon the blood of atonement, having a heart renewed by the divine Spirit, and living continually in prayer and in the hope of immortal blessedness. If any one could have witnessed the grateful welcome with which, in many a subsequent year, Mr. Codman was ever received at Londonderry, it might awaken in his heart the desire of gaining the same inestimable reward of an act of kindness.

After visiting this afflicted family in the month of May, Mr. Codman, with his friend, prosecuted his journey from Londonderry to Windsor, Vt., and Dartmouth College. At Windsor, he met with a number of his highly esteemed Boston friends, who were called thither by reason of the ordination of the Rev. Bancroft Fowler. Among them were Rev. Dr. Eckley, Rev. Mr. Channing, and Mr. Josiah Salisbury, whose sister resided in Windsor.

The candidate was minutely examined, for as yet it was deemed important that the forms of examination should be rigidly observed, though a wider latitude of faith was tolerated; and it was not required of the candidate that he should be so explicit, on some mysterious points of Christian faith, as was soon afterwards found to be necessary. Mr. Channing made the introductory prayer. Dr. Burton, of Thetford, preached. Mr. Rowell, of Cornish, gave the right hand of fellowship, and Dr. Burroughs, of Hanover, a plain, unpolished, honest old gentleman, presided and gave the charge. Dr. Burton is known as the supporter of the Taste Scheme in theology, retaining the old and correct division of the mental faculties, the intellect, the affections, and the will. He maintained, that all holiness consists in a good taste, or a right state of the affections; and that volitions have no moral quality, except as indicating the state of the heart. As we are depraved beings, it is necessary, in order to holiness, that a new taste be implanted by divine grace; a benevolent, holy disposition, which finds happiness in imparting happiness. At a subsequent period he published a volume of Essays, in which he unfolded and vindicated his moral theory.

From the beautiful village of Windsor, Mr. Codman journeyed to Hanover, where he was received by President Wheelock, into a family afterwards peculiarly endeared to the writer. At this time there was one wooden college-building and a small chapel, near which was the pleasant mansion of the President. The next Sabbath was spent by Mr. Codman and his friend at Londonderry; and they had the pleasure of listening to the preaching of President McKeen, a native of Londonderry, and the first occupant of the presidential chair of Bowdoin College.

As illustrative of the character of Mr. Codman, it may not be improper for the writer here to introduce an extract from his own journal, of May 31st: "How great is the goodness of God in giving me such a friend as John Codman! He has presented me with an interleaved Bible, Cruden's Concordance, and Brown's Dictionary of the Bible. He has requested me to consider his property as my own. 'God,' said he to me, 'has blessed me in giving me more money than I want to use; you have but two hundred dollars a year; you cannot live upon it; let my money be your own.' Never have I known a friendship so pure and fervent. May God reward him; and may our friendship, which is founded on the religion of Jesus, be lasting as eternity."

At the time he offered me Cruden, I hesitated in receiving it, saying that he conferred obligations which I could never repay. He wrote on a piece of paper as follows:—"I am surprised to hear you speak of the reception of favors which cannot be repaid. If I have ever conferred a favor upon you, it has been amply and fully repaid. I enjoy, what is to me of infinitely more value than silver or gold, the pleasure of your society, and, I must hope, of your friendship. Let me, I beseech you, return a little of the debt, by sharing together what a merciful God has been pleased to give me. It would be my highest happiness, if we were so intimately united as to supersede all those ideas of obligation; that we were one in heart, and life, and in all our interests."

CHAPTER III.

HIS STUDIES WITH REV. HENRY WARE — DIFFICULTIES OF HIS SOCIAL POSITION — VOYAGE TO ENGLAND — HIS MORAL INDEPENDENCE AND THE INFLUENCE OF RELIGION UPON HIS LIFE.

At this period, 1805, there was no public seminary, with teachers devoted to the instruction of students in theology; although some young men, resident at Cambridge, were assisted by the professor of theology in their pursuits. The candidates for the ministry in general availed themselves of the teachings and the libraries of private clergymen; and it must be said, to the honor of those ministers, that they devoted much time and labor to qualify those under their care for the sacred office. It was considered a part of ministerial duty, to receive and educate those young men who desired to consecrate themselves to the service of Christ and the church. As the fruits of their self-denying labors, many clergymen of great eminence and piety were thus theologically educated, and became the means of extensive good to the community and the world.

Accordingly, we find Mr. Codman pursuing his studies with Rev. Henry Ware, then of Hingham. The decline in matters of religious faith, and of Christian feeling and practice, which for some years had been noticed, was now disclosing a strong opposition to Calvinistic theology. Mr. Codman was surrounded by his own family connections, and by the many friends of his early youth, who belonged to the "liberal party," so called, and was thus brought under the full influence of the new opinions. These opinions had not then taken the name of Unitarianism, but their advocates were men of the world, greatly opposed to the excitement of religious feelings, which had in them anything of anxiety for the soul, or any deep solicitude for the salvation of others. The doctrines of grace, if preached at all, were only alluded to in Scripture language, or in terms so general, or so ambiguous, as to make little or no impression. Men were exceedingly afraid of being righteous overmuch; hence there were few prayer meetings, very little religious conference, and Sabbath evening services were by many considered reproachful or unnecessary. Happily for Mr. Codman, he resolved to take his opinion, in matters of such infinite moment, from the word of God. Not "conferring with flesh and blood," in that noble independence for which his whole life was remarkable, he determined to "choose affliction with the people of God," and to enlist the ardor of his youth, and the influence of wealth and station, and all the powers of his mind, to promote a gospel, which was despised and rejected of men. He believed it to be the gospel of the Son of God. In his own joyful experience, he had found that divine peace which no other gospel could give; and neither the pride of the world, nor the accomplishments of life, nor the love of friends, nor any or all the combined and powerful influences which were brought to bear upon his mind, could shake his high and holy resolution. He was ready to "count all things but loss for the excellency of the knowledge of Christ Jesus his Lord;" and in the prayer meeting, the conference room, and private devotional duties, he found his supreme satisfaction and never-failing springs of delight. Far from being bigoted or misanthropic, a more cheerful Christian was rarely seen. He was most remarkable, even at this early period, for a sound judgment and practical wisdom; and he united the accomplishments of the gentleman with the meekness and sincerity of the Christian, in such a manner as to call forth the respect and admiration of those who were most opposed to his religious faith.

Few men, at this day, can have any conception of the embarrassments and trials which Mr. Codman endured, as the fruit of his religious convictions.

Among his early acquaintances and friends were two young men, of great eminence as scholars and of most attractive eloquence as preachers, — Mr. Channing, who was ordained in Boston, in 1803, and Mr. Buckminster, who was ordained in 1805, and who died in about five years afterwards. Mr. Channing was the beloved minister of Mr. Codman's mother-in-law. In his preaching there was a pious fervor, in connection with literary excellence, which rendered it extremely interesting. He lived to be the head of the whole party in America, which, though very diverse in their views concerning Jesus Christ, the Son of God, is classed together as one by the title of Unitarian.

Mr. Channing was by some years the senior of Mr. Codman. At this time, the tendencies of his mind to the evangelical faith were undoubtedly strong. It was his practice to dine, on every Saturday, with the family of Mrs. Codman; and he therefore became familiar with Mr. Codman, whom he always regarded with esteem and affection; and although, in after years, their views of Christian doctrine placed them in widely different relations, yet their mutual friendship and regard were never interrupted. As an evidence of the strong evangelical feelings of Mr. Channing at this period, we would state that, while Mr. Codman was pursuing his studies with Dr. Ware, he was spending a few days at home, on one of which Mr. Channing dined with the family. After dinner, he requested Mr. Codman to ride with him a few miles, and, during the ride, after much serious conversation, he expressed his fears that the religious speculations of the times were leading many astray; and he earnestly desired that his young friend might guard his mind from the prevailing errors, and that, by a prayerful study of the word of God and an implicit faith in its teachings, he might be prepared for the solemn duties of the ministry. Mr. Channing was not, at this time, ready to give up the evangelical doctrines; doubtless they were more or less modified in his view; but yet they exerted a powerful influence over his preaching and his life. Nor is it believed that this influence was wholly destroyed, in any stage of his subsequent departures from the faith of the New England churches.

We have already seen the active operation of divine grace upon Mr. Codman's mind. Under all the peculiarities of his situation, far more unfriendly to the growth of piety than if his position in life had been obscure, we find him advancing in all the graces of the Christian; but a higher maturity was soon after attained, in circumstances more congenial to his Christian advancement. In the belief that his theological studies could be pursued with greater benefit in Scotland, he resolved to avail himself of the advantages which the older institutions of that country afforded. Accordingly, he embarked for Liverpool in the brig Superb, Captain Bosworth, and sailed from Boston on Tuesday, July 30, 1805. His fellow passengers were, a gentleman of Boston and his wife, and two young ladies.

The following are extracts from his journal:

Sunday Night, August 4.—I have had to lament one of God's holy days spent in a very indifferent manner, being very sick and unable to fix my mind on devotional subjects.

Tuesday, August 6.—This morning, read to the ladies on deck an excellent little pamphlet by Andrew Fuller, on the question, "What shall I do to be saved?" Read two of Smalley's Sermons, and spent a very pleasant afternoon on deck. The evening was uncommonly fine, and Mr. T. obliged us with some excellent songs.

Wednesday, August 7.—In the afternoon, read to the ladies

several pieces from the Assembly's Missionary Magazine, and from the Panoplist.

SUNDAY, AUGUST 11.—Fine weather and fair winds. On this day, when thousands are uniting throughout the world in praising God, I sensibly felt the deprivation of public worship. There is an inexpressible pleasure in uniting with the congregation of the people in keeping holy day, of which those who are not at a distance from the house of God cannot conceive. In the morning read some of Smalley's Sermons, and in the afternoon Mr. and Mrs. T., the Misses E., and Captain B., assembled in the cabin to attend my imperfect services. After prayer, reading of the Scriptures and singing, I delivered a discourse from Isaiah xli. 10. I hope and pray, that the Lord will assist my weak endeavors, and that these exercises may be beneficial to the souls of my hearers. I have much to bewail and lament before God, my many and aggravated sins, particularly my coldness and indifference to things spiritual, during my passage thus far. The delightful exercise of prayer has in a great measure abated, and I am too inclined to relapse into the habits of my companions. How often and how deeply have I regretted the absence of those dear friends, whose eminent piety and religious attainments served to animate my endeavors and strengthen my Christian zeal; and more especially do I feel the absence of one who has so often accompanied me to a throne of grace, with whom I have spent so many agreeable hours, and to whom, under God, I owe much spiritual edification. May his life, health, and usefulness, be ever precious in the sight of the Most High.

SUNDAY, AUGUST 18.—I pray God not to take his Holy Spirit from me, nor to suffer me to be led away by the temptations of the great world upon which I am about to enter. In the morning, read to the ladies a sermon from 2 Kings v. 13; and in the afternoon, my usual auditors being assembled in the cabin,

I again performed divine service. My discourse was from 1 Corinthians xi. 28.

SUNDAY, AUGUST 25.—To our great joy, we discovered the Irish coast. My usual hearers being assembled in the cabin, after having returned thanks to God for his kind care and protection during the voyage, I delivered a sermon from Romans i. 20, in which, it being the last Sabbath we shall probably spend together, I took notice of our situation, in an occasional address to my hearers. God grant, if there be any thing of good in my sermons, they may make a serious impression on the hearts of those who have heard me.

TUESDAY, AUGUST 27.—An English man-of-war, of thirty-two guns, boarded us with three or four hardy looking seamen, and one haughty, insolent officer, who, after inquiring whence we came and who we were, called for our men; and after examining their protections, took a young man from us, who had the appearance of an Irishman, but with a regular American protection. Poor fellow! almost in sight of port and perhaps of friends, to be forced on board a man-of-war, subjected to the tyrannical insolence of his superiors. Such are the tyrants of the ocean! How grateful ought I to be to Almighty God, for preserving me from the situation of the Irish lad! How unsearchable are his ways, that one should be taken, and another left!

WEDNESDAY, AUGUST 28.—Arrived at Liverpool. Praised be God, that I can now close my journal under such favorable circumstances,—a pleasant passage of twenty-eight days and good health. This evening, thanks to the Giver of every good and perfect gift, I enjoyed some little freedom in prayer, and was enabled to pour out my soul in thankful adoration to the Preserver of mankind for his sparing mercy in bringing me safe to this foreign land. Oh, may I never be unmindful of the God of my salvation.

These extracts from Mr. Codman's journal give us a pleasing idea of his religious disposition and feelings, and of his Christian courage. A young man, a student in theology but not a licensed preacher, amidst the discomforts of his first voyage, with a small company, not sympathizing with his views and emotions, yet, in his zeal for the glory of God and their spiritual benefit, he undertakes to be their religious teacher and persuade them to devote the Sabbath to religious services. Of the two men of this company, one was much opposed to Trinitarians and Calvinists, and the other was a disbeliever in any revelation to man from the Supreme Ruler of the universe. Of the latter, Mr. Codman said, "A man, so benevolent and kind, as he appears to be, and yet a stranger to Jesus Christ, is much to be pitied. I had a very interesting conversation with him, in which I endeavored, to the best of my ability, to explain to him the scheme of salvation through a crucified Saviour. He heard me with attention, and seemed to be interested in the conversation."

It is not thus that the men of the world occupy their time and talents. It is sufficient, in their view, to pursue the gains and to enjoy the pleasures and honors which the world offers. How striking is the contrast between their pursuits and the noble aims of this young servant of Christ! For *them*, there is no hour of secret prayer, no communion with God, no lively apprehension of those eternal realities upon which they must soon enter. For *him*, the morning and evening altar are the symbols of that high fellowship, which he hopes to enjoy hereafter with his adored Redeemer. For *him*, no scene of pleasure has any attractions, which does not comprehend some foretaste of those joys which "eye hath not seen nor ear heard." His Bible, his Sabbath, the conversion of immortal souls, are the objects dearest to his heart; and, though surrounded by the wealth and flattery of the world, he remains uncorrupted and undeceived. Pressing forward in the path of duty, he gives his example, and all his energies, to that cause which, though it be "a stumbling-block and foolishness" to the world, is, to them that believe, "the power of God and the wisdom of God."

It is exceedingly rare, that the religion of the cross achieves its noblest victories amid the scenes of uninterrupted prosperity. Yet some such examples are found; and, in the subject of this Memoir, we have one which invites the most serious contemplation of those who enjoy in profusion the blessings of Providence. It is a picture of moral beauty, in which we may see the divine excellence of the Christian graces, and their superiority to all the motives which govern the worldly and unrenewed mind. It was not the incapacity of tasting earthly pleasures that turned him to God; it was no disgust with the world; it was no love of singularity, no eccentric action of disordered sensibilities; but it was the calm decision of a well-balanced mind, that, under the guidance of the gracious Spirit, enabled him to triumph over the snares of youth and the blandishments of the world. It was from the survey of the interests and of the future destiny of the soul, that he derived the mighty power of reducing the prominent and gaudy objects of time to their own littleness, and of investing with dignity and unappreciable worth the realities of eternity.

CHAPTER IV.

LIVERPOOL AND LONDON — PREACHING OF JOHN NEWTON — CHRISTIAN FRIENDS IN LONDON — VARIOUS PREACHERS — EDINBURGH — STUDIES AND LECTURES — DRS. HOPE AND HUNTER — DUGALD STEWART — SCOTCH "BAPTISTS" AND "INDEPENDENTS" — RELIGIOUS REFLECTIONS.

It was in the spirit of constant and fervent prayer, that Mr. Codman entered upon the new and interesting scenes to which he was now introduced. He was perfectly aware of the powerful temptations in his path, and he deeply felt the need of restraining and supporting grace. He did not intend to turn away from those various objects, which are so worthy of the attention and call forth the admiration of men of taste and genius, but he resolved that everything should be subordinate to the higher purposes of his mind. He knew that the holy duties, to which he had consecrated his life, demanded his first and supreme attention; and it was to qualify himself for the most extensive usefulness, and not for personal gratification, that he had sought the land of his ancestors.

Upon his arrival at Liverpool, he therefore eagerly repaired to several places of public worship; but in some of the pulpits of that city he did not find the dignity and decorum, to which he had been accustomed in his native country. In fact, he was often disgusted with the familiarity, vulgarity and levity of some preachers, which led him to say, "God grant, if he ever permits me to preach the everlasting gospel, he will restrain me from all appearance of levity." While in Liverpool, he heard Mr. Yates, the celebrated antagonist of Wardlaw, and in his journal says of him, "Mr. Yates is a pleasing man, but he appears to be incorrect in religious sentiment; probably of Socinian views. His preaching, although it may gratify the man of taste, is not calculated to afford sustenance to the hungry soul." The School for the Blind, in Liverpool, was an object of especial interest. He was particularly gratified with its highly religious aspect; and, on an occasion for catechetical exercises, he listened with pleasure to recitations from the Catechism by seventy-five members of the school, of both sexes, and of widely different ages.

After a solitary ride of two nights, in the mail coach, he reached London, and had the pleasure of meeting his old friends and relatives, John Lowell,

Esq. and family, of Boston. He took lodgings in Norfolk Street, Strand, which was then the American rendezvous of London, and gave him opportunity to hear often from his friends at home.

In his journal of September 8, he writes as follows:

This was another of the days of the Son of Man, and I hoped at last to hear some serious, evangelical preaching. Called on Mr. and Mrs. Bromfield, whom I found waiting to accompany me to church. To me, the occasion was one of deep interest. I expected to hear the excellent John Newton, but my friends thought it doubtful whether he would preach. On entering the church, we were agreeably surprised by seeing his venerable form in the sacred desk. His interesting life, his uncommon piety, his remarkable conversion, and his friendship for Cowper, had created an indescribable interest in my mind. I had frequently and most ardently desired to see that man of God. The wish was at last accomplished. His figure was rather short, and he wore a dark wig; his countenance was strongly marked, and his features were bold and commanding. He had his servant with him, in the pulpit, to name his text; for his memory generally failed him in that particular.

After the text was given, which was from Acts xxvi. 28, "Almost thou persuadest me to be a Christian," he repeated it, and, leaning over the pulpit, began his sermon. It was not so connected as might have been expected from him in early life; but it was a train of fatherly counsels and good sayings, so that the most abandoned sinner might have left the church with the text on his lips, and deeply fastened in his memory. Every now and then the good man would hesitate and falter, and I was in great anxiety for him, lest he should not be able to proceed; but he recovered himself and spoke with considerable facility. Upon the whole, he is a wonderful man and a most impressive preacher, considering he is upwards of eighty years of age.

After dinner, I went to hear Mr. Burder, author of "Village Sermons," who preaches in a small chapel in Feather Lane. His sermon was pious and his manner impressive.

September 11.—Dined with Mr. Henry Bromfield. He is one of the most agreeable and best Americans I have yet met. He retains much of the manners of New England, is an excellent merchant, and a very pious man. At dinner, I met with two of my countrymen, Mr. Otis, and Mr. James Everett, an old friend and class-mate, who came to England on business last fall, and had been confined by sickness all winter in London.

September 12.—This day I was engaged to dine with Mr. Robert G. Steele, of the house of Chalmers and Cowie; and, as Mr. Burder lived in Colebrook Row, Islington, I called there on my way to Mr. Steele's, with a letter of introduction from Dr. Morse. I was received with great kindness by this truly excellent man, and found him preparing to go to Mr. Steele's to dinner. As we were conversing, a Mr. Frey, a German Jew, recently converted to Christianity, came in. I was much pleased in seeing this worthy man. His preaching has been attended with great success among his countrymen in this city. We all went together to Mr. Steele's, and I found one of the best and most agreeable families I had ever been acquainted with. It consisted of Mr. Steele, (Mrs. Steele being absent,) his mother and sister, and three very interesting children. Several ladies were there, and also Mr. Lewis, pastor of a chapel in Islington, of which Mr. Cowie is the great support and patron.

Rev. Mr. Bogue, of Gosport, was also there, and the conversation turned on my excellent friend, Mr. Allen,* who gave me the letter to Mr. Cowie, and to whom I shall always feel under the greatest obligation for introducing me to this society.

September 14.—Dined with Mrs. Gordon, at Islington. It being a most delightful morning, I walked thither over the City Road. It is very large, wide and beautiful, bordered, as is usual in England, with hedges. Mrs. Gordon lives in a very neat little house, quite in the country, and is a native of Charlestown, near Boston. She appears to be a very pious lady, and treated me with great affection and kindness. In the evening, I heard Mr. Frey preach an excellent discourse on the subject of the Brazen Serpent. There were many Jews present, although at the risk of their lives. I pray God that he may be abundantly useful to his countrymen. After service, several young Jews called on him; and we had some very interesting conversation on the state of their souls.

In a letter to his friend, dated at Edinburgh, November 1, 1805, Mr. Codman says:

I have now to inform you that, at Cambridge, I heard Mr. Hall, so justly admired for his sermon on "Infidelity," at Oxford; Mr. Hinton, a celebrated and most excellent man; and, subsequently, at a Baptist ordination, Dr. Ryland, and our much admired Andrew Fuller. I had the pleasure of seeing Mr. Fuller, and of receiving a warm invitation to visit him. The Baptists of this country are highly intelligent and respectable, and they unite with the most evangelical sentiments the true spirit of charity. I have had the pleasure of communing with a Baptist church, and with the pious of all denominations.

---

* Rev. Thomas Allen, of Pittsfield.

Cambridge is a very inferior town; Oxford, one of the most beautiful in Europe, remarkable for the elegance of its Gothic buildings and the best collection of paintings in England. I spent ten days in that delightful place, and left it unsatisfied. I have likewise visited the manufactories at Birmingham and Manchester, and also Bristol, where I have an uncle; and have seen the romantic lakes of Cumberland and Westmoreland.

In comparing our government with this, perhaps it may be dangerous to hazard many observations across the Atlantic. Of this, be assured; that more federalists return republicans, than the reverse. There are twenty Americans in Edinburgh, all republicans. John Gorham, whom you may remember at college, is now here. He has visited England and France, and is more and more satisfied of the policy and good sense of our government, in their pacific measures. These sentiments, you know, are not in compliment to you, but are the result of the little observation I have made since I have been here. So much for politics. Perhaps it is best for ministers not to meddle with them; but no true American can help rejoicing when he considers the blesssings of his government, and dreading the exertions of those, who attempt an imitation of a system of which they do not know the evils.

I arrived here only last week, and the lectures have not yet commenced. There are nearly a thousand medical students. I shall attend the Professor of Divinity, and the lectures on Church History and Hebrew; also, Dugald Stewart's lectures on Moral Philosophy, and the lectures on Chemistry, which are very excellent.

The mode of living, in this country, is entirely different from that in America. We find our own provisions, and breakfast and dine in each other's rooms. Four o'clock is the hour of dining, fixed by the University, it being the only one in which there is not a lecture.

The following are extracts from his journal :

Edinburgh, January 1, 1806.—Another year is past without much improvement; oh, may the ensuing one be marked with greater progress in knowledge, virtue, and holiness. The Scotch have a singular custom of ushering in the new year. Between twelve and one o'clock this morning, we were aroused by shouts of festivity and rejoicing. The people crowd the streets, with liquors of various kinds, which are freely distributed. This morning I walked with Mr. Ross, Mr. Silliman,* and Dr. Gorham. After visiting Parliament House and the Courts of Judicature, we proceeded to Edinburgh Castle, apparently one of the most impregnable fortresses in the world. It is situated at the west end of Edinburgh, and commands a most delightful view. On the south are seen the meadows, Arthur's Seat, Salisbury Crag, and a beautiful intervale, bounded by majestic hills, rising in sublime confusion one upon another. On the north, is a most enchanting view of the new town and the Frith, with ships at anchor, and mountains on the opposite side covered with snow. On the east, is a view of the old town, the Tolbooth, and other churches.

January 2, 1806.—This day the lectures commenced. Dr. Hope, it is said, gives one of the best courses on Chemistry. His manner is rather stiff and pompous, and his style diffuse and tautological. He is chiefly remarkable for the neatness of his experiments. Dr. Hunter is the Professor of Divinity. He is remarkable for his uncommon piety and a strict adherence "to the faith once delivered to the saints," united with great charity and benevolence towards those who differ from him in sentiment. As a professor, he is not so much distinguished for his talents as for fervent zeal, pious simplicity, and Christian liber-

* Now Professor Silliman, of Yale College.

ality. On Mondays, he expounds a portion of the Epistles; occasionally, he examines the class; and Friday is devoted to the purpose of reading discourses. Dr. Hunter gives out the subjects, which are critical, practical, or for lectures. Each student, who reads a discourse, makes one or two prayers. Critical observations are made by the professor and students. I presume there are upwards of eighty students. An attendance on this course, the Hebrew and Church History classes, together with those on Natural and Moral Philosophy, and the dead languages, is requisite to a license to preach in the Church of Scotland.

From Dr. Hunter's, I proceeded to Professor Dugald Stewart's lecture on Moral Philosophy. I dare not undertake to describe the wonder of Europe, the boast of metaphysicians, the pride of literature, the ornament of polished life,—DUGALD STEWART. The riches of the ancients are at his command. The advance and improvements in literature and science, among the moderns, are perfectly familiar to him. The graces of eloquence, the flowers of poetry, serve in his hands to adorn and elucidate the abstruse science of metaphysics. His manner is energetic and lofty, his style nervous, beautiful and glowing. He commands the most profound attention. Once, indeed, a student made some little disturbance in his class. Mr. Stewart cannot submit to the least noise or inattention. As Gouverneur Morris says of Washington, "His wrath was terrible." He made a solemn pause, and, fixing his eye on a particular part of the room, was silent for two or three minutes. He then renewed his lecture, but the noise recurring he paused again, with his eye directed to the same spot. In the most emphatic manner, he desired the person who made the disturbance not to leave the lecture room without speaking to him. After proceeding with his lecture for some time, he stopped again and observed that, in order to prevent mistake, he requested that gentleman to give him his name. No answer was given. He then said, "I have my eye upon him. He sits in the last seat, the fourth person from the end. He shall not leave the room without my speaking to him; and I promise myself that the like shall never happen again." All eyes were directed to the poor student, who had been so unfortunate as to excite the wrath of Dugald Stewart. I know not who he was, nor do I know what disturbance he made, as my seat is at a distance from the offender. It must have been a very heinous offence, to have justified such language.

In the evening, Mr. Silliman and myself supped with Mr. Black, one of the ministers of Edinburgh, and one of the best of men. He is a man of uncommon piety and great meekness of deportment. His manners are remarkably easy and polite, and his preaching truly evangelical. We met a great number of very worthy and pious young men there. Before supper, we attended family worship. All the family and strangers being assembled together, including three or four maid servants, a short blessing was asked, followed by singing, in which the servants took a part; the Scriptures were read, and all, falling on their knees, united in prayer to the common Parent. It was a most delightful scene.

January 4.—Dined with Mr. D. Dickson, Jr., colleague pastor with Sir H. Moncrieff Welwood, in the West Church. He is a sensible, pleasant young man, and we found there some very agreeable company. In the evening, called on Rev. Mr. Campbell, who has lately succeeded Dr. Kemp in the Tolbooth church, and there united in the delightful duties of family worship. How sweet, how pleasant it is to praise God in a social circle of Christians!

JANUARY 5.—This morning I went to the Baptist church. The Scotch Baptists are remarked for great illiberality of sentiment. They hold no communion with Christians of other denominations. The church is in the Cowgate, and the celebrated Dr. McLean is one of the pastors. The sermon was a good essay upon the vanity of the world, but was grossly deficient in what Dr. Doddridge thinks indispensable for a sermon,—some mention of our Lord Jesus Christ and of the influence of the Holy Spirit.

JANUARY 6.—This day I called on Mr. Robert Haldane, with a letter from Mr. Burder. There are in Edinburgh two brothers of this name, both of considerable fortune.* Mr. Robert Haldane was once a violent politician, and was very obnoxious to the ministerial party. Within a few years he has become a religious man, and is now as obnoxious to the friends of Presbyterian government. He has a large fortune, which he devotes to pious purposes, principally for educating young men for preaching. Mr. James Haldane has likewise become a religious man and a preacher. These two gentlemen are the leaders of the Scotch Independents. It seems that two ministers of the established church, a Mr. Ewen and a Mr. Inness, from some disgust quitted the church, and, with the Messrs. Haldane, set up Independency. There is a large tabernacle, at which Mr. Haldane is the preacher. They never license to preach, and they administer the Lord's supper every Sabbath afternoon. Upon entering the room, Mr. Haldane received me with considerable cordiality; and the first questions he asked were, "What I thought of a gospel church?" "Whether I had inquired and consulted my Bible

* Mr. Robert Haldane died in 1842, and Mr. James Haldane in 1851. The biography of both has been recently published in this country.

on the subject?" "What church I belonged to in America?" "What church I communed with here?"

The following extract from a letter to his friend Allen, dated February, 1806, will exhibit the nature of his religious impressions at that time:

Like you, I have been attending lectures on Chemistry, and my time has been fully employed in my various pursuits. O, my friend, while we increase in useful human knowledge, I hope we shall not decrease in that knowledge, which will alone be useful to us in the day, when we must appear before the judgment-seat of Christ. Since I have been in this country, my mind has been not a little distressed at my lukewarmness and coldness in the spiritual life. The Lord, who knows all things, I humbly hope knows that I *desire* to love him; but with all my desire, my heart still remains cold and languid. The effects of indwelling sin are constantly rising in my heart and appearing in my life. The temptations of the world, the flesh and the devil, are constantly attracting me; and I am daily exclaiming with St. Paul, "O wretched man that I am, who shall deliver me from the body of this death!"

In the preceding pages, we have seen the careful and judicious observer of the passing events connected with his entrance upon the world, and upon his preparation for active usefulness. Mr. Codman was now in his twenty-fourth year, and his remarks upon the society and circumstances, among which he moved, exhibit a wise discrimination, a just caution, and remarkable maturity of judgment. The reader will not fail to see, that in his religious experience he speaks with great humility and self-distrust. The attractions of the world were exceedingly strong, and the conflict between his convictions of duty, his remembered vows, his high obligations, and the opposing influences of fashion and the world, was often sharp and distressing; but he had not yet attained to that high Christian principle which, in after life, sustained him in yet fiercer conflicts, and enabled him to rejoice that he was "counted worthy to suffer shame for the name of Jesus." He was now hopefully in the Christian life; yet he does not seem to have partaken largely of its consolations. He loved the people of God, the place of prayer, and the worship of the sanctuary, more than all other objects; but he longed for a holier zeal, a more lively faith; and, as his standard of Christian feeling and duty was high, his felt deficiencies, his apprehended want of conformity thereto, often excited his fears and checked the aspirations of his heaven-directed hopes. But, though rarely attaining those more elevated Christian enjoyments, which are often afforded to the disciples of Christ, he was rapidly maturing those vigorous principles of piety, which best exhibit the calm and cheerful aspects of the Christian hope, and which enabled him in after life so signally to overcome the world, and to 'endure hardness as a good soldier of Jesus Christ.'

CHAPTER V.

JOURNAL AT EDINBURGH—DIFFERENT PREACHERS—REV. MR. BLACK, HIS SICKNESS AND DEATH—STATE OF RELIGION IN SCOTLAND—LONDON—VISIT TO MR. WILBERFORCE—COMMENCEMENT OF MINISTERIAL LABORS—LETTERS FROM HIS MOTHER AND REV. MR. CHANNING—TOUR ON THE CONTINENT—RETURN TO EDINBURGH.

EDINBURGH, FEBRUARY 3, 1806.—Engaged in study all day. In the evening, I went to the prayer-meeting for supplicating the Almighty to extend the limits of the Redeemer's kingdom, and to succeed all missionary exertion. This meeting is held once a month, and the pious of all parties in the church unite in it. O may the prayers that have this evening been offered at the footstool of Mercy, be heard and graciously answered; and may the happy time soon come, when Jesus Christ, our Lord and Saviour, shall "have the heathen for his inheritance, and the uttermost parts of the earth for his possession."

FEBRUARY 4.—Nothing to interrupt my studies. The weather here is quite variable. To-day was the coldest day I have experienced in Scotland; thermometer at 21°.

FEBRUARY 8.—Attended the Philo-Theological Society, of which I am a member. Heard a very good essay on the comparative merit of the Christian and Mohammedan religions. The question for debate was, Whether there are errors in the Church of Scotland sufficient to justify a secession? It was decided unanimously in the negative.

February 9.—Attended, as usual, the Tolbooth church, and heard Mr. Campbell preach upon the office of ruling elders. He asked the elders, who sat before him, several questions: "Do you believe in the Scriptures? Do you believe the doctrines of the Westminster Confession to be the doctrines of Scripture? Do you believe the form of Presbyterian government to be according to Scripture, and promise to support it? Do you promise to perform the duties of your office to the best of your abilities?" To which they assented, by an inclination of the head. After the ordination prayer, he added some advice, in which he urged the frequent perusal of Scripture and other duties. In the afternoon, I went to hear Dr. Jamieson, a Burgher minister, celebrated for his controversy with Dr. Priestly, on the divinity of Christ. He preached a very excellent sermon from Isaiah lvii. 17. He observed, that no one was stationary in religion; that if he was not making progress, he was going backward. I have very great apprehensions, that this is my case. Little, very little progress have I made in religion since I have been in this country. My heart has backslidden from God. O Lord, "take not thy Holy Spirit from me. Restore unto me the joy of thy salvation, and uphold me with thy free Spirit." Not till then, shall I be able to fulfill the duties of a Christian minister. Not till then, shall I be able to "teach transgressors thy ways, that sinners may be converted unto thee."

February 14.—This evening, for the first time since I have been in this country, I went to a place of public amusement. It was a funeral concert on the death of Lord Nelson, Mr. Pitt, and the Marquis Cornwallis. The room was hung in black, and was very crowded. The gentlemen were all dressed in black, and the ladies in black or white. The music was sacred, from Handel.

February 16.—Heard Dr. Balfour, of Glasgow, preach an excellent sermon from Psalm lxxxiv. 11. His manner was easy and graceful, his style rich and glowing, his sentiments just and evangelical, and the whole discourse one of the best I have heard. Again I heard him in the afternoon and in the evening, at the Tron church, for the Sabbath School Institution. Never did I hear a more eloquent discourse. What rich means of grace do I enjoy, and how little do I improve them!

February 21.—Dined in company with Mr. Silliman, at Dr. Buchanan's. We met there a Scotch Baronet, Sir John Stirling, his lady and daughter. Lady Stirling is an American, and was born near New Haven. Mr. Silliman remembers a story of a Scotch nobleman falling in love with the daughter of a mechanic, at church, in a place not far from New Haven. This is probably the very person. Her father still lives, and continues his trade.

Monday, February 24.—Every one appears interested about the Rev. Mr. Black, who is dangerously ill. His door is thronged, and in the evening the pious from all parts of the city crowded to his church, to supplicate Almighty God to spare his valuable life.

February 26.—Sent a messenger to inquire for Mr. Black, who brought me word, that 'he was at his rest.' Supposing that he was better, I went light-hearted to my duties. Seeing Mr. Dickson, he gave me the melancholy intelligence of Mr. Black's death, and told me that the phrase, 'He was at his rest,' was usual in Scotland to express death. O God, how unsearchable are thy judgments, and thy ways past finding out! His spirit has ascended to those heavenly mansions, prepared for him by his blessed Saviour. It is our loss, but his unspeakable gain. He was a man of the most gentle and affectionate disposition, of great zeal in the cause of Christ, and a most useful and excellent minister. He has left a disconsolate widow and five young children. The God and the Judge of the widow, and the Father of the fatherless, will provide for them. Never did I see more general sorrow than is expressed on this melancholy occasion; for he was universally beloved, and is universally lamented. He died in the forty-fourth year of his age, of a nervous fever, after a short illness.

Sunday, March 2.—Hail, sacred day of rest! In the morning I went to church, accompanied by one of my countrymen, a very pleasing and amiable man, but I fear a stranger to the blessed gospel. May the Holy Spirit constrain him to the truth.

Monday, March 3.—To-day, Mr. Black was interred. The funerals in this country are conducted in a very different manner from those in America. There are no prayers at the house, or at the grave. No person attends, unless formally invited by letter; and he must then appear in full mourning. The mourning of the Scotch, is deep black with crape on the hat, generally very long, and with the cuffs of their coats trimmed with white; which trimmings are called *weepers*. The people, after taking refreshment, attend the corpse to the grave, which is sometimes carried on shoulders, but most commonly in a hearse. This is drawn by two, four, six, and sometimes eight horses, the lower part being decorated with various colors. The upper part is covered with black velvet and black trimmings, and ornamented with plumes. After the hearse, followed ten mourning carriages and six private gentlemen's coaches.

Sunday, March 9.—In the morning I attended at Mr. Black's church, to hear the tribute of affection and love. The church was exceedingly crowded, and many could not obtain admittance. After service, I went to Lady Glenorchy's chapel to partake of the sacrament, unworthy as I am, and so little deserving of the crumbs that fall from my Master's table. What a privilege, to sit down at the marriage supper of the Lamb!

Friday, March 14.—It being a beautiful morning, I took a ride into the country on horseback. The scenery was quite American. The hills were covered with snow, and the ground just parting with the frost. As I jogged along, I overtook a fellow-traveler; and, according to the good old Yankee custom, we fell into conversation. I must here observe, that I noticed in this plain, good Scotchman, the same curious spirit for which New England has been so frequently ridiculed. Perceiving I was a stranger, he inquired from what country I came, what my business was, &c., &c. He was, apparently, a sensible, judicious and pious man. I make not this observation to condemn such curiosity as impertinent, for I really did not consider it so; but merely to show, that it is not peculiar to my Yankee countrymen.

Saturday, March 15.—I attended, as usual, the Philo-Theological Society, and heard a very good essay on moral agency from Mr. Brotherston. Some of the society, however, did not think so highly of it; and rudely attempted to pull it to pieces. No good Calvinist could possibly have objected to the essay, but these gentlemen pretend to be Calvinists; that is, they are told they must be so, their church confession obliging them to it; and they are much offended if you insinuate that they are not so. The fact is, that very many of the members of the Church of Scotland are Arminians, although they all sign the most complete Calvinistic confession of faith in the world. Many of the students of divinity, now at the hall, are *at heart* Arminians, though they think it a most opprobrious title. "The heart is deceitful above all things, and desperately wicked; who can know it!"

Sunday, March 16.—There is much real religion among the lower classes of people in this country. The churches, where the gospel is preached in its purity, overflow with hearers; but in the other churches, there is little more to be seen than the bare walls. Happy Scotland! while the most woful degeneracy exists in every part of Europe and in my favored country, thou still retainest, in a great measure, the piety and virtue of our forefathers! Never shall I forget the good I have received in thy churches.

In a letter of April 25, 1806, he says:

I have spent the winter very pleasantly, and considerably to my satisfaction. The session is now over, the lectures are closed, and I am starting again to see a little of Europe. I expect to visit the Highlands, thence proceed to London, and after crossing the channel, if it should be safe, to return to Edinburgh to devote another winter to my books.

The following extract from a letter to his friend, will show the temper of his mind at this time, and his love to the cause of his Saviour. After alluding to a project of going, with other ministers, into the woods of the Genesee country, to settle the trackless wilds, he adds: "Have you forgotten your plans on this subject? Do you remember how we used to talk it over together? For my own part, I would not hesitate to sacrifice all the favorable prospect I might have, of a pleasant settlement among my friends, were I persuaded that I might advance the interests of our dear Redeemer."

He arrived in London, June 1, 1806; and, that

he might be near his friends, took up his residence in Islington for a few weeks. In his journal, he thus speaks of his friend, Mr. Robert Cowie: "He is a father to a numerous circle of pious friends in Islington, and is the principal supporter of a place of worship. How delightful is Christian intercourse! In this country, to be a Christian, is a sufficient recommendation to Christians. The fashionable world, the literary world, the mercantile world, the idle world, are cold and ceremonious; but the Christian world is the reverse, warm and friendly,—a temper truly becoming the disciples of Christ."

SATURDAY, JUNE 14.—Supped with Mr. Lewis, the minister of Highbury Grove chapel, a very amiable, pious and useful man. After tea, I went with him to a prayer-meeting at the chapel. How unworthy I am to be favored with such privileges, and, particularly, to lead the devotions of others.

SUNDAY, JUNE 15.—After morning service, the sacrament was administered, first in the Church form, and then in the Dissenter's; at the last of which I had the privilege of partaking. In the evening, it was announced that I was to preach the next Thursday evening. Gracious God, prepare me for this entrance upon my ministerial duties! O Lord, I trust in thee; to whom should I go, but unto thee!

WEDNESDAY, JUNE 18.—This morning, I received a note from Mr. Wilberforce, to whom I had a letter of introduction, informing me that he was much pressed with business at present;

but if I would come and take a beef-steak with him, between three and four, to-day or to-morrow, he would be very happy to see me. When I reached his door, at the time appointed, I found it so surrounded with coaches of style, that I could hardly make my way up. I knocked, and was informed by the servants that Mr. Wilberforce was not at home. He had written me, if he should not be in, to wait till he came. The servants accordingly ushered me into the parlor, where were five or six gentlemen waiting for Mr. Wilberforce. I took a seat, but no one knew me, and I knew no one; no one spoke to me, and I spoke to no one. In this awkward dilemma I sat for about half an hour, when the servant came in and said, "Gentlemen, Mr. Wilberforce will not be in to dinner." The gentleman who presided at the table was polite enough to take a glass of wine with me, but not another word was exchanged. When dinner was about half over, we heard a most violent rapping at the door. One of the gentlemen exclaimed, "That is Wilberforce!" The door opened, and in ran a very small man, who, in Scotland, would be called a *wee wee mannie*, hopping about here and there. "How do you do, my lord!" "Most obedient, gentlemen!" in a prodigious hurry; and obliged to back a friend's motion in the house. "Excuse me, gentlemen; must be gone!" I rose and bowed; but the little man was near-sighted, and could not distinguish the features of a stranger. Presently, one of the party said, "Mr. Wilberforce, here is a gentleman who wishes to see you." I went up to him, bowed, and told him my name. "Oh, Mr. Codman," he exclaimed, "I did send you a note this morning. I should beg a thousand pardons, and will send an apology to my friend, Mr. Banks, immediately." "By no means, sir," said I. "Will you excuse me, then?" "Certainly." And out he flew, without introducing me to a single person in the room. I suppose however, in the entry, he had told the gentleman who presided, that I was from America; for I was asked some questions at table concerning America, and some conversation ensued. The company, I found, were Lord Teignmouth, Mr. Henry Thornton, a clergyman, who I believe was Mr. Owen, author of the "Fashionable World Displayed," and other gentlemen. They were polite and affable to each other, though not to me; for it is a standing rule, in this country, to take no notice of a person to whom they have not been regularly introduced. Our Boston gentlemen, who are in the habit of giving such splendid entertainments, would be surprised at the dinner given by Mr. Wilberforce. Some slices of cold beef, and a small piece of roast mutton only, were provided for noblemen and members of parliament. The most common white plates were on the table, and every thing in the same style.

THURSDAY, JUNE 19.—The evening of this day forms one of the most interesting periods of my life. I entered upon the arduous duties of a preacher of the gospel, and consecrated myself to the service of God, and of his Son Jesus Christ. My public labors were commenced before a few chosen friends, the congregation not exceeding two hundred. I preached from Romans xiv. 10. After having done all in my power to prepare myself for this solemn undertaking, I left the rest to God; to his grace, to support me under the trying situation; and, praised be his glorious name, I never had more presence of mind, nor was I ever so regardless of man. To him be all the glory.

As yet, however, he had not been licensed as a preacher.

JUNE 25.—Accompanied Mr. Lewis to Hoxton, a village about two miles from Islington, to attend an anniversary of the academy. The academy is for Dissenters, and from this place preachers are continually issuing. It has a master and a few tutors. The students are taught Latin, Greek and Hebrew, and a smattering of Philosophy. They are sent out to preach almost immediately upon their entering on their studies, first to the almshouses and then to the villages. There is no regular course of study required; but the students may preach as soon they please, and whenever they are invited. Dined with the excellent Mr. Cowie. O how delightful is Christian communion! a foretaste of the joys, which are prepared for those who love the Lord Jesus, in another world.

It may be proper to introduce, in this place, a few extracts from letters received, during his residence in Scotland, from his step-mother, Mrs. Catharine Codman, which may show the mutual esteem and affection which subsisted between himself and that excellent lady, as well as throw some light on his domestic character.

May, 1806.—I have already written you by Mr. B——, since which I have received yours; and as I believe he has not yet sailed, I must thank you for it. In doing this, however, you will not expect me to describe the feelings it has excited. If you have reason to thank God for the event, which gave me to be your mother, how much have I to bless him, that it gave me you for a son! In my peculiar state, what can be so consoling as your friendship? On what object can my affection so naturally fasten, as on the counterpart of him who has been taken from them? My gratitude for the blessing is still more excited, when I view you as the father of my children; and this is augmented by reflection on the sacredness of the profession you have chosen, which will add such weight and influence to parental advice. . . . . . .

This is the first time I have attempted to write you in my new house; and it seems to me, that I should write in an improved state of heart, and produce something which should evince a sense of that peculiar goodness which has followed me all my days, and which sometimes breaks out in such fresh instances of favor, as to create astonishment that it is bestowed on so unworthy a creature. On the evening of my entrance into this house, I asked Mr. Channing, with two or three pious friends, to assemble here and unite with me in prayer, that I might wait upon God in it better than I had ever done, and thus consecrate the house to his private service. But alas, after all, I find this body of sin still about me, weighing me down to earth, while receiving blessings which should attract me to the skies.

As the children advance in years, their conduct becomes of so much more importance as greatly to increase my anxiety. I have need, as well as you, to trust in Him, who can give me grace that shall be sufficient for me; and it is with earnestness, my dear son, that I solicit your prayers that I may receive divine support. You need not, as you say, ask for mine. They are what you have always had. Your happiness, and especially your advancement in the Christian life, never presses more forcibly and tenderly on my heart, than when it is lifted up to the throne of grace; and I trust that my petitions for you, will be answered in your safe return and useful subsequent life. With what pleasure do I look forward to that period, when the influence of your precepts and example will so greatly aid me in rearing my children, and when we shall realize all the fond wishes expressed for them in your last! Let me again thank you for that precious letter.

The following is an extract from a letter, which he received about this time, from Rev. Mr. Channing:

Your last letter increased my interest in your welfare and improvement. You seem to be full of doubts and fears respecting your sincerity. It is good to doubt and to fear, when our minds, instead of sinking into despondency, are excited by painful uncertainty to self-examination, to careful inquiry into the nature of true religion, as exhibited in the Scriptures, and to humble, fervent prayer. I believe, my friend, we are apt to expose ourselves to much needless pain, by forming loose and vague opinions of our characters; by condemning ourselves on account of something which we cannot define. I am here speaking of my own experience, rather than yours. I have often felt gloom overspreading my mind, without being able to tell on what account I felt it. I believe we may indulge this general indefinite depression and fear without becoming, in any degree, better acquainted with our real characters, without perceiving more distinctly what change must be wrought in us, without distinguishing the true Christian spirit from its counterfeits, and without seeking from divine grace the temper we need to qualify ourselves for heaven. I have suffered so much from indistinctness of views, that I wish to guard you against it. Be not contented with general views of religion. Analyze your heart, and seek to obtain from the word of God just views of the distinguishing exercises of a child of God; and if then you have reason to fear for yourself, you cannot be too much impressed with your danger. On this point, we cannot be too faithful. May God, who searches us, save us from deceiving ourselves on the infinitely interesting concerns of eternity.

In July, Mr. Codman left London for a short tour on the continent, and returned to Edinburgh in the following November. In a letter to his friend he says: "I remained six weeks in Paris, and left it on the 3d of October, after having seen everything that was deserving the attention of one of my profession. I brought three very dear little children of a Mr. White with me, from Paris to England, whose story I shall reserve for a winter's evening. I embarked from Rotterdam, and arrived safe in a land of gospel light and liberty. O, my friend, until you have been deprived of the institutions and ordinances of religion, you can never sufficiently appreciate their value. After spending a few days with our Islington friends, I went to Bristol, on a visit to my uncle, and preached for Mr. Lowell, a Dissenting minister, on the first Sabbath of November. From Bristol, I came immediately to Edinburgh. Before my arrival here, I had received very pressing invitations from my excellent friend, Rev. D. Dickson, Jr., to make his house my home during the winter. He would not allow me to decline; and I am now living on the truly generous hospitality, for which this favored part of the island has been so long distinguished. I cannot be sufficiently grateful to Almighty God, for raising up such kind friends in a foreign land. Surely, goodness and mercy have followed me all the days of my life."

CHAPTER VI.

HIS RETURN TO AMERICA — ORDINATION AS PASTOR OF THE SECOND CHURCH IN DORCHESTER — SERMON OF DR. CHANNING — PARISH DIFFICULTIES — THE "DORCHESTER CONTROVERSY."

In the spring of 1807, Mr. Codman left Edinburgh. At Bristol, he obtained a license to preach, dated April 29, and signed by three ministers of Bristol and Bath,—Samuel Lowell, William Thorp, and William Jay. He was soon invited to preach in the Scotch church of Swallow Street, London, where he continued his labors for about a year. Returning home in 1808, he arrived at Boston in the month of May. In August, he first preached to the Second Church in Dorchester, which had been recently organized. The new meeting-house was dedicated, October 30, 1806. After preaching here on two Sabbaths, the Church and Parish invited him to become their Minister. Before accepting their call, he sent to them a communication, of which the following is an extract:

To the Members of the Second Church of Christ in Dorchester.

My Christian Friends and Brethren,—I have received your unanimous call to settle with you as your Pastor, with sentiments difficult, indeed impossible for me to express. The entire unanimity of the call demands my most devout acknowledgments to the great Head of the Church, and my warmest gratitude to those who have thought it proper to give me their votes.

I have endeavored to lay this very important subject at the footstool of the throne of grace; and to seek that wisdom which cometh from above, which is profitable to direct. It has also been my endeavor to advise with pious and judicious friends, upon a subject so intimately connected with my future happiness. But, before I give a definite answer to your application, I think it my duty to make a few remarks, and to enter *into some explanations*, which are highly important and interesting, both to you and me.

You must be sensible that the office of a Minister of the Gospel is, in the greatest degree, important and responsible. Immortal souls are committed to his charge; and we are assured that the Lord will require their blood at his hands. It becomes him, then, as he regards the commands, and values the favor of the great Jehovah, as he regards his ordination vows, as he values immortal souls, to declare the whole counsel of God, to deliver his message with boldness, to be faithful unto death. He will necessarily sometimes speak of *doctrines* that may not be altogether *congenial* to his hearers. It therefore appears to me highly important, *to prevent future difficulties*, for the people, and especially the Church, in their choice of a Minister, to be fully acquainted with his views, with regard to the peculiar doctrines of the gospel.

The Second Church and Society in Dorchester, before they

gave me a call, had but little opportunity to form an opinion of my theological sentiments, having heard me only two Sabbaths and one lecture. On those occasions, however, I endeavored to be plain, explicit, and decided in the avowal of my religious opinions.

Lest, however, there should be a *doubt* in the mind of any one upon this subject, I think it my duty, in the presence of a heart-searching God, and of this Church, to declare my firm, unshaken faith in those doctrines, that are sometimes called the doctrines of the reformation, the doctrines of the cross, the peculiar doctrines of the gospel.

These doctrines, through the help of God, I intend to preach ; in the faith of these doctrines, I hope to live ; and in the faith of these doctrines, I hope to die.

It gives me great pleasure to have it in my power to say, that I believe my faith is the same with that of our venerable forefathers ; and particularly with that of the former Pastors of the Church of Dorchester, Warham, Maverick, Mather, Burr, &c., &c., &c.

As *Arian* and *Socinian* errors have of late years crept into some of our churches, I think it my duty to declare to that Church of Christ, of whom I may have the pastoral charge, that I believe *the Father, Son, and Holy Ghost, to be the one living and true God;* and that my faith, in general, is conformable to the Assembly's Catechism, and to the Confession of Faith drawn up by the Elders and Messengers of the Congregational Churches in the year 1680, and recommended to the Churches by the General Court of Massachusetts.

With regard to the Discipline of the Church, I shall be guided by that excellent Platform of Church Discipline, drawn up at Cambridge, principally by the Rev. Richard Mather, formerly Minister of Dorchester.

I have thus discharged a duty, which I thought I owed to the Great Head of the Church, and to you, his visible members.

On the 31st October, 1808, it was voted by the Church and Parish to accept the communication of their Pastor elect. Of the same date, was a letter of the Parish Committee, of which the following is an extract:

Dear Friend and Brother,—Although there may be a difference in opinion among us, respecting some parts of the Holy Scriptures, your communication is received with pleasure and general satisfaction; and we venerate the principles of our forefathers, especially the pious and worthy Pastors of the Church of Christ in Dorchester, who have been as shining lights in the golden candlestick; and are happy to find you agree with them in sentiment.

We are sensible that the office of a Minister of the Gospel is, in the highest degree, important and responsible; but if you accept that office, and we are the people of your charge, we hope it will not be rendered difficult or unpleasant, by the want of candor or propriety of conduct on our part, and that no root of bitterness will spring up to trouble us.

In our present imperfect state, various opinions and discordant sentiments will exist, and occasions occur for the exercise of a spirit of condescension, patience and toleration. This spirit we wish to cultivate, as we all acknowledge the same Great Head of the Church, and in him are all brethren; and if we follow his example, shall be all friends.

We all have important duties to perform, and may reasonably

expect many difficulties to encounter; but we hope the guidance and blessing of the Father of lights will attend us, and bring us at last to the knowledge of the truth, and enjoyment of himself, through the merits of our glorious Redeemer.

The way being now prepared, Mr. Codman sent the following answer to the call which he had received:

To the Second Church and Society in Dorchester.

My Christian Friends and Brethren,—The moment has now arrived, when, in the providence of God, I am called to accept the solemn and responsible charge of immortal souls. When I consider the importance of the ministerial character, and the nature and extent of ministerial duty, and when I reflect on my own weakness as a worm of the dust, and on my guilt as a sinner, condemned by the righteous law of a holy God, I am ready to exclaim, "Who is sufficient for these things!" and to wonder at the goodness and grace of God "in counting me faithful, putting me into the ministry."

Sensible, however, that God can employ the weakest instrument to advance his cause, and the chief of sinners to promote his glory, and relying on the promises and encouragements of his holy word, I desire to go forward in the strength of the Lord, to the arduous work of the gospel ministry. I accept the friendly and affectionate call, which you have so unanimously given me, to be your Pastor; and shall endeavor, with a humble reliance on Divine assistance, to discharge with faithfulness the important duties of the pastoral office. The satisfaction with which my communication has been received, and the readiness with which my requests have been granted, are considered by me, as proofs of your attachment, and will always be remembered with lively emotions of gratitude.

The promotion of THAT PEACE, which is founded on *true Christian principle*, and not on *carnal* security; and of *that unanimity*, which is the *effect of the general reception of evangelical truth*, and *not of indifference to religious opinions*, will be the subject of my prayers and the object of my life.

It will be my earnest endeaavor, *as far as consistent with the faithful discharge of ministerial duty*, to promote peace and friendship among the people of my charge, to do all in my power to continue and confirm it among our sister Churches and their Pastors, and to promote the best interests of the University, of which I shall be an overseer.

And now, my Christian friends and brethren, I look to you for encouragement, countenance and support, in the arduous work in which I have engaged. After the explicit declaration which I have made in a late communication, you can be no strangers to the articles of my faith; and I trust you will unite with me 'in holding fast the form of sound words in faith and love, in contending earnestly for the faith once delivered to the saints, lest any man spoil us through philosophy and vain deceit, after the tradition of men, after the rudiments of the world, and not after Christ.'

I ask an interest in your prayers. Frequently think of your Pastor at a throne of grace. Earnestly pray that God would grant him those gifts and graces, which are so essential to a Minister of the Gospel; and that he would make him faithful in declaring the whole counsel of God, and successful in winning souls to Christ.

Accept my prayers for you. Brethren, 'my heart's desire and prayer to God for you is, that you may all be saved.' If I know my own heart, I have no other motive in coming among you than to promote your eternal happiness. 'For what is my hope, or joy, or what will be my crown of rejoicing? Will not even ye, in the presence of our Lord Jesus Christ at his coming? I trust ye will be my glory and my joy.' "And now, brethren, I commend you to God, and to the word of his grace, which is able to build you up, and to give you an inheritance among all them which are sanctified." Believe me to be your willing servant in the gospel of Christ.

Mr. Codman was ordained December 7, 1808, by a Council consisting of the following clergymen of Boston and vicinity:—Rev. Drs. Osgood, Eckley, Porter and Morse, and Rev. Messrs. Huntington, Harris, Pierce, Channing, Bates, Buckminster, Lowell and Gile, all of whom are now deceased excepting Rev. Drs. Bates and Lowell. The following is the *Confession of Faith*, which was presented to the Council:

In conformity to ancient usages in our Churches, and with a dependence on the Spirit of God for illumination and direction, I desire humbly and reverently, in the presence of Almighty God, and before this venerable Council, to make a confession of my faith in the great doctrines of revealed religion.

Existence of God.—I believe in one God, self-existent, immortal, invisible, unchangeable, infinite in wisdom, power and goodness, without beginning of days or end of years.

Holy Scriptures.—I believe that God, out of his sovereign pleasure and boundless goodness, has been pleased to reveal his mind and will in the Scriptures of the Old and New Testament; and I believe that "all Scripture is given by inspiration of God, and is profitable for doctrine, for reproof, for correction, for instruction in righteousness."

I take the Holy Scriptures to be the standard of my faith, and the rule of my practice; and not from the traditions of men, but from that inspired volume alone, I desire to form the articles of my creed.

Trinity.—I believe that the Scriptures reveal, as a *fundamental* doctrine, that there are Three in the Godhead; the Father, the Son, and the Holy Ghost; and that these Three are the One living and true God, the true Jehovah, the Christian's covenanted God, the only proper object of religious worship; and although this doctrine is above my reason, I believe it is not contrary to it, but is to be received with meekness and humility, to be spoken of with reverence and godly fear, and always to be considered as a mystery, which to attempt to explain, is presumption; and which to comprehend, is above the capacity of finite beings.

Decrees of God.—I believe that God, from all eternity, has foreordained whatsoever comes to pass; yet in such a manner as not to be the author of sin, nor to affect the accountability of man. I believe that God has elected some to everlasting life, while others are left to suffer the just punishment due to their sins.

I believe that this doctrine is not without its practical uses, in making us humble, under a sense of our entire insufficiency, and in leading us to attribute our salvation, not to our own works, but to the free and sovereign grace of God.

Creation and Providence.—I believe that God, the Father, Son, and Holy Ghost, created the world and all things therein, visible and invisible, in the space of six days, and that He upholds the same by the word of his power, exercising a general and particular providence over the work of his hands.

Covenant of Works.—I believe that God created man upright, and gave him a law as the rule of his obedience, when he said, "Of every tree of the garden thou mayest freely eat; but of the tree of the knowledge of good and evil thou shalt not eat of it; for in the day that thou eatest thereof, thou shalt surely die." I believe that it thus pleased God to enter into covenant with man, and that the first covenant made with man was a covenant of works, "wherein life was promised to Adam, and in him to all his posterity, upon condition of perfect obedience."

The Fall.—I believe that, enticed by the craft and subtilty of the devil, our first parents disobeyed the command of their Maker, broke his covenant, fell from the estate in which they were created, and thus exposed themselves, and all their posterity, to the penalty of God's most righteous law, temporal, spiritual, and eternal death.

Original Sin and Actual Transgression.—I believe that, in consequence of Adam's transgression, all his posterity are, "by nature, children of wrath;" and, in addition to this original pollution, every one, who arrives at an age to distinguish good from evil, is guilty of actual transgression; and I believe that God might have left our first parents, and all their posterity, to have perished eternally, and his justice have remained uninfringed and unimpaired.

Covenant of Grace.—But I believe that, out of his free and sovereign grace, he has been pleased to have mercy on man, and to enter into another covenant with him, commonly called the covenant of grace, wherein he freely offers sinners life and salvation by Jesus Christ, requiring of them faith in him, that they may be saved.

Jesus Christ.—I believe that God the Father, in his eternal purpose, hath appointed the Lord Jesus Christ to be the only mediator between God and man; and I believe that, in the fullness of time, the second person in the glorious Trinity, who is God over all, blessed forevermore, and who thought it no robbery to be equal with God the Father, condescended to take upon himself the human nature, to be subject to all its infirmities, yet without sin. I believe that he was conceived by the Holy Ghost, born of the Virgin Mary; that he was truly God, and truly man; and I believe that this glorious person, mysteriously uniting the divine and human natures, is the true Christ, the only sure foundation upon which sinful man can build his hopes. I believe that he fulfilled the violated law by a perfectly holy life, and by offering himself on the cross as a sacrifice for sin, thereby satisfying the justice of God, and making an atonement for the sins of men; so that 'God can now be just, and justify every one who believeth in Jesus.' I believe that he descended into the grave; that he rose the third day from the dead; that he ascended into heaven, and now sitteth at the right hand of God the Father, and ever liveth to make intercession for his people.

Holy Ghost.—I believe that the Holy Ghost is the third person in the Godhead; and that it is his office, in the plan of redemption, to renew the hearts of the elect, and to carry on the work of sanctification until the day of Jesus Christ.

Regeneration.—I believe that Regeneration is the immediate work of the Holy Spirit; opening the eyes of the spiritually blind, taking away the heart of stone, and giving a heart of flesh; renewing the will, and changing the disposition from the love of sin to the love of holiness, and from the power of Satan unto God.

Sanctification.—Sanctification, I believe also to be a work of the Spirit, and to be a continuation of the work of regeneration.

Saving Faith.—Saving faith I believe to be the gift of God; and to be that grace by which a sinner receives Christ as offered to him in the gospel, and relies upon his merits for salvation.

Justification by Faith.—I believe that, by the deeds of the law, no flesh shall be justified; but I believe that all God's people are justified by faith in the Son of God, the righteousness of Christ being imputed to them, and they receiving the same by faith.

Adoption.—I believe that those whom God justifies, he adopts into his family, and makes "heirs of God and joint heirs with Christ."

Repentance unto Life.—Repentance unto life I believe to be that grace, by which a sinner mourns for his sins, as offensive to a pure and holy God, and turns from them unto God, resolving, in the strength of the Lord, to keep his commandments.

Good Works.—I believe that good works, a holy life, and blameless conversation, and a general conformity to the moral law, is a requisite evidence of a sincere faith and repentance.

Perseverance of the Saints.—I believe that those who are renewed, justified and sanctified, notwithstanding all the assaults of the world, the flesh and the devil, shall persevere unto the end, and obtain everlasting life.

Invisible and Visible Church.—I believe that Christ has a Church in the world, and that the "gates of hell shall not prevail against it." I believe that this Church is invisible and visible; that the invisible Church consists of all those who are, have been, or ever shall be, gathered into one, under Christ, its head; and that there is a visible Church, consisting of all those who have made a profession of their faith in Christ, with their children. I believe that Christ has instituted two Sacraments in his Church, Baptism and the Lord's Supper.

Baptism.—I believe that Baptism is the mode which God has

been pleased to appoint for admission into the visible Church; and is to be considered as a sign and seal of the covenant of grace, and that it is to be administered to believers and their offspring only.

Lord's Supper.—I believe that the Lord has been pleased to institute the Sacrament of the Lord's Supper, in perpetual commemoration of his death and sufferings, to be observed by all his disciples, and his disciples only, to the end of the world.

Resurrection.—I believe that, after death, the dust shall return to the earth as it was, and the spirit unto God who gave it; and that, at the sound of the last trump, the dead shall be raised, incorruptible, and they which are alive and remain, shall be caught up in the clouds to meet the Lord in the air.

Judgment.—I believe that God has appointed a day wherein he will judge the world in righteousness, by Jesus Christ; when all men shall appear before the judgment-seat of Christ, to give an account of their thoughts, words and actions, and to receive according to what they have done in the body, whether good or evil.

Final State of the Righteous and the Wicked.—I believe that there are distinct states prepared for the righteous and the wicked. A state of endless felicity for the righteous, and of endless torments for the wicked; and that, after sentence is pronounced, the wicked "shall go away into everlasting punishment, but the righteous into life eternal."

JOHN CODMAN.

The Ordination Sermon was preached by the late Rev. Dr. Channing. His subject was, "The importance of a zealous and affectionate performance of ministerial duties." It was an earnest and eloquent exhortation to faithfulness in the office of a minister of the gospel. The following are a few extracts:

"The salvation of man is a leading object in the providence of God. For this, the Son of God himself left the abodes of glory, and expired a victim on the cross! For this, the harmony of creation was disturbed, and stupendous miracles were wrought to attest the gracious promises of God. For this end a church has been erected, and its interests guarded, amidst the convulsions of a sinful world. Heaven is gladdened by the tidings, that a sinner has repented. Angels are sent forth to minister to the heirs of salvation. . . .

"Of all the frowns of Providence, perhaps none is more threatening than the settlement of a cold-hearted, uninstructed minister. . . . Negligent minister! look forward to the tribunal of God. Behold a human being there condemned, whom thy neglect has helped to destroy. In that countenance of anguish and despair, which might have beamed with all the light and purity of heaven; in that voice of weeping and wailing, which might have sung the sweet and happy strains of angels, see and hear the ruin which thou hast made! And canst thou yet be slothful and unconcerned?"

After his settlement, Mr. Codman labored for about a year in quietude and with great success; but the three following years were years of anxiety, controversy and trouble. The origin of these difficulties cannot be explained, except by a declension, among the people, from the faith of the primitive Christians of Dorchester and of the first settlers of New England. Dorchester was the third settled town in Massachusetts, as distinct from Plymouth Colony, being next after Salem and Charlestown. It was settled by a church gathered at Plymouth, in England, which arrived at Nantasket, or Hull, May 30, 1630, having two pastors, John Maverick and John Warham. The former died in 1636, and in the same year the latter removed with the church to Windsor, in Connecticut. A new church was formed in Dorchester, August 23, 1636, of which Richard Mather was the teacher for thirty years. He furnished the model of our Congregational Platform, adopted by the Synod in 1648. His colleagues, for a short time, were Jonathan Burr and John Wilson, Jr. The subsequent ministers were, Josiah Flint, who died in 1680; John Danforth, who died in 1730; Jonathan Bowman, from 1729 to 1773; Moses Everett, from 1774 till his dismission, in 1793; and Dr. Thaddeus M. Harris, who was ordained October 23, 1793, and died in 1842.

In the Right Hand of Fellowship, delivered at the ordination of Mr. Codman, Dr. Harris said, in speaking of the inhabitants of Dorchester, who had been under his pastoral care for fifteen years: "Standing fast in one spirit, and striving together for the *faith of the gospel*, they have paid little attention to lesser matters and words of doubtful disputation, and have been indoctrinated rather in those important truths of religion, in which all agree, than in those speculative topics about which so many differ. The modern distinctions of sect and party are scarcely known, and have never been advocated among them. To be disciples and followers of the LORD JESUS, has been their only endeavor; and to be called CHRISTIANS, the only appellation by which they have aimed or desired to be distinguished. Enter, MY BROTHER, into these my labors. In this portion of the vineyard, may you find the vines flourishing and the clusters fair, and gather fruit unto everlasting life!"

If, in his subsequent experience, Mr. Codman was tempted to say, "Their grapes are grapes of gall, their clusters are bitter," yet he could hardly doubt, that it was in consequence of his plainly preaching those doctrines, of which he expressed his belief in his 'Confession of Faith,' and earnestly enforcing them upon the conscience.

The controversy which ensued, assumed at the outset the ostensible form of a question, 'Whether he had the right of refusing to exchange pulpits, indiscriminately, with the neighboring ministers, with some of whom he did not agree in religious sentiment, and whose teachings he did not think would be profitable to the souls of his people?' At a parish meeting, it was voted, that he "be requested to exchange with the ministers who compose the Boston Association." His reply was in accordance with his reserved rights in his letter accepting his call, that he could not "pledge himself to exchange pulpits with any man, or any body of men whatever." He added: "At the same time you may rest assured that, in my exchanges, as in every part of ministerial duty, it will be my endeavor, as it always has been, to conciliate the affections and to promote the peace and happiness, but especially the spiritual welfare of the people committed to my charge."

In consequence of this reply, the parish voted, by a small majority, that the connection between them and their minister, "become extinct." This, of course, was not in itself an effective measure. In the progress of the proceedings at this period, seventy-three male members of his parish presented to him an affectionate address, in which they said: "Nearly all your parishioners appear satisfied with your performances, and acknowledge you have conformed to the doctrines and principles held out to us in your communication, previous to your ordination; and the foundation of the difficulties, professedly, is your declining to exchange ministerial labors with the Association of Ministers to which you belong." They also acknowledge, that the right was vested in him, "by the custom of ages, to decide in respect to exchanges." This was followed by an address, admirably written, from one hundred and eighty-one female members of his parish, which must have been most consoling and refreshing to his heart. They say: "We, beloved sir, when you were settled as our pastor, echoed the voice of joy that proceeded from our husbands, fathers, brothers and friends; and, although we could not become public advocates for your settlement, the eye of approbation disclosed the happiness of the heart. The power of sympathy has never been denied us; the virtue of sincerity we hope is not withheld. With affectionate sympathy and Christian sincerity, we beseech you to bear up against the host of troubles that beset you, and, like a good soldier of Christ, having on the whole armor of the gospel, we hope you will fight manfully, and come off conqueror, and more than conqueror, in this important conflict."

These women added in their address: "You have this consolation, and our hearts gratefully bear witness to the truth, that your preaching has not been in vain; but that, by a blessing attending your faithful and affectionate administrations of the word, many of us have been awakened, comforted, animated and strengthened."

In the course of this controversy, the parish instructed a committee to write to the ministers, with whom Mr. Codman had been in the habit of exchanging, to request them not to preach in his pulpit again, until difficulties were settled. The ministers written to were, Rev. Drs. Morse, Bates, Griffin and Strong, and Rev. Messrs. Greenough, Homer, Gile and Huntington. But the committee fell into the blunder of thus addressing two members of the Boston Association, when the very complaint against their pastor was, that he would not engage to exchange with the ministers of that Association. It was thus betrayed, that the real objection was to the *religious faith* of the ministers exchanged with.

Rev. Dr. Bates, in his reply, inquired by what right he was interdicted from preaching in exchange with a brother minister, and why he was thus censured and proscribed, and his ministerial character impeached? For his refusal to yield to their request, he assigned four reasons: that his compliance would lend a sanction to such irregular proceedings as the interference of a parish with matters purely ecclesiastical; that it would be taking a part in a parochial controversy; that it would be, in fact, a denouncement of a brother in the ministry, whom he esteemed and loved, and regarded as a faithful minister of Jesus Christ; and that it would have no tendency to promote their lasting peace and happiness.

Rev. Dr. Morse, in his reply, alluded to the fact of his being a member of the council which settled Mr. Codman, and also a member of the same *Boston Association*, saying, "There is an obvious inconsistency in requesting *me* not to preach in his pulpit, merely because, in his exchanges, he selects members of other Associations in preference to those of his own." . . . . "In conformity to the usages of the churches, from time immemorial, he maintains the right of inviting whom he pleases into his pulpit."

When, in the course of the controversy, it was agreed that a mutual council should be called, six of the ministerial members were chosen by the pastor, and six by the parish committee. By the pastor the following ministers were chosen: Rev. Dr. Prentiss of Medfield, Rev. Dr. Lyman of Hatfield, Rev. William Greenough of Newton, Rev. Dr. Austin of Worcester, Rev. Dr. Morse of Charlestown, and Rev. Dr. Worcester of Salem; and by the parish committee, Rev. John Reed of Bridgewater, Rev. Richard R. Elliot of Watertown, Rev. Thomas Thacher of Dedham, Rev. Dr. Bancroft of Worcester, Rev. Dr. Kendall of Weston, and Rev. Nathaniel Thayer of Lancaster.

The council met, October 30, 1811. The cause, on the part of the parish, was conducted by Hon. Samuel Dexter and Benjamin Parsons, Esq., and on the part of Mr. Codman, by Dr. Bates and Daniel Davis, Esq., Solicitor General. There were various charges of imprudence or immorality, but their inventors did not seem to attach any importance to them; and the agents of the parish declared, in the public hearing, that, if the affair of exchanges was yielded, all other difficulties could be settled in five minutes. In the result, the charges in general were pronounced "not supported," or unimportant. The great question was, 'Whether Mr. Codman should be censured for his course in regard to exchanges?' And on this, the council were equally divided.

That the six ministers, chosen by the parish, should vote for this censure, showed very plainly their sympathy with their employers, and that a marked and well understood division, at this early period, existed among the ministers of Massachusetts.

The arguments on each side were, in substance, as follows: on the part of the parish, it was claimed, that, to decline so long to exchange with the members of the Boston Association, was a refusal which amounted to a denial of their ministerial character, a condemnation of a respectable body of men, an impeachment of their fidelity, and tended to stigmatise them as heretics; that it was a needless scruple, for none of them, in *his* pulpit, would enter upon controverted topics; that it was an interruption of the harmony, peace and charity, which should prevail among neighboring societies and their ministers; that a diversity in opinion was no ground for a refusal of communion; and that although the minister had the control of his exchanges, yet the people, too, had their rights, and, if their wishes were not regarded, it was a reason for the dismission of their minister.

On the part of Mr. Codman, it was said, that he had given no pledge and made no promise in regard to exchanges, yet he was always ready to perform what he should find to be his duty; that there was now an attempt to impose upon him a compulsory system of exchanges, unknown in the history of the Protestant churches; that, even in the Boston Association, there is no such compulsion, for some of its members have exchanged with the others, and therefore, by joining that Association, there was no implied engagement as to exchanges; that a minister is responsible for the religious instructions which, by his means, are given to his people, and, therefore, he would be criminal in introducing a preacher of pernicious error; that he may have very good and satisfactory reasons for neglecting to exchange, when the public announcement of these reasons might be improper; that if he himself preaches the true doctrines of the gospel, and exchanges with ministers who preach the same, his people have no reason to complain; that to allow of a parish interference on this subject would lead to contention and incalculable evil, for it would be impossible to satisfy individual preferences and wishes, and even a vote of a majority might be variable from time to time, as had already been experienced; that the clamor in favor of liberality, charity, candor and harmony, was very absurd, for charity "rejoiceth in the truth," and the minister is set for the defence and the promotion of the truth, nor was there any charity and candor in allowing that all others were preachers of the truth, against the most notorious evidence to the contrary; that Mr. Codman brought no charges, however, against any one, but only maintained the right of private judgment in regard to his duty on the point of indiscriminate exchanges; and that it was indeed most wonderful, that in a region deemed the most liberal and free, enlightened and catholic, in the world, there should be this attempt to subject a minister to a system of compulsion.

The precise form of the motion, on which the ministers and delegates were equally divided, was as follows: "That, in the opinion of this council, the aggrieved brethren and the majority of this parish, have just cause of complaint against the Rev. Mr. Codman, for having neglected to exchange ministerial labors with the ministers of the Boston

Association generally." Had this motion prevailed, the purpose was avowed of introducing another motion, advising the dismission of Mr. Codman, unless he would pledge himself on the subject of exchanges.

After this first council, the opposers of the pastor, instead of sitting down quietly under his ministerial labors, persisted in their efforts to effect his removal. They demanded another mutual council, on the failure of which proposition the parish committee was instructed to call an *ex parte* council, and submit to it two questions: First, "Whether Mr. Codman had not given just cause of complaint in regard to exchanges?" Secondly, "Whether his dismission should not take place, on account of the divided and unhappy state of the parish?"

As the parish were determined to prosecute the controversy, the church took measures to give their minister all the support in their power. In a report of their committee, they say: "After three years have elapsed, we are not able to perceive that he has deviated from the course of conduct which he then so explicitly prescribed to himself. On the contrary, we feel ourselves constrained to declare that, in the services of the pulpit, he has laboriously and zealously inculcated those doctrines which he then professed, and has followed them by pressing on the conscience and the heart the duties of Christianity. In his private intercourse with the members of his church and parish, we recognize the disinterested, self-denying, beneficent spirit of the gospel. Large additions have been made to our number under his ministry, the attention of our youth has been directed to religion, and the fruits of the Spirit have appeared, as we conceive, in the increase of vital and practical piety."

Among the reasons which they assign for not consenting to the dismission of their pastor, one is, that they believe the complaint against him, "with respect to exchanges, has been, with many, only ostensible; and that opposition to his religious doctrines is the radical cause of complaint and dissatisfaction, which, we have reason to fear, would not cease or become more tolerable, unless his friends would sacrifice their own principles and feelings, and become entirely subservient to those, whose high professions of liberality do not preserve them from the greatest intolerance."

CHAPTER VII.

THE CONTROVERSY CONTINUED — A SECOND COUNCIL — DOCTRINAL ERRORS OF THE TIMES — VIOLENCE OF THE OPPOSITION — CLOSE OF THE DIFFICULTIES — LETTER OF REV. DR. MILLER — MARRIAGE OF MR. CODMAN — FAMILY AFFLICTION AND ILL HEALTH.

ALL attempts for the settlement of the controversy having failed, another mutual council was agreed upon. This second council, which met May 12, 1812, consisted of nine ministers, four of whom were chosen by Mr. Codman and his friends, and four by his opponents. Rev. Dr. Lathrop, of West Springfield, was chosen moderator and umpire, by mutual agreement. Those chosen by the friends of Mr. Codman were, Rev. Daniel Dana of Newburyport, Rev. Samuel Stearns of Bedford, Rev. Drs. Prentiss of Medfield, and Worcester of Salem; and by the parish, Rev. Dr. Barnard of Salem, Rev. Dr. Reed of Bridgewater, Rev. John Allyne of Duxbury, and Rev. Nathaniel Thayer of Lancaster. The direct question was now proposed, 'Whether the dismission of the pastor was expedient?' The eight ministers, with their delegates, being equally divided in their vote, the moderator, Dr. Lathrop, gave his decision in the negative. At the same time, in explanation of his vote, he stated, that he gave it in the belief that Mr. Codman "would open a more free and liberal intercourse with his ministerial brethren, and thus remove the only objection alleged against him, and the only reason urged for his dismission. Failing to do this," he said, "if again called to vote, he should vote for his dismission."

To many of his friends and those of Mr. Codman, this expression of his views was very unsatisfactory. It was attributed to his mistaken judgment concerning the actual state of religious opinion among the members of the Boston Association. It has been stated, that he supposed they agreed with him in receiving the doctrines of grace, particularly the doctrines of the atonement, of justification by faith, and of the renewing and sanctifying operations of the Holy Spirit. Had he been aware that they differed in sentiment among themselves, from rigid Calvinism down to the lowest Socinianism, it is highly improbable that he would have approved of an indiscriminate exchange; and, by "a more free and liberal intercourse," he must have intended only an exchange with a part of them. In such a condition of things, it is evident that every minister must be left to his own judgment and conscience in the matter of exchanges.

The parish committee still insisted that Mr. Codman should exchange with twelve ministers, whom they named. Although he actually exchanged with two of them, this did not satisfy his opponents. In a letter to him, they asked: "Are one or two stars, though of the first magnitude, to content us for the light which might be derived from all the planets of our system, revolving in regular succession?" Mr. Codman might, perhaps, have had reason to think, that some of these "stars" were not the regular and useful lights of heaven, but distant, wandering planets, reflecting but few rays from the fountain of light in our Christian system.

As to this variety of opinion, and the extreme errors into which some of the members of the Boston Association had fallen, the following remarkable statement was made in a review of two pamphlets relating to the Dorchester controversy, which was published in the Panoplist, in 1814, said to have been written by Jeremiah Evarts, Esq., a delegate from the church in Charlestown to the first council.

"The following opinions," he says, "are held by one or another of that Association, viz: That Christ was a mere man; that no such doctrine as that of the atonement is taught in the Scriptures; that the idea of an atonement is perfectly ridiculous; that the common opinion of conversion is fanatical; that reason is superior to revelation; that the religion of nature is of higher authority than book religion; that repentance of sin is all that is required for the enjoyment of happiness, here or hereafter; that men are justified by their works; that those who do not repent in this world, will become wiser and repent, and be happy in the future world; that there will be no general judgment; that the soul sleeps with the body from death to the resurrection; that Christ made but two considerable additions to the religion of mankind, viz., the *fact* of the resurrection of the body, and the institution of the Christian ministry; that the soul of man is material; and many other unscriptural notions. This description is not given without consideration. With respect to every one of these opinions, we have either heard it delivered from the pulpit, in unequivocal terms, by some member of the Boston Association, or have been assured by competent witnesses, that it was so delivered, or that it was clearly and expressly maintained in conversation. All but two of these opinions have been delivered from the pulpit; and most probably they have also."

On the subject of exchanges, the council unanimously agreed in the following declaration: "While they view it an important privilege of the Christian minister to regulate his exchanges with his brethren, according to the unbiassed dictates of his own mind, they are sensible that this right ought to be exercised with prudence and tenderness. If he treat with wanton disregard, either the wishes of his people or the sensibilities of his ministerial brethren, he is undoubtedly culpable. Errors of this kind, however, are of different degrees, and are not all to be treated with the same severity."

The difficulties were not ended, but matters soon came to a crisis. At a meeting of the parish November 24, 1812, it was again voted by the parish to dismiss their pastor. On the following Sunday, they placed another minister in the pulpit, with a guard on the pulpit stairs, so that Mr. Codman was obliged to preach from the platform below the pulpit; and, after preaching, he retired with his congregation. The parish preacher then went through his services, and, in the afternoon, performed a second service, at the close of which Mr. Codman regained his pulpit and went through his usual labors, having some hundreds of hearers; while the other preacher, much to the confusion of the opposition, had only about fifty.

This strange and unheard-of outrage was so revolting to the public sense of decorum, in the minds of men of all religious denominations, that the opposers of Mr. Codman, by this step, annihilated at once their own power and gave to him the triumph. They soon agreed to sell their pews and to retire from the parish. And thus was the pastor left perfectly free on the subject of exchanges; and the parish now voted as follows: "As it is the important privilege of the Christian minister to regulate his exchanges with his brethren according to the unbiassed dictates of his own mind and conscience, we think it expedient that the parish should agree, that Mr. Codman should not be confined in his exchanges, the advice of any council or member thereof notwithstanding; as the advice that was given was upon the expectation, that the disaffected were to continue active members of the parish, which is not now the case; and that the exercise of this privilege shall not again be made the subject of complaint before an ecclesiastical council in this parish."

It appears that, at this time, of one hundred and fifty church members, all but seven or eight were anxious to retain their pastor; which may show how very unjust and oppressive, in respect to the church, would have been the triumph of the opposers of the minister in the parish.

In arranging the terms of compromise, it was agreed by those who were disaffected towards Mr. Codman, that they would sell their pews and cease to act in the concerns of the parish. The value of the pews purchased was about ten thousand dollars; and of these there remained in the hands of Mr. Codman, after a year or two, pews to the value of about three thousand dollars, which were readily rented. The seceders, in 1813, built a new meeting-house, and became a distinct and Unitarian parish.

Thus ended this protracted controversy. "It was conducted," says the Rev. Dr. Storrs in his funeral discourse, "on the part of the youthful pastor, with a moderation and Christian heroism, rarely exhibited on the broad arena of ecclesiastical strife, even by men of riper years. It was the cause of Heaven and of vital Christianity, which he defended; it was to maintain the faith of the Puritan fathers and their descendants, the Warhams, the Mavericks, and the Mathers, who had preceded him in this fair field, that he strove; it was to win souls to Christ and prepare them for the heavenly city, to the exclusion of every personal consideration and private interest, that he hazarded reputation, endured reviling, and emulated in fortitude the martyr at the stake."

Beyond all doubt, this was a very important controversy in respect to the interests of truth, the honor of the pure gospel, the character of the evangelical ministry, and the rights and the welfare of the churches. It was so felt beyond the bounds of New England, as is evinced by the following letter, written in the period of this controversy, by the Rev. Dr. Miller, who, after the lapse of nearly forty years from its date, recently died at Princeton, where he had long been one of the eminent professors in the theological seminary there established.

New York, November 19, 1810.

My Dear Brother: — I have heard of your troubles. Strange that a set of men who profess to cultivate the spirit, which *may* be called *liberality* itself, should be so illiberal and intolerant towards an orthodox brother! But we may cease to wonder. If it were not so, neither the conclusion of reason nor of Scripture would be fulfilled.

I hope and believe, my dear brother, from what I hear, that you are determined, whatever may occur, to adhere to your original resolution respecting EXCHANGES with ministers of heterodox or doubtful sentiments. I am as firmly persuaded that it is your duty to do so, as I am that it is your duty rather to suffer martyrdom, than to deny the Lord that bought you. I know that some good men are of a different opinion, or at least feel doubtful on the subject. But the more I have reflected on it, the more my mind has become fixed in the conclusion, that no minister, situated as you are, can possibly recede from the ground you have taken, without yielding a most important advantage to the enemy, and without inflicting a deep and lasting injury on the cause of truth.

Exchanging with ministers of known or suspected heterodoxy, appears to me inconsistent with fidelity to our Master in heaven. With the principles which we hold, we should not dare to preach to our people a *false Gospel.* We should consider ourselves, in this case, as falling under the awful denunciation of the Apostle, Gal. i. 9: "If any man preach any other Gospel unto you than that ye have received, let him be accursed." But if we dare not preach another Gospel ourselves, can we be innocently accessory to this sin being committed by others? And is not deliberately sending a man into our pulpits, whom we suspect and more than suspect of heresy, fundamental heresy, something very like being accessory to the propagation of that heresy? It is by no means a sufficient answer to this argument to say, that the persons thus sent to our pulpits, may not openly preach their peculiar sentiments. Even if the *fact* were so, it by no means relieves the difficulty; because the very circumstance of our people seeing us receive a heretic and practically bid him God-speed, will tend exceedingly to diminish their abhorrence of his heresy, and to make them suppose, either that we consider it to be a very small evil, or that we are very inconsistent if not dishonest men. But the *fact* is not commonly so. These men generally preach in such a way, that attentive hearers may readily perceive that they reject every fundamental article of evangelical truth. They are not only betrayed by their omissions, but also, at every turn, by their phraseology and by their theological language; so that, in fact, they seldom enter our pulpits without holding out to our people false grounds of hope. And is this a small evil? I must conclude that the minister, who views it in this light, has not well considered the subject.

But solemn as this consideration is, there is another, which appears to me in every respect equally solemn. It is the tendency of the system of exchanging with heterodox ministers, to banish the peculiar doctrines of the Gospel from our own sermons and our own pulpits. I assume, as the basis of this argument, that preaching the peculiar doctrines of the Gospel in a plain, pointed and pungent manner, is the duty of every Christian minister; and that, without this, he cannot expect the divine blessing on his labors, or hope to see real religion flourishing among the people of his charge. I verily believe, that if an orthodox minister could, in conscience, leave out of his sermons all the peculiar and fundamental doctrines of the Gospel; if, without preaching anything contrary to them, he were silent respecting the total depravity of our nature, regeneration, the divinity and atonement of Christ, &c. &c.; or if, to put the case in the most favorable light, he sometimes advanced those doctrines, but always did it in a *concealed, wrapped up* manner; I verily believe, that by pursuing this course for twenty years, he would banish religion from his church and prepare his people for becoming Arminians, Arians, Socinians, Deists, or any thing that the advocates of error might wish and endeavor to make them. If I wished to banish religion from my church in the most effectual manner, I certainly should not come forward openly and preach heresy. This would excite attention, inquiry, and opposition. But I would endeavor to lull my people asleep by simply withholding the truth; and should expect to succeed, by this method, with the least trouble and in the shortest time possible. Now this negligent, spiritless, smooth kind of preaching, is precisely that which frequent exchanges with the heterodox is calculated to produce. The most pious and faithful minister living, when he goes to the pulpit of a heretical brother, is under the strongest temptation, if not absolutely to *keep back* truth which he supposes would be offensive, at least in a considerable degree to soften and polish it down, that it may be received with as little irritation as possible. Accordingly, he will be apt to take with him to such a place, a discourse prepared upon this plan. If his exchanges be frequent, he will often prepare such discourses. If they become habitual, he will habitually preach those. The consequence is as evident, as it is dreadful. To expect that a man who prepares *many* such sermons, will preach none of them to his own people, is an expectation not to be entertained. And to hope that the mind of that man who preaches frequently in this strain, will suffer no diminution either of evangelical zeal or of ministerial faithfulness, is certainly an unreasonable hope. I think there can be no doubt, that the Apostle Paul, with all the ardor of his zeal for the truth and with all the tenderness of his love to the souls of men, could not, without a miracle, have withstood the influence of such a habit; and that, if he had indulged in it for one or two years, he would have been found at the end of that time a less pointed, a less faithful, and less successful preacher, than before.

You will perceive then my impression to be, that exchange in ministerial services with the heterodox, is not only unfaithfulness to our Maker and his cause, but that it also tends to produce the most unhappy effects on the mind and in the strain of preaching of the orthodox themselves; that, if habitually practiced, it can scarcely fail to lower the evangelical tone of their ministry; to destroy that sacred unction from the Holy One, which can only attend the simplicity that is in Christ; and to produce such an accommodation of their discourses to the tastes and feelings of their heretical hearers, as to render them, in fact, no longer preachers of the Gospel. I think it would not be difficult to point out living examples in conformity to these remarks.

The question has often been asked, What has led to that awful degeneracy of Boston with respect to evangelical truth, which the friends of the faith once delivered to the saints have so long observed and deplored? Various reasons have been assigned for this phenomenon, which has been nearly if not entirely unparalelled in ecclesiastical history; but I acknowledge, that none of these reasons have been satisfactory to me. The licentiousness and derangements of the war were known, and exerted an influence in other places, as well as in Boston. The literary character and inquiring spirit of the clergy have been quite as much distinguished in some other places, as in that town. The same remark might be made with respect to several other considerations usually offered to assist in solving the difficulty.

I have scarcely any remaining doubt, that the principal cause of the effect in question, is to be sought in the subject of this letter, viz: indiscriminate exchanges with all classes of heterodox ministers. And there probably never was a place, in which this system has been carried to such a length, as in Boston. I certainly know of none. These exchanges have almost unavoidably led to a strain of general, pointless, inoffensive preaching, in which all may be disposed to agree. This strain of preaching has of course banished the knowledge and the life of the peculiar doctrines of the gospel from the churches. The greater part of the present race of clergy, bred under such ministrations and finding them most popular, have become their friends and advocates. And the great body of the people, as might have been expected, are distinguished, not so much by their adherence to any distinct, avowed form of heresy, as by a general belief of the innocence of error, and of the almost equal excellence of all modes of faith. The more I reflect on the subject, the more I am persuaded that this has been the principal cause and the natural course of the Boston apostasy; and the stronger conviction do I feel that, wherever the same practice is admitted, similar effects will follow.

Believe it my friend, that practice, whatever it may be, which induces ministers to preach seldom, or superficially, on the peculiar doctrines of the blessed Gospel,—which places the ambassadors of Christ in circumstances in which they consider delicacy as forbidding them to speak often, fully and pointedly, on the great, distinguishing truths of the word of life,—will never fail to have a most unhappy effect on their own souls, and to lay a foundation for irreparable mischief among the people of their charge.

The man who feels willing, or allows himself to be compelled in the composition of every discourse, and especially in those which he is preparing for exchanges, to inquire and balance in his own mind, how far a gay and polite world will allow him to go in declaring his Master's message, degrades his character, dishonors his Master, is treacherous to his trust, and will soon find himself to be left to be filled with his own devices.

I know that there may be a rash and indelicate mode of declaring the truth. I know that a man may be rude, boisterous and violent, in the sacred desk, and call it fidelity. I consider it as the duty of every minister to endeavor to find out acceptable words, by means of which to convey the truth as it is in Jesus. But I would not, for my life, put myself into a situation in which I should habitually or often be tempted to keep back, or accommodate to human prejudices, those great and essential truths which I dare not alter or modify to please any man. I hope, therefore, my dear brother, that you will adhere to your purpose with unalterable firmness. Let neither the frowns nor smiles, the threats nor persuasions, of opponents move you. I know that it is a trying thing, to resist the wishes of those whom we respect, and who respect us. But, in this case, it really appears to me that the cause of truth and righteousness, for generations to come, is involved; and in such a cause, I take it for granted, you are of the opinion that a minister ought to be willing to make any sacrifice, rather than turn to the right hand or to the left. It would afflict me more than I can express, to hear that my friend had become an Arian or Socinian. But, believe me, I should be little less distressed to hear that you had abandoned your original ground with respect to the subject of this letter, and had consented to exchange with the advocates of fundamental error. I should really consider you, in one sense, as having delivered your God to the enemy. I am more and more convinced, that the friends of evangelical truth in Boston and its neighborhood must consent, at least for a time, to be a little and comparatively a despised flock. They must form a little world of their own, and patiently bear all the ridicule and insults of their proud and wealthy foes. If they do this; if, instead of despairing or being impatient in the day of small things, like a band of brothers they humbly wait on God, and, when he tries their faith, instead of being discouraged, still trust in him; if, in short, they take for their model the conduct of the Apostles, when all the wit, and learning, and wealth, and power of the world were leagued against them, they will as certainly finally triumph over the enemies of Christ, as there is a King in the holy hill of Zion. But if they suffer themselves to be distracted and divided; if they are impatient under abuse and contumely; if they are discouraged when difficulties arise; and, especially, if they suffer the desire of emulating their opponents, in worldly wisdom and worldly grandeur, to gain the ascendency in their minds, it is certain that they will be scourged and depressed, if not, as a body, ruined.

My dear brother, I have written in extreme haste. I have not time to be shorter, and scarcely to read over what I have written. I have poured out, however, the feelings of my heart on the subject; and if what I have said should tend, in the least degree, to strengthen your hands, it will afford unfeigned pleasure to your sincere friend and affectionate brother,

SAMUEL MILLER.

There were other friends of Mr. Codman who took a different view of this affair, and who were disposed to say to him: "You are an orthodox preacher; you know and love the truth; you are set for the defence of the gospel. Then preach the gospel honestly, pointedly, and with all the energy of Christian zeal in every sermon, in every pulpit. You are placed in circumstances of peculiar advantage for accomplishing the great work of staying the progress of declension, perhaps of reforming our corrupted and declining churches. You are a native of Boston, of a most respectable family, and this gives you influence. You have property, and are entirely independent as to pecu niary matters. Even the loss of a parish, in this respect, will be nothing to you. Let it be, that fatal errors have been embraced by many ministers around you; yet the errors are, for the most part, concealed. There is no honest boldness, as yet, on the side of heresy. Preach every where the truth, and you may arrest the downward progress. Besides, there are many good Christians in the heretical churches. You may enlighten them and strengthen them, and keep them from being carried away. Imitate the Apostle Paul, who feared not the face of the bigoted Jew, of the besotted idolater, nor of the learned philosopher of Athens. Confine not your labors to congregations already enlightened, but carry a blazing torch into the midst of darkness. This is your duty, and it is also the best policy. If you undertake to judge your brethren, where sentiments are not distinctly known, and select the ministers with whom you will not exchange, you will be accused of uncharitableness and will make difficulty among your own people. But be ready to exchange, and always preach the most solemn and important truth, and you will throw the odium of refusing to exchange upon the men of error. Nor need you fear, that the number of your exchange pulpits will not be soon reduced. If not, you should rejoice that you may go on in the good work of saving those who are in great peril. The time has not yet come, though it will come, for the division of the ministry and the churches; but now is the time for benevolent and earnest labor in every field around you, that you may gather into the fold of truth those who otherwise might be lost. If you are in danger of being corrupted yourself, then consider the example of Paul, of Luther, of Edwards, of Whitefield. Catch more of their burning zeal, and more earnestly seek the grace of God, which can make you faithful even unto death, and then bestow upon you a crown of life."

But this advice would seem to savor somewhat of self-confidence and presumption, and to partake less of deliberate wisdom, and to be less adapted to the peculiarities of the crisis than the advice of Dr. Miller, and of the great body of evangelical ministers whose judgment was the same. The special field of a minister's labor, unless he be a Whitefield, is his own church and parish; and to instruct, guard and guide them, must require all his efforts. To introduce into his pulpit a teacher of error, or of a corrupted gospel, is to counteract his own most earnest purposes. It is not office which makes a minister, but character; the belief, the love, and the inculcation of the pure truth as it is in Jesus Christ. It does not appear, that Mr. Codman was ever dissatisfied with the course which God enabled him to pursue in his difficult situation; and in the close of the Review, already referred to, it is remarked, "that his character has not suffered by the long trials through which he has passed; that his parish is now very flourishing, as more persons attend his ministry than has been the case at any previous time; and that he and many of his friends, in every part of the United States, think there is abundant cause to bless God that the controversy has been brought to so favorable a termination."

In respect to this controversy, the wonderful wisdom of Divine Providence, which brings good out of evil, and makes the depraved passions of the human heart subservient to his purposes of mercy, ought not to be overlooked. A young minister, of a distinguished family, endowed with a plentiful estate, accustomed to the tokens of respect and esteem, would not be likely to choose for himself to enter upon his ministerial course under a cloud of obloquy and abuse, obliged, as he was, to struggle for years against a powerful ecclesiastical party, in the maintenance of his rights, and for the honor and success of the gospel which he preached. But doubtless this unwelcome and severe discipline was precisely the discipline which he needed for his own humiliation, the perfecting of his virtues, and the improvement of his character. In several respects he was peculiarly fitted to be a champion of the cause to be asserted and maintained. He was firmly established in the faith which he professed; he had zeal and courage; and his very wealth, which in other circumstances might tempt to self-indulgence, was here a source of strength, a muniment in the conflict. He waged a weary battle of three years; but he fought wisely, and manfully, and prayerfully, and achieved a very important triumph. Thus he gained a wide reputation and influence, which he could not otherwise have acquired. Had he not been a soldier, he would not, in his age, have had the satisfaction of remembering the conflicts of his youth.

Had he been overcome in the contest, and, driven from his field of labor, succeeded by a preacher of a different system of faith, it is easy to imagine what would have been the result in his own particular parish. The people might have heard from the pulpit many sweet words concerning liberality and charity, the progress of light and exemption from the bigotry of past ages; discourses on the moral virtues, and on the pure and holy example of Jesus; on his death as a martyr to the truth; on his resurrection also, as a proof that our bodies will be raised; exhortations to good works, that the higher rewards of virtue may be obtained, with perhaps some soothing suggestions to the immoral and impious that, in the end it might be well with them and with all men, and that they might hope to reach a humble place in heaven. Under such preaching, there would have been a deep spiritual slumber, or under such guidance immortal men, ignorant of the truth, misguided and deluded, would have traveled to the grave and to the judgment seat of Christ.

But they would not have had a preacher describing their depravity and ruin, teaching the necessity of the renewing of the Holy Ghost in order to their salvation, calling them to repentance and to the exercise of faith in Jesus Christ, that they might be redeemed by his blood, and to the practice of all goodness; warning them of the terrors of the great day of doom, and holding up to their view the glorious, everlasting destiny of the friends of God, and of the true disciples of his crucified

Son, who has gone to prepare mansions for those that love him. They would not have had a preacher discoursing of these things with deep earnestness, and solemnity, and affection, manifesting in every way his solicitude for their religious improvement and immortal welfare. Nor would their minister have had the happiness to welcome, to the table of the Lord Jesus, hundreds of immortal souls, enlightened, through God's blessing on his instructions, renewed and sanctified; and who, as he hoped with unutterable emotions, would be his crown of rejoicing in the day of the Lord.

In the course of this controversy, Mr. Codman formed an intimacy with the family of William Coombs, Esq., of Newburyport, an eminent merchant, and a gentleman of rare and exalted piety, who acted as delegate on the council for his settlement. The intimacy thus formed, led to an acquaintance with a grand-daughter of Mr. Coombs, the eldest daughter of Ebenezer Wheelwright, Esq. of Newburyport, with whom he was united in marriage, January 19, 1813. Of this lady, who still survives, well known and appreciated by a large circle of affectionate friends, we need only say, that she was eminently qualified to fill the important and, in many respects, difficult station, which she was for so many years called to occupy.

In the year 1817, Mr. Codman wrote to his friend, the author, in reference to afflictions which each had experienced: "Those who sleep in Jesus, God will certainly raise to life and glory. With peculiar satisfaction I learned, from Professors Hall and Hough, the excellent and respectable character and rising eminence of your brother in Middlebury College. But God's ways are not as our ways. My friend, we have always been peculiarly united. For nearly twenty years, we have traveled together in the journey of life. We were married within a few days of each other, and have each been blessed with three dear children. But, alas, two of mine are not, and but one boy remains. Oh, my friend, although you have met with severe domestic afflictions, you have not yet lost a child; and I pray God, of his infinite mercy, to spare you the painful stroke."

January 27, 1822, he wrote in reference to the commencement at Cambridge: "I am particularly desirous that you should attend this year, so as to meet the class on the evening preceding. You will recollect, that twenty years have passed since we took leave of our alma mater. It is quite an epoch in our class history, and we hope to have a very general attendance of the class. It is remarkable that, in a class of sixty, but fourteen are deceased during that period. Before the expiration of such another era, how many of us will have taken our leave forever of all human associations!* In the light of eternity, my dear friend, how trifling, how insignificant do all human honors appear. How important that honor which cometh from God only!"

In regard to the title of Doctor of Divinity about to be given him by Princeton College, he says: "Of the distinction to which you allude, I had already received some hints from another quarter. I trust I can truly say, that the longer I live the less important do such things appear. I most sincerely reciprocate your wish, that we may be more *divine* and heavenly in our temper and lives, and be excited to teach others with greater fidelity and pleasure the grand principles of the gospel."

March 12, 1823, he writes: "My health has been very indifferent all winter. In October last I

* The writer, and seventeen other classmates of Dr. Codman, passed Commencement Day together in 1852, half a century after their graduation at Cambridge. They did not forget their recently departed friend.

had a fall from my horse, striking my head, which deprived me of my recollection, and I felt myself in danger of inflammation of the brain, or extravasation of some of the vessels in the head. I have never been brought so near, in my apprehension, to the eternal world; and may God grant that I may be the better for this correction of his providence. Bleeding and a general system of depletion reduced me very low, and sensibly affected my nervous system. I am now, blessed be God, in comfortable health, and, as the physicians assure me, out of danger from the fall. I am still subject to seasons of depression, and have been advised to take a voyage to Europe for the recovery of my health and spirits."

Alluding to another accident of a similar nature, he writes, April 13, 1824: "Since we last met, I have passed through a long and painful confinement, occasioned by a fall in attempting to mount a horse. I dislocated my right shoulder, and injured my left arm to such an extent that it is doubtful if I shall ever recover the perfect use of it. For nearly three months, I was prevented from the customary discharge of ministerial duty. My general health and spirits suffered much, but, through divine mercy, are now restored. In a little while, my dear friend, our boys will be taking our places, and we shall be gone. I have had much occasion to familiarize my mind with the solemn thought of death. Oh that we may be prepared for that great change! I ask your prayers for me, that I may be found faithful. It is a delightful consideration, that friendship, which has religion for its basis, will continue through eternity."

The life of the pastor of a country parish offers but little of stirring incident to interest the public. Happy in the faithful and diligent discharge of the duties of his office, and in the devoted affection of his flock, he exercised over them that silent and yet powerful influence by which the character of a people is generally moulded. In the children belonging to his charge, he ever took a deep and lively interest, often assembling them, according to the custom of 'the good old time,' for catechising; delighting to lead them in the way of truth, and looking forward to the period when those, whom he had consecrated to God in baptism, should rise up and take the places of their fathers. He was highly fitted to enjoy domestic life; and, surrounded by a large circle of affectionate relatives and friends, living in the midst of the most attractive charms of nature, and exercising an unbounded hospitality, the sun of earthly prosperity seemed to shine upon him with almost unclouded brightness. He was remarkable for a grateful appreciation of all the mercies which surrounded him, delighting to trace, in all the rich bounties of Providence, the hand of an indulgent Father, and ever ready to employ all the means in his power for doing good.

CHAPTER VIII.

JOURNEY TO THE SOUTH—A CHRISTIAN PLANTER—SAVANNAH AND FAIRFIELD—VOYAGE TO ENGLAND—INTERVIEWS WITH OLD FRIENDS—REV. DR. CHALMERS—MRS. HANNAH MORE AND "BARLEY WOOD"—ROWLAND HILL—THIRD VISIT TO EUROPE—LETTERS—LAST VISIT TO ENGLAND—RELIGIOUS ANNIVERSARIES.

Dr. Codman's health and spirits had suffered so severely from the effects of the accident, to which he alludes, that a sea voyage was considered by his physician indispensable to their restoration. Accordingly, on the 11th of November, 1824, accompanied by Mrs. Codman and a female relative, he embarked in the ship Emerald, Capt. Howes, for Savannah. In that city, and in Charleston, he passed a few months in very pleasant intercourse with ministers and excellent Christians of his acquaintance, occasionally preaching for his brethren. A visit to Richmond, the seat of Mr. Clay, gave some insight into the management of a slave plantation by a kind and Christian master. We have the following account of it: "At a short distance from the house is a small village of negro huts, (which they call the street,) consisting of thirty or forty buildings, all of which, with their inhabitants, are the property of Mr. Clay. As we entered the street, we found the different families employed in assorting cotton. Each house has a small coop for poultry attached to it, and a portion of land is set apart for each family, which they are at liberty to cultivate for themselves after they have fulfilled their tasks. As we stood talking with some of the children, an old black man came up to us, by the name of Scipio. He is upwards of seventy years old, and we soon discovered, that he was pious and intelligent, acting the part of priest, physician and nurse, in the village. Mr. Clay told us that he was in the habit of collecting all the blacks together, every evening, to attend prayers,—a duty which he himself performed in their behalf."

The following account of a Sabbath passed at Fairfield, the seat of Colonel Law, may be read with interest. The church alluded to was at a place called Midway,* and was built by emigrants

* Of this church an uncle of the writer, Rev. Moses Allen, a native of Northampton, was the pastor when his meeting-house was burnt, in the war of the Revolution. In attempting to escape by swimming from a prison-ship at Savannah, he was drowned February 8, 1779, aged thirty years.

from Dorchester, Massachusetts: "Soon after breakfast we prepared ourselves to attend church about nine miles distant from Col. Law's. On our way, which was principally through a thick wood, we passed many negroes, neatly attired, walking to the house of God in company. As we approached the church, a great number of carriages were coming in every direction to this sacred spot, which is far from the habitations of men, and surrounded only by the grave-yard and a few little houses and arbors, erected for the convenience of the congregation, who come from such a distance that, in some instances, they take their whole families with them. There is an intermission of about half an hour, and this interval is spent by the whites in the buildings and arbors around the church. The blacks, meanwhile, retire with their leader or watchman to the woods, where they are reminded of the truths to which they have been attending, by one of their own number, whom they call an 'exhorter.' I preached morning and afternoon to a very attentive audience. The singing was performed in the old-fashioned style, and without any select choir. The members of this church retain the primitive faith which their ancestors embraced, and are extremely fearful of innovations. There are about six hundred communicants, including the blacks, and the ordinance is administered once in three months. The blacks have watchmen, as they are called, whose duty it is to see that they walk circumspectly; and, in case of deviation, to report the same to the church, which has ever maintained a wholesome discipline. Thus has passed this interesting Sabbath, which may truly be called a 'Peep at the Pilgrims,' and carries one back in feeling to the early settlement of our country, when the church was indeed in the wilderness, and the disciples of Christ a distinct and peculiar people."

On the first of February, Dr. Codman and his companions embarked again on board the Emerald, for Liverpool. Little occurred to vary the monotony of a sea voyage. Dr. Codman performed divine service in the cabin, whenever the weather would permit. They arrived at Liverpool on the morning of February 28; and, after a few days occupied in viewing the objects of interest there, they proceeded to Manchester. Their visit to that place was rendered peculiarly interesting, by some circumstances connected with an acquaintance which Dr. Codman had formed, during his previous visit to Europe, with Mr. White, of Manchester, who was then residing in Paris, to which he alludes in a letter written about that period. He always retained a most affectionate interest in the family of Mr. White; and, in after years, delighted to relate to his own children the story of his little adopted ones, as he always called them.

The following is the interesting account of the circumstances connected with this family:—When Dr. Codman visited Europe, in the year 1806, he was introduced to an English gentleman in Paris, by the name of White, whose lady had recently died and left him with the care of five small children. The friends of Mrs. White, who resided at Seven Oaks, in Kent, on hearing of her decease, requested that, if it were possible, the three eldest children might be sent over to them, and they would adopt them as their own. But the difficulties then existing between France and England, seemed to render such an arrangement quite impracticable. It was about this time that Dr. Codman was introduced to Mr. White and his lovely little family, in whom he became much interested. Mr. White stated to him the difficult situation in which he was placed with regard to the children, and his desire to get them over to their friends. Dr. Codman was about leaving Paris for England, by the way of Holland; and, being an American, there was not much difficulty attending his return. After considerable deliberation, he told Mr. White that if he would intrust him with the care of his children, he would endeavor to take them safely over to their friends. The proposal was gratefully acceded to; and in a few days the children, with an attentive nurse and a man servant, under the care of their new protector, left Paris in the diligence for Rotterdam. The eldest of the children was about eight years of age, and the youngest, four. They were familiar with but few words of the English language, excepting a hymn which their mother had taught them, and the Lord's prayer. They would kneel and repeat this on every evening of their journey, and then unite in singing that sweet hymn:

> "My God, how endless is thy love,
> Thy gifts are every evening new," &c.

Their party occupied all the seats in the diligence excepting one, which was taken by a Frenchman, who was very inquisitive to know something about the children, remarking to Dr. Codman, that he was quite a young man to be the father of such a family. Dr. Codman discouraged any conversation, on the ground that he was but little acquainted with the French language, so that the gentleman suppressed his curiosity for the remainder of the journey. The nurse accompanied them as far as Antwerp, and then returned to Paris. When they reached Rotterdam it was late in the evening, and the children were put into their beds very weary. In the mean time, there was a report in circulation, that the children were the offspring of English parents. On being informed of this, Dr. Codman hardly knew what course to pursue; but finally concluded to take the children from their beds and go with them himself to the French commandant, and let his servant state all the circumstances of the case and plead in their behalf. This the servant managed so well that, before he had finished his story, the commandant burst into tears, took the children in his arms and kissed them, saying, "If they were the children of King George, I would let them go." He at once signed their passports, and in the morning they set off for the Briel, and took passage in a vessel bound for England. Dr. Codman flattered himself that he had no more difficulties of this kind to encounter; but on presenting his passport, he was told that it was defective, not having been signed by the commandant at the Hague. All entreaty was vain; and, finding that the children would be permitted to go, he committed them to the care of an American gentleman on board, and returned to the Hague. Having succeeded in obtaining the necessary signature to his passport, he set off again for the Briel. Day was just beginning to dawn, as he approached the landing; and, to his great joy, he found the vessel still detained by a head wind. He was soon on board; and, the wind changing in the course of an hour, they set sail for England, where the children were safely delivered to their friends.

It was the recollection of this adventure, which gave a peculiar interest to Dr. Codman's visit to Manchester, after the lapse of so many years. He found Mr. White still living in that town, though quite an invalid. He had suffered from several attacks of paralysis, which had so weakened his mind that it was a long time before he could be made sensible with whom he was conversing. But when he was convinced that it was indeed Dr. Codman, he extended his hand with all the warmth of friendship, and gave an account of the state of his family and situation of his children. He promised that the two eldest should pass the evening with Dr. Codman at his lodgings, without informing them whom they were to meet. They accordingly came; and, though twenty years had elapsed since they had seen their protector, the eldest had a perfect recollection of him, and mentioned a number of circumstances that took place on their journey, which Dr. Codman had forgotten. This interview was the more delightful to Dr. Codman, when he found that both the young men were pious, and had made a profession of their faith in Christ. One of them had been engaged in the early part of the evening at a charity school, and he produced from his pocket "Janeway's Token for Children," which Dr. Codman had given him when he was four years old, and from which he had been instructing the poor children connected with the charity school.

Mrs. Codman's journal, written in the familiar style of letters, contains many interesting incidents of this journey; but, passing over much that might otherwise engage our attention, we make such extracts only as may seem most appropriate to our present purpose. Their visit to Scotland, and the renewal of Dr. Codman's intimacy with early friends in Edinburgh, were among the most delightful reminiscences of this tour.

On the fourth of April, Dr. and Mrs. Codman made a visit to St. Andrews, where they were received with great kindness by Rev. Dr. Chalmers and his lady.

We dined with them, and then proposed going to Cupar to pass the night, to which Dr. Chalmers would not consent; and, after we had concluded to stay, he introduced us to a young gentleman, who offered his services in showing us about the place. In the evening, we went with Dr. Chalmers to an obscure part of the town, to attend the first missionary concert for prayer that was ever held in St. Andrews. This gave us an opportunity of seeing Dr. Chalmers to the best advantage. He is, at present, exceedingly interested in the subject of missions, and had taken great pains in preparing for the exercises of the evening. His object was to give the people a history of missions from the beginning, in as concise a manner as possible; and for this purpose he had condensed a great body of materials, so that he might exhibit the whole subject, in all its important bearings, at one view. In doing this, he made large extracts from his own sermons, which he delivered in a very animated and energetic manner, so as to give us a perfect idea of his mode of preaching. After our return home, which was between nine and ten o'clock, he devoted his whole time to us; and, as we were seated around the supper table, partaking of minced collops and oatmeal cakes, he entered into conversation in the most lively and animated manner, using at the same time various gestures, expressive of the interest which he felt in the subject of conversation. *Edwards* was one part of his theme; and, after pronouncing an eulogium upon this great and good man, he lifted both hands and exclaimed: "Oh, he was the glory of America."

In person, Dr. Chalmers is of middling size. His complexion is light and pale, and his face is deeply marked with the small-pox. His eye is of a filmy blue, and devoid of animation. He has a fine broad forehead, but it is not until he speaks, that one can discover any thing in his countenance to interest or please. It is seldom that the mouth gives the whole expression to the face, but it is remarkably so in this case; and one can hardly be said to have seen Dr. Chalmers, who has not seen him smile or heard him speak.

At Rothsay, in the Isle of Bute, Dr. Codman visited his old friend Mr. Denoon, the parish minister, who preaches partly in the Gaelic language, having the charge of the whole parish, or island, of six thousand souls. The living is in the gift of the Marquis of Bute, who is much attached to Mr. Denoon and frequently visits him, patronizes Sabbath schools in the parish, and offers to remunerate any expense that may occur in the establishment or continuance of them.

Passing over a visit to many objects of interest in Ireland, we come to the following account of an interview with Mrs. Hannah More.

May 4.—The events of this day have been of a peculiarly interesting nature, and such as will long be remembered. After breakfast, Mrs. B—— proposed taking us in her carriage to "Barley Wood," the residence of Mrs. More. We were informed, at the door, that she was not so well as usual to-day, but that she would see us with pleasure. We were then conducted to her bed-chamber, where we found her seated in an easy-chair. She rose at our entrance, extended her hand, and gave us a most cordial reception. Her person interested us exceedingly. She has a fine countenance, full of animation, and expressive of every thing kind and benevolent. She wore a plain lace cap, with a wreath of white ribbon in front, and her hair was slightly powdered. Dr. Codman took the chair next her; and, while conversing with him, her countenance brightened, and she occasionally laid her hand upon his arm,—a gesture expressive of the interest which she felt in the subject of conversation. When Dr. Codman remarked that he had not seen her last work, she at once handed him a copy of it, saying, "I will make you a present of it. It was compiled during my late illness, and was intended as a death-bed present to my friends." She then wrote his name on the leaf, without using her glasses, for which she said she seldom had occasion. She remarked, that it had pleased God to deprived her of both taste and smell, "which," she said, "you may think somewhat afflictive; but no, for I have been doomed for the last eight years to live upon medicines, and I can see the kindness of my Heavenly Father in continuing to me the two intellectual senses, seeing and hearing, while he has deprived me only of those which, under existing circumstances, would have been a source of misery." On a table before her lay a box made of mulberry wood, which, in her youth, she had taken from a tree, planted by the hand of Shakespeare. We read aloud, at her request, the lines she had inscribed upon it:

"I kissed the ground where Shakespeare's ashes lay,
And bore this relic of the bard away. 1767."

The room in which she received us was furnished in a very simple manner. One part of it contains her library, and in the other part there is a bow with three windows, down to the floor. In this bow, a large number of beautiful plants and flowers were arranged. Beside her was a table composed of parts of the different kinds of trees, growing at Barley Wood, all of which she had planted with her own hand, excepting one, which was put into the ground by her friend, Bishop Porteus, and was distinguished from the rest by its peculiar color and texture. Some ladies, who were present, introduced the Catholic question, a subject in which her feelings were warmly interested, and she inquired of Dr. Codman, with great earnestness, whether he had read the speech of the Duke of York, and expressed much anxiety lest the bill for the emancipation of the Catholics should pass the House of Lords. Something had previously been said on the subject of slavery in our southern States, and Mrs. More remarked, that if she could live to see that evil remedied in our country, and the question above alluded to settled according to her views, she could say, "Now let thy servant depart in peace." As we were leaving, Mrs. More begged us to walk about her grounds, and visit the monuments which she had erected to the memory of Locke, and of her friend Porteus. We walked through a winding path, bordered by shrubbery, with here and there a little rural house, which had been erected for the accommodation of Mrs. More and her friends, in their rambles through this delightful solitude. Near where we stood, on the top of the hill, was the monument to Locke presented by Lady Montague to Mrs. More; and the birth-place of this distinguished man may be seen in the village over against it.

May 11.—The great missionary meeting of the Dissenters was held to-day in Surry Chapel. Dr. Morrison, of China, preached a very appropriate sermon; after which, Rowland Hill rose in the desk below and made an address. He concluded by saying, that he hoped a large collection would be made, and that the people of Surry Chapel would not be backward in the good work; that he should hold one of the plates at the door, and hoped his hearers, as they passed out, would heap up his plate full. As we went out by way of the vestry door, we saw the old gentleman standing and presenting his plate to those passing him, and at the same time gathering up in his hand a few stray half-pence, which had fallen in among the silver, saying, in a low voice, "I will take up all these as fast as they come and put them into my pocket, lest others, seeing them, should drop in theirs also instead of silver."

May 16.—We went to Queen Street Chapel, to hear Mr. Irving. He gave us a sermon nearly three hours in length, from the seventh chapter of Daniel; but confined his discourse principally to the Book of Revelation, which he represented as one great drama, divided into a number of scenes, interspersed with choruses sung by the heavenly hosts. His manner was very terrible, and well accorded with some parts of his subject.

On the sixth of June, Dr. Codman and his friends made a journey to Paris; and, on their return, visited the Isle of Wight, lingering with great interest among the scenes associated with the memory of Leigh Richmond. In July, they sailed from Liverpool, in the Emerald, for Boston, with several very agreeable passengers, and arrived on the 30th of August.

After a lapse of about ten years devoted to his pastoral labors, Dr. Codman was again induced to cross the Atlantic. At the meeting of the General Association of Massachusetts, in June, 1834, he was appointed a delegate to represent that body at the annual meeting of the Congregational Union of England and Wales, in London. With the intention of passing the preceding winter on the continent of Europe, he embarked at New York for Havre, in the ship Silvie de Grasse, October 16, 1834, accompanied by a part of his family. It will be unnecessary here to give the particulars of this journey, as, on his return, he published an account of the religious anniversaries in London, together with a rapid sketch of his tour on the continent, in a small volume, entitled, "Visit to England." He returned to America in September, 1835. His people received him with a most warm and affectionate welcome, and he engaged anew in his ministerial labors with undiminished usefulness. In about five years, one hundred members were added to his church; and the demands upon his time, in various fields of labor, for the advancement of the kingdom of Christ, continually increased. In a letter dated October 20, 1841, he writes:

Things go on with us very quietly. All we need is more attention to the subject of religion, and this we need greatly. "Pray for us, that the word of the Lord may have free course, and be glorified." I feel that I have great reason for gratitude, for the innumerable blessings I enjoy; and for none more so, than the blessing of health with which I have been highly favored. Though approaching to threescore, I am still able to discharge all my ministerial duties with comfort, and can scarcely realize that I am growing *old;* but it cannot be denied. My dear friend, may God grant that we may both bring forth fruit in old age, and that our friendship may continue firm and ardent, as it was in the days of our youth.

To show his tender and affectionate interest in the spiritual, as well as temporal welfare of those whom he loved, a few extracts of letters, written to a beloved sister-in-law, whose attention had been called to the subject of religion, may here be introduced:

JUNE 3.

I am obliged to you, my dear sister, for the freedom with which you have written respecting the state of your mind. It would give me the greatest delight to be the instrument of helping you on your way to Zion. You ask me if, by approaching the table of the Lord, you may hope to have your heart warmed, &c. I can only say, that I have found this ordinance a source of comfort and joy which I cannot describe; and though I have often lamented my coldness and insensibility, and have been deeply sensible of my unworthiness to sit down at the table, yet I have never regretted being united with the church of Christ. Far be it from me to urge you to make a profession of religion. I would not do so upon any consideration. My object in my last letter was only to call your attention to the subject, and I should not have done even this, had I not entertained a hope that you had experienced the power of religion; in which case I conceive it is the duty of every one openly to profess Christ before men. Whether this is your case, my dear sister, you may form some opinion. Let me advise you to examine yourself faithfully by the rules contained in the word of God. At the same time that you are strict and close in the examination, remember that we must not despise the day of small things; that the *weakest* believer is a suitable guest for the table of the Lord, and that a merciful Saviour will not break the bruised reed nor quench the smoking flax. May the Lord direct and bless you. May he discover to you your duty, and enable you to perform it.

JUNE 23.

I know that you have it in contemplation to make a profession of religion, to enter into an everlasting covenant with the Lord your God; and I feel it my duty to write to you freely upon this subject, in the hope of removing any difficulties which you may feel, and of confirming you in the path which you have begun to tread.

I presume that the principal difficulty which now lies in your way, is a consciousness of not being prepared for such an important and solemn duty. You feel that you have so many corruptions, which are yet unsubdued; that you are afraid, in your present state, to approach the table of the Lord. My dear sister, you must remember that sanctification is a progressive work, and that the ordinance of the Lord's supper is one of the means which God has appointed for carrying it on in our souls. It is sufficient, if we have reason to entertain the hope, that God has begun the good work in us. We are encouraged, without delay, to connect ourselves with the visible church; to avail ourselves of all the privileges it affords, in order that we may grow in grace, and in the knowledge of our Lord and Saviour Jesus Christ. The table of the Lord is spread, I conceive, for *babes in Christ* as well as for the more advanced and experienced Christian. There we may hope to have our faith increased, our love excited, our hope animated, and all our graces nourished. It is true, that much will be expected of those who make a public profession of religion; but I trust this does not operate as an objection in your mind. If I am not greatly mistaken, you have forever renounced the world, and are willing to come out and be separate, to take up your cross and follow Christ. You will from this time, I have no doubt, be a companion of those who fear God, and will never choose for intimate friends those who are strangers to the power of religion.

In this day of delusion and error, when the enemy has come in like a flood, and when men will not endure sound doctrine, I have no doubt that you will be decided in your attachment to those doctrines which are calculated to debase the sinner and exalt the Saviour. You will not for a moment listen to the insinuating arguments of those who wish to be considered liberal Christians, but who "deny the Lord who bought them." My dear sister, may you never cease to be attached to the peculiar doctrines of the gospel. Let it always be the language of your heart: "God forbid that I should glory, save in the cross of our Lord Jesus Christ, by whom the world is crucified unto me and I unto the world."

In the year 1845, Dr. Codman made his last visit to Europe. He sailed from Boston, accompanied by his youngest son, on the first of April, in the steamship Cambria; and was absent from home about six months, spending most of his time among his early friends in England and Scotland. This frequent renewal of intercourse with those whom he had known and loved in former years, was tinged with sadness by the changes wrought by the hand of time, and the breaches made in the pleasant circle during each successive separation. Some, who very dear to him, had been called to their reward since his last visit; and it was with a full heart that he offered, to their surviving families and friends, the tribute of his affectionate sympathy. He had the happiness of seeing again his old friends at Islington, and Drs. Reed, Matheson, Burder and Raffles. He went one morning to Swallow Street Chapel, where he had preached thirty-six years before; but the condition of this Scotch Church was now changed, for, in the Free Church movement, many of its excellent members had seceded and formed a new congregation.

It was his privilege again to be present at the interesting anniversaries of the benevolent societies in London, in the month of May. At the meeting of the British and Foreign Bible Society, Lord Teignmouth, son of the first president, presided, and Dr. Codman, as delegate from the American Bible Society, made a speech, which was very favorably received, and was afterwards published. Other addresses were made by the Bishops of Norwich and Chester, Dr. Cumming of Scotland, and others. Dr. Codman was also invited to address the Religious Tract Society, on its forty-sixth anniversary. He spoke again at the fifty-first anniversary of the London Missionary Society, at Exeter Hall. One of the most eloquent speakers on these occasions was Dr. Cumming, a zealous supporter of the National Scotch Establishment, in an interview with whom, Dr. Codman was happy to learn that, notwithstanding the secession of the

Free Church, in Scotland, there yet remained in the Establishment many evangelical ministers, who knew, and loved, and preached the truth, as it is in Jesus Christ. At the meeting of the Congregational Union of England and Wales, he met with two or three hundred ministers, among whom he was happy to be introduced to Dr. Harris and Mr. Jenkyn, and to greet again many of his old friends.

Dr. Codman made a rapid tour through France, Italy, and Germany. At Hamburg he passed a few days, and enjoyed the opportunity of very pleasant intercourse with the relatives of his son-in-law, to whose kindness and hospitality he was very much indebted. On the seventh of August, he breakfasted with Dr. Chalmers, in Edinburgh, and had an interesting interview with him. At parting, the latter inquired, when they should see each other again. Dr. Codman replied, that he hoped to visit Europe again in 1848. "O, then," said Dr. Chalmers, "we shall meet again in '48." Little did either of them imagine that, ere that period arrived, their glorified spirits would indeed meet, unrestricted by the limits which bound our earthly intercourse, in that world where they should together receive the reward promised to the good and faithful servant.

Dr. Codman preached at the Free Church in Kenmore, near Taymouth Castle, the seat of the Marquis of Breadalbane, on Sunday, August 10. In the evening, he dined at the Castle, and was very hospitably received by the Earl and his Lady. On the nineteenth of August, he sailed from Liverpool in the Caledonia; and after an unusually rough and stormy passage, arrived in Boston, September 3, 1845.

CHAPTER IX.

HIS LAST SICKNESS AND DEATH.

The closing scenes in the life of every true minister of Christ are of deep interest. He is now about to put off his armor, and to rest from his labors. Like the holy Apostle, he can say: "I have fought a good fight, I have finished my course, I have kept the faith. Henceforth there is laid up for me a crown of righteousness, which the Lord, the righteous Judge, shall give me at that day."

The faithful pastor is now standing on the outposts of life. He has heard the summons, which warns him that his work is done; and he solemnly reviews his ministry. He is conscious that he has declared the whole counsel of God. He sees around him many who have listened to his warnings, and, through his instructions and persuasions, have turned from the love of the world to the love of God. He looks back to the scenes of his early ministry, to the friends who have counselled him in his difficulties, and supported him by their prayers; but they have gone before him to the world of spirits. He attended them with a pastor's love to the borders of death, and cheered their departing moments with the hopes and consolations of the gospel. He wept with surviving friends, and performed the last sad offices of burial. A new generation has risen in their places; but they are the children whom he baptized, and whom he has instructed and guided in the path of life. The bond of love, which united him to the fathers, and which was broken in death, has been twined around the hearts of the children. They loved and venerated the man of God. His deep solicitude for their temporal and eternal good, had filled their hearts with gratitude. Under his counsels, his watchfulness, and his prayers, they were trained for God and heaven; and it was their delight to gladden his declining years with tokens of unwavering confidence and increasing love. But they, too, heard the voice of God, and saw the approaching messenger of death. A deep gloom gathered over the church and congregation, as the hour drew near when they must part with their beloved pastor. Their beautiful sanctuary was filled with mourners for weeks before the symbols of death were hung upon its walls. Many a tear flowed, many an earnest prayer was offered for the pastor's life; and a solemn pause in the eager pursuits of the world attested the general sorrow.

But how was it with the pastor himself? The time of his departure was at hand; and he was ready. Those holy doctrines which he had so faithfully preached, and which had gathered around him the fairest fruits of evangelical faith, were now his trust and confidence, and the foundation of his own hopes. In the midst of the severest trials of his youthful ministry, when urgently pressed to yield to the liberal influences of the day, he publicly declared, "In the faith of these doctrines I desire to live, and in the faith of these doctrines I hope to die." And he died in the faith of them.

The closing events in the life of our departed friend, are now to be briefly narrated. In the month of June, 1847, he was admonished, by a violent illness, that he was liable to sudden and speedy death. He soon recovered partially from this attack; but the symptoms of his disease left little doubt, in his mind, that his life was near its close. He hoped, nevertheless, by suspending his labors for a time, to recover strength for yet more service in the cause of his Master. He was able, in the month of September, to attend a meeting of the American Board of Commissioners for Foreign Missions, at Buffalo, of which he had for many years been a member.

In a letter, of November sixth, to his friend, he says: "I returned from Buffalo in excellent health, and had a pleasant journey; but immediately after my return I was seized with a severe influenza and cold, the effects of which remain, in great difficulty of breathing, so much so that I am obliged entirely to suspend for the present the labors of the pulpit. I am this morning going into the city to consult Dr. Jackson." After speaking of some occurrences in his family, he added: "I have reason to be thankful for domestic blessings, but am admonished, by present symptoms, that I may be suddenly removed from them to another world. O that we may be prepared for that great change which awaits us."

On the third of December following, he wrote to the same friend, as follows: "Since I last wrote you, I have been entirely laid aside from preaching, and it is doubtful whether I shall ever be able to preach again. Very laborious breathing, arising from some difficulty in the heart, occasions at times great distress; and, although my physician assures me that there is no immediate danger of a fatal result, I feel admonished to prepare for the event. It would give me great pleasure to receive a visit from you, could you spare time from other engagements. Our old and constant friendship affords me great comfort in the review, and I trust that we may be prepared to renew it in a better world."

In compliance with his wishes, his old friend immediately made him a visit, and passed a few days with him,—the last days of their intercourse on the earth. Dr. Codman was now very ill, though able to walk, and occasionally to ride out. It was the wish of his physician and his family, that his feelings of discouragement, as to the recovery of his strength, might be counteracted, so that the aid of hope might accompany his medical treatment. His own judgment, however, seemed to be fixed, that he was near the close of his days; and his great desire was, evidently, that he might set his house in order, and obey the summons of his Lord. His friend assisted him in arranging his affairs, and particularly in disposing of the books of his valuable library, in order that these unfinished matters might no longer weigh upon his mind.

He had preached for the last time, in the pulpit, on the forenoon of Sunday, October 17, from the text, "As for me and my house, we will serve the Lord." At this time there was no want of his usual energy; but, though after this he occasionally took part in the services of the sanctuary, he did not again attempt the more difficult and exhausting duty of preaching. His last service was at the communion table, on the Sabbath, December 5, when he dispensed the elements and offered one of the prayers. In this devotional exercise, he alluded with deep sensibility to the death of Mr. Lemuel Withington, a member of the church, aged ninety years. His emotions, on this occasion, were doubtless deepened by the thought, that his own departure was at hand. His first sermon, nearly forty years before, was on "the gospel of Christ," and his last service was the commemoration of the Saviour's death.

It was a great satisfaction to Dr. Codman, that the young licentiate, who assisted him on this day, was one on whom he had fixed his eyes as his desired successor in the ministry, and whom his people seemed to regard with much favor. This gentleman, soon after the decease of Dr. Codman, was ordained as pastor of the church.

As he rode one day, with his friend, to a distant part of his parish, they stopped before the house of an aged pair, the members of his church, and long his friends. They came out to take once more by the hand their much respected pastor. It was an interview, full of admonition and instruction, between those who had long been intimately associated in the service of God on the earth, but who must have regarded themselves as all not far distant from the scenes of a better and glorious world. He frequently spoke of his approaching death with great calmness, yet with deep humility, aware of his own unworthiness, and relying on "the only name under heaven" whereby he could be saved. So deeply were his thoughts absorbed in the contemplation of eternity, that, when looking out from his dwelling where the beautiful prospect extended in every direction, he said that it occasioned him no disquietude to think of parting with objects so pleasant, and with which God had so long refreshed his eye.

Soon after his friend left him, the symptoms of his disease became more alarming. "On the Friday preceding his death," says the Rev. Mr. Dyer, "I was sitting by his side, when, after he had made some grateful remarks respecting the intimate and uninterrupted pleasure of our friendship, I spoke to him of the precious consolations of the gospel he had preached to others. He replied, 'They are precious, and I feel that they are enough.' I subsequently mentioned to him an expression of the late Rev. Dr. McAll, who, as a brother minister asked him a few hours before his death, if he felt that his hope of heaven was securely laid, replied, '*Aye, in oaths, and promises, and blood.*' As I finished the sentence, he took up the two last words, and clasping his hands said, with an emphasis and satisfaction I shall never forget, 'AND BLOOD!' I replied, 'The atonement is very precious.' He answered, '*Oh it is, it is.*' On the following Sabbath evening, I was privileged again to see and pray with him. He was at the time suffering greatly, and could scarcely speak; still, as I spoke to him of the sympathy of Jesus, he affectionately pressed my hand, and thus signified his assent. The same night, when a little relieved from pain, he exclaimed, 'Bless the Lord, O my soul,' and repeated several verses of the one hundred and third Psalm. Subsequently, as a member of his family finished the quotation of some Scripture promises, unable to speak, he looked up with an imploring smile for her to continue and repeat others. And when desired, the day before his death, to give some sign if he felt the Saviour precious to his soul, he readily and firmly pressed the inquirer's hand."

The Rev. Dr. Storrs, in a discourse at his funeral, gives some notices of his last hours. "On one occasion, adverting to the public labors he loved so well, he said, 'I have endeavored to preach in the demonstration of the Spirit,'—and there paused. He soon added, 'In my Father's house are many mansions.' To his wife in tears, as she stood over his bed of agony, he earnestly said, 'Let not your heart be troubled! You believe in God; believe in Christ. I am willing to be in God's hands.'" He died in calmness, and in the confidence of Christian hope, on the morning of Thursday, December 23, 1847, aged sixty-five years.

"On Friday morning," writes another friend, "I learned that Dr. Codman was no more. I had endeavored to prepare myself for the sorrowful tidings; but when I heard that he was gone indeed, the sad reality overpowered me, and, seeking where I might weep, I entered into a chamber, and wept there. The remembrances of nearly forty years swept before my mind, and images of gladness and grief, of kindness and love, of sweet communion and hallowed hours, deepened the tide of sorrow, and cast a dreary shade over the world. But it was not for him I wept. Thanks be unto God, he had gotten the victory. Death had no more dominion over him. He was landed on that blissful shore, where the conflicts of life shall agitate him no more ; and the blessings he so richly shared on earth, have expanded into the felicities and glories of the heavenly world.

"In the afternoon, I went to the house of mourning. As I passed up the winding pathway, which led to that dwelling where I had enjoyed so many tokens of welcome and friendship, the signs of desolation and grief were everywhere visible. It was winter ; and the wild gusts of the bitter wind shook the trees, and sighed among the leafless branches. Silence and sadness rested on the village, the church, and among the habitations of men. The great master was gone. It was grief in that expressive stillness, which is only marked by the habiliments of death.

"I entered the chamber, where the form of the departed pastor was laid. There, in its calm and peaceful aspect, its manly proportions and its countenance serene, as in the quiet embrace of sleep, it attested his victory over death. He had indeed fallen in the conflict, but his spirit had triumphed over mortality, and the gloom of the grave had been exchanged for the chariots of Israel and the horsemen thereof. Who would have wished him back to the conflicts and storms of this mortal life? Who would desire to 'revive the troubled dream of life, in a sleep that was now so peaceful?'"

On Monday, December 27, the solemn offices of burial were performed. The day was severely cold; but, in the sanctuary, the warm love of a devoted people had thronged its pews and aisles with sincere mourners. His friend, Dr. Storrs of Braintree, preached a fervently eloquent discourse from Hebrews xi. 16: "But now they desire a better country, that is, an heavenly," &c.; after which, a long procession followed his remains to the south burial ground, where they were placed in a tomb as a temporary place of repose.

Dr. Storrs, in his funeral discourse, has given a faithful delineation of his character, and account of his labors. After speaking of the wisdom and heroism manifested during the ecclesiastical controversy at the outset of his ministry, he adds: "Through the whole of his remaining days, his course exhibited a bright pattern of pastoral fidelity in the services of the pulpit, the lecture room, the prayer meeting, at the bedside of the sick and dying, in the cottage of the poor, and the mansion of the opulent. . . . . .

"On the broader fields of ministerial labor, his calls were multiplied almost beyond a parallel. Few ecclesiastical councils have been convened, within a wide region around, of which he was not a chosen member, and commonly the presiding officer. His uniform urbanity of manners, the well known tenderness of his heart, his quick discernment of the right and the wrong, the promptness with which he accepted, and the facility with which he performed every duty assigned him, inspired universal confidence. Few men have so rarely erred in judgment, and fewer still have found their decisions so justly appreciated; while to none has been more freely accorded, at all times, the high praise of just and unprejudiced attention to the business before him.

"His warm devotion to the prosperity of Zion, and his known liberality in the use of his ample means for extending her boundaries, brought him, of course, into close communion with the various benevolent associations of our age and country. What enterprise of benevolence has ever urged a just claim on the advocacy and pecuniary support of the church, that met not a cordial response from him? What association of unquestionable character enrolls not his name among its benefactors, and its elected or honorary members? And where is the man, who has poured forth more freely and acceptably the strains of eloquence, and faith and prayer, in the annual convocations of those who labor for the world's conversion? Of his private charities, no account is kept in human records, for even his right hand knew not what his left hand did; but that they were abundant and free, ten thousand witnesses on earth can testify, and the opened books of heaven will hereafter declare."

As an instance of his liberality, Mr. Dyer mentions that, after the formation of the Village Church in Dorchester, he provided a preacher at his own expense, between one and two years, and assisted in the erection of the house of worship. His whole contribution to the support of an evangelical ministry in this village, and to the erection and enlargement of this house, during a period of five years, was above three thousand and five hundred dollars.

Dr. Codman's manner in the pulpit was dignified and serious. His voice was clear and impressive; and his sermons, sometimes very forcible, always well arranged and perspicuous, were at times delivered in a style of remarkable pathos and eloquence. He was singularly happy in the adaptation of his subjects to the circumstances of his hearers. Few ministers have excelled him on communion occasions. When the love of Christ was his theme, all his sensibilities were awakened; and when he gathered his flock around the table of the Lord, many a disciple has exclaimed, "How dreadful is this place; surely, this is none other than the house of God, and this is the gate of heaven!"

"It is difficult to understand," says Dr. Storrs, "how our dear brother found leisure and ability to meet the claims of the study and the pulpit, with all these demands on his time and resources; with the additional demands of literary and theological institutions on his supervision, and the numberless calls of family connections and personal friends from all parts of this and other lands, and a widely extended correspondence of business and friendship. Yet he failed not, from week to week, to bring from his treasures things new and old; to preach instructively 'in season and out of season;' and to satisfy the wants of his own and the expectations of other congregations. And the secret of this lay not so much in the originality or depth, as in the transparency of his thoughts; not so much in the extensiveness of his theological researches, as in the purity of his soul's breathings; nor so much in his power of rich and diversified illustration, or closely woven argument, as in the scriptural simplicity and pathos of his discourses, and the perfect adaptation of his style and manner to his well-chosen subject."

It is probable that the usefulness of Dr. Codman as a minister, was much increased by a prominent trait of his character, which greatly endeared him to his friends. We mean his ardent social feelings; his ready sympathy; the warmth and benignity of his heart; the true, unaffected interest, which he took in the welfare of others. His was no austere dignity; though never failing in a just regard to his ministerial character, yet a genial glow of kindness was visible in his countenance, and his feelings of sympathy and gladness have mingled in many a scene of happiness, and dispelled the gloom from many a desolate fireside. He delighted to minister to the comfort of those who were less favored than himself, and gathered from the afflicted, those salutary lessons which chastened and moderated the worldly tendencies of his own prosperity.

If he possessed, in an uncommon degree, the

power of disarming prejudice and of commending to others the faith which he preached, it was because his own life bore the fruits of goodness, and because he gave evidence of perfect sincerity and of honest zeal for the highest welfare of those whom he addressed. That, through the efficiency of the Divine Spirit, he was so successful in his labors, seems to be a testimony of Heaven to his faithfulness in preaching the gospel. He doubtless felt much satisfaction, in his last days, in reflecting that, after a ministry of nearly forty years, he should leave his church in such a prosperous and happy condition, familiar with the peculiar doctrines of the gospel, reverencing the Sabbath, observing the ordinances of religion, training up their children in the right way, and showing, in all the methods of holy living, the power of Christian principle. He had taught them the duty and necessity of persevering to the end, in order that they might inherit the immortal blessings which, as he hoped, he was about to possess. How might he have associated, in his thoughts, their unfaltering faithfulness with the expansion of religion in future times on the earth, from this one point of the Redeemer's Zion; with the kindling up, from this holy light, of an increasing, widening splendor, from age to age, till its radiance should be lost in the full millennial glory?

Whatever might have been his dear and cherished hopes, he has gone from his much-loved field of labor. He is dead; yet he only sleepeth. He will awake again. In the morning of the resurrection, he and his beloved friends, and every faithful pastor, with his people, will awake to a new and blessed never-ending life. Let the people of his late charge, then, and the people of every faithful pastor, be persuaded to examine themselves, and to determine whether they are likely to share in the resurrection of the just, and to be their pastor's "hope, and joy, and CROWN OF REJOICING, in the presence of our LORD JESUS CHRIST, at his coming!"

REMINISCENCES

OF THE LATE

JOHN CODMAN, D. D.

WITH

BRIEF NOTICES OF THE PROMINENT TRAITS OF HIS CHARACTER.

BY JOSHUA BATES, D. D.

REMINISCENCES.

THE name of JOHN CODMAN, belongs to the ecclesiastical history of New England; and will, unquestionably, occupy a prominent place in that history when, at some future period, it shall be written by a faithful hand, and be made to embrace in its records all the leading events and distinguished men connected with the organization of churches in this land, and their progress to this time. It is no part of my intention, however, to write such a history, nor even to give a full biography of the subject of these reminiscences. The former of these tasks must be performed by some future historian, who shall be able, after the results of present movements and changes shall be seen, to take a retrospective and comprehensive view of the whole ground, with an impartial and discriminating eye;

and shall be so far removed from the exciting influence of the scene, as to be able to delineate characters, and record events, with a steady and impartial hand. And the latter has been assigned to a familiar friend, capable of doing justice to the subject.

It is my purpose simply to record my own recollections of Dr. Codman, and present the record to his family and the public, with a few brief notices of such distinguishing traits of his character as fell within my own observation, and with such reflections and practical hints as are naturally suggested by the narrative. I shall, therefore, refer to the history of the times no further than is necessary to illustrate the transactions in which he was engaged, and to exhibit the prominent traits of character which were developed by them.

For the sake of convenient reference, however, I subjoin to these prefatory remarks two chronological statements.

John Codman was born in Boston, August 3, 1782, and died at Dorchester, December 23, 1847, in the sixty-fifth year of his age, and fortieth of his ministry; leaving the beloved wife of his youth and six children, three sons and three daughters, with a large circle of friends in this country and in Europe, to lament his death, but admire his character and cherish his memory.

"Calm resignation, patient endurance, undoubting confidence in the covenant-faithfulness of God," we are assured, "were the bright features of his closing earthly experience."

"*Blessed are the dead who die in the Lord.*"

RECOLLECTIONS OF MR. CODMAN IN COLLEGE, AND DURING THE TIME OF HIS PREPARATIONS FOR THE MINISTRY.

With Mr. Codman, I had no familiar acquaintance before his settlement in the ministry at Dorchester. I knew him, indeed, at Cambridge, where we often met during the period of our co-residence at that seat of learning. But as we were connected with different classes in the University, he with the class which was graduated in 1802, and I with that of 1800, our meetings were transient, our personal intercourse was slight, and our acquaintance with each other was, of course, neither intimate nor familiar. I knew him only as an amiable young man, and a highly respectable member of one of the most distinguished classes which ever received the nurture and honor of our venerated alma mater. I knew him, not so much individually, and absolutely, as relatively; as viewed in connection with his classmates; as a companion and associate in letters with such men as Dr. Allen, late President of Bowdoin College; the Hon. J. T. Austin of Boston, formerly Attorney General of Massachusetts; Dr. Crocker of Providence, R. I.; Dr. Flint of Salem; Professor Frisbie, deceased; S. Greele, Esq. of Boston; R. D. Harris, Esq. of Boston; Hon. S. Hoar of Concord; J. N. Knapp, Esq. of Walpole, N. H.; Gov. Lincoln of Worcester; Hon. W. Minot of Boston; Dr. Nichols of Portland; A. Ritchie, Esq. of Boston; E. Rockwood, Esq., deceased; and the late Hon. L. Saltonstall of Salem.

As a scholar, my impression was that young Codman held a medium rank in this highly distinguished class. And a singular fact, connected with the conferring of the literary honors of the institution,—the fact that an honorable part was assigned to him, subsequently to the public announcement of the arrangements for the commencement exercises of his class,—shows that this impression was in accordance with "the second, sober thoughts" and final decision of the governors and instructors of the college.

Whether he was a professor of religion or not, while an under-graduate in college, I have no means of ascertaining. My belief is, that he had not, at that period, made a public profession, by becoming a member of any organized church. He did, however, as far as I had opportunity to observe, maintain a high moral character, and exhibit a reverential respect for religion and its institutions.

From the time of my leaving Cambridge, in 1800, till the time of Mr. Codman's ordination, December 7th, 1808, when he became one of my nearest neighbors and most intimate associates in the ministry, we had no opportunity for personal intercourse with each other. I did, indeed, occasionally hear of him, and learn something of his movements. I knew the fact of his engaging in the study of the law, preparatory to his proposed professional pursuits for life. And I heard, with great interest, that the death of his father, with the peculiar feelings and strong desires of that honored and beloved parent, expressed in his last hours, had become the occasion of young Codman's changing his purpose as to his professional pursuits, and of his commencing the study of theology. Whether he dated his hope of acceptance with God, and his consecration of himself to the service of his Redeemer at this period, or whether this was simply the time and occasion of renewed and peculiar consecration and self-devotion to this service, and of his adopting this new mode of glorifying his God and Saviour, I never heard him say, nor ever distinctly learned. But the fact of his change of purpose and course of life, and the occasion of the change, were known and spoken of, with interest, by those who loved the cause of Zion, in all the region about Boston.

Another recollected incident I state here, not on account of its intrinsic importance, but because it recurs to mind as a reminiscence connected with the religious usages of the day, and because it furnishes opportunity for a conservative remark on the customs of our Puritan fathers, and the importance of adhering to "the good old ways" of piety in which they walked. On the 28th of July, 1805, I preached, on exchange, in Boston; and, as I was entering the door of the church, a note was handed me, of this import: "A young man, about to cross the ocean, desires the prayers of this congregation to Almighty God, that he would protect and bless him, and, in due time, return him in safety to his friends and country." This young man, as I afterward learned, was John Codman, who sailed on the Tuesday following, in a ship bound to Liverpool, with a view of proceeding to Edinburgh, and there of pursuing studies connected with his newly chosen profession. The note was read; the prayer was offered; and the petition was granted.

This incident, as I said, may appear to some of small importance; but to him and to me, it was one of pleasing recollection. It is recorded here, however, principally for the purpose of introducing the following remark:—Our Puritan fathers made it a fundamental principle of their religion to follow the directions of the Scriptures, as fully and precisely as possible. They made them, indeed, the rule of their faith, and the guide of their lives; embracing the doctrines which they teach, without gainsaying or distrust, and obeying the precepts which they contain, without perversion or reluctance. Accordingly, it was their custom to make everything, pertaining to life and to godliness, a subject of prayer and thanksgiving; to acknowledge God in all their ways, ask his blessing on all their pursuits, and give thanks to him for all his mercies, through Jesus Christ. As social beings, required to meet in the name of Christ and pray for one another, and believing the special promise made to those who thus unite in prayer, and agree as touching the thing that they ask, they often offered prayers and gave thanks, in their public assemblies, for individuals and communities, by special appointment or particular request. In accordance with this general principle and uniform practice, it was customary, when any person or family, belonging to a congregation, had received special blessings, or were passing through severe trials, or were about to commence some important enterprise, to send a note to the sanctuary, requesting their fellow-worshipers to unite with them, as the case might be, either in prayer or thanksgiving, to him "from whom all blessings flow." This custom of our pious ancestors, observed by them with great reverence, and continued, till recently, in most of our evangelical churches, was surely a good custom, founded on Scripture authority; and I am afraid that the growing neglect of it, in these days, is connected with a diminution of a proper sense of dependence on the providence and grace of God. I wish, therefore, that the practice could be revived, and observed with all the seriousness and faith which characterized the worship of former days.

HIS ORDINATION AND SETTLEMENT IN DORCHESTER, AND MY SUBSEQUENT FAMILIAR ACQUAINTANCE AND INTERCOURSE WITH HIM.

When Mr. Codman returned from Europe, in the Spring of 1808, I heard of him as an interesting and impressive preacher; and, with great satisfaction, I soon learned that there was a prospect of his being settled in the second parish, then a newly organized society in Dorchester. The prospect was pleasant to me, because this parish was adjacent to the first parish in Dedham, with which I had then been connected for five years, and because I had already become somewhat acquainted in Dorchester, and deeply interested in the prosperity of this new society. Indeed, the known difference of sentiment, which prevailed in the parish, created an apprehension that no candidate could obtain a united call of the church and people to become their pastor and teacher; or, if any one should be called and settled, that the settlement would soon be disturbed, and the position of the incumbent be rendered one of disquiet and severe trials. Mr. Codman's frankness, connected with the kind manner in which he announced his sentiments, however, prevented the first of these apprehensions, and secured an apparently harmonious action of the church and the parish. But it was not in the power and wisdom of man, as will be seen in the sequel, to prevent the occurrence of the second, and preserve peace and harmony among such discordant elements.

From the time of Mr. Codman's ordination, till the time of my removal to Middlebury, Vermont, in 1818, our acquaintance with each other was intimate, and our social and ministerial intercourse uninterrupted and confidential.

This intimate acquaintance and familiar intercourse between us, commenced immediately after his ordination. Our exchanges were frequent; and we both wished to have it so, that we might often see each other, and have opportunity to converse together on the great subjects of our professional duties and high responsibilities. On my part there were additional inducements, because I had become acquainted with many of his people, and felt an interest in their spiritual prosperity; and especially, because the people of my charge were highly gratified, and, as I believed, greatly edified by the arrangement.

But, when the difficulties in his parish, which tried his wisdom and patience and firmness, for three long years, began to appear, I saw him still more frequently than before; and had opportunity to observe more minutely, and mark with more accuracy, the prominent traits of his character. Especially, when called to sit by his side during the long session of the memorable Dorchester Ecclesiastical Council, and to see his meekness, fortitude and self-possession, under accusations cruel and unfounded; and to observe with what forbearance he spoke of his revilers, and with what composure and success he vindicated his character and justified his ministerial course, I had opportunity to learn 'what spirit he was of,' and discover the discriminating traits of his character, as they were thus fully developed.

That, however, which gave me the best opportunity to know him as a preacher of the gospel, 'a scribe well-instructed unto the kingd m of heaven,' a man of high social qualities, and a Christian of deep experience and warm-hearted piety, was our union, together with Dr. Gile of Milton, in what may not improperly be denominated a Special Association. For eight or nine years, we three maintained such an association; visiting each other (often with our wives, always indeed when practicable) once every two weeks, dining together at each other's houses, and in succession preaching each other's preparatory lectures. The arrangement was one of deep interest, furnishing opportunity for sweet Christian and ministerial intercourse and mutual improvement. Of this delightful and profitable association, the memory is precious. Three of the members, Mrs. Bates, Dr. Gile and Dr. Codman, are now gone, but not forgotten. The latter, who died December 23, 1847, lived to write for the Boston Recorder, a biographical sketch of the former, who died February 7, 1826; and to preach at the funeral of Dr. Gile, who died October 16, 1836.

Perhaps it may be thought, that I should have omitted the record of this reminiscence, as inapposite in this connection; but it is full of interest to myself, and I doubt not to the two other surviving associates and companions of the deceased. And I could not omit it here, without concealing the ground on which the credibility, of many of the following statements of facts and notices of character, must depend; especially with those who had no personal acquaintance with Mr. Codman. Besides, I was unwilling, while recording my recollections of one deceased and beloved ministerial friend, to omit the name of another, so intimately and endearingly associated with ours, as that of the late Rev. Samuel Gile. He was, indeed, a dear friend, possessing a lovely spirit, eminently a man of prayer, and a faithful minister of the Lord Jesus Christ.

When I was called away from Dedham, and became connected with Middlebury College, my personal intercourse with Mr. Codman was necessarily interrupted and greatly diminished. Still we were permitted to hold correspondence by letter, and frequently to see each other 'face to face.' Twice he visited me at Middlebury; and in my frequent visits to Massachusetts, during my residence in Vermont, I never failed to visit him and spend a portion of the time allotted, at his friendly and hospitable mansion. On my return to the active duties of the ministry, in our native State, he consented to preach at my installation at Dudley, just forty years from the time of my ordination at Dedham, and thirty-five from the time of his induction into the pastoral office in Dorchester. Nor did our friendly and confidential intercourse cease, till his death. Most of the reminiscences and notices of character which I have to present, however, must be drawn from our ten years' intimate intercourse, between 1808 and 1818. During this period, as already stated, I had opportunity to see him and hear him, and converse with him often, and under circumstances fitted to exhibit his character in all possible attitudes, and in the clearest and strongest points of view.

STATE OF THE CONGREGATIONAL CHURCHES AND MINISTRY, IN BOSTON AND THE VICINITY, AT THE COMMENCEMENT OF THE NINETEENTH CENTURY.

I should now proceed to exhibit the traits of character and characteristics of mind, which these opportunities of intercourse enabled me to discover in my deceased and lamented friend; — but the fact, that so many of these characteristics were developed, and so many of these traits formed or matured by the trials through which he was called to pass, during the first three years of his ministry, and especially during the time of the session of that great and long protracted ecclesiastical council, held at Dorchester, in October and November, of 1811, seems to require of me a brief statement of my recollections, of the scenes and circumstances connected with those trials, and of the proceedings and results of that council. Of the twelve ministers, who constituted the clerical part of the council, no one now survives; and the same, as far as my knowledge extends, may be said of the delegates who sat and acted in council with their respective pastors, with the exception of John Punchard, Esq., of Salem, now in the ninetieth year of his age. Of the four advocates of the parties before the council, I only remain to tell the story, and to speak, as a living witness, of the character and conduct of Mr. Codman, while under the pressure of such crushing cares and overwhelming responsibilities as he, then a young man, was called to endure.

Nor can I render the narrative of these facts and proceedings intelligible, without briefly adverting to the state of the Congregational churches and the character of the Congregational ministry, at that period, in Boston and the vicinity. Such a reference seems to be absolutely necessary, to a correct understanding of the Dorchester controversy, since the whole difficulty, involved in that controversy, grew out of the peculiar condition of the churches and the ministry in that region,—a condition which imposed on Mr. Codman, as he believed, the duty of pursuing the course which he adopted, and which involved him in severe trials, and resulted in effects of momentous consequence to the cause of evangelical religion.

Originally, the Congregational churches in and about Boston, and indeed every where in New England, were strictly Puritan—Puritan in doctrine and Puritan in practice. Like the Puritans whom they left behind them in England, when they came to this country, they professed their faith in the plenary inspiration of the Holy Scriptures, and received them as their rule of faith, and their guide in life. Of course, they observed the same rules of organization, and forms of worship, on both sides of the Atlantic, and agreed substantially in the same articles of faith. As far as Congregationalism admits of any authoritative standard, as an explanation and summary formula of Scripture doctrines and duties, they adopted the same standard. In the year 1648, the elders and messengers of the Congregational churches of Massachusetts assembled at Cambridge, and sanctioned the Westminster Assembly's Shorter Catechism, as in their view a correct summary of the doctrines and duties of Christianity. This summary, which had been adopted by the General Assembly of the Presbyterian church of Scotland in 1647, subsequently by the Puritans of England and those of Connecticut at Saybrook, and more recently by the several branches of the Presbyterian church in the United States, as an authoritative standard of faith, became such therefore, as far as united action could render it so, to the Congregational churches of New England. For it was unanimously sanctioned, not only by the Synod of 1648, at Cambridge, but afterward, by an authority of equal weight, at Boston itself, in 1680.

Although, therefore, the principles of union among the Congregational churches are truly republican, leaving every church free and independent in forming its own articles of association; bound by no authority but that of Christ, and no book of discipline but the Bible; yet, for a long time, all the Congregational churches in the region of Boston, as well as all the churches which assumed that name, in all parts of New England, acknowledged the advisory rules and sanctioned the ecclesiastical decisions of the Synod of 1648, at Cambridge, or of that subsequently held at Saybrook. For they continued, everywhere, to use the Assembly's Shorter Catechism as their approved symbol of faith and bond of union; to teach it to their children, and to select their ministers according to its true spirit; choosing such, and such only, for their pastors and teachers, as they believed would preach, substantially, in accordance with its teachings.

But, in process of time, a departure from the faith and practice of 'the fathers' took place,—gradually, indeed, and sometimes covertly, but really and substantially affecting the character of the churches and the ministry,—so that, at the close of the eighteenth and the commencement of the nineteenth century, it came to pass that the churches of Boston and the vicinity, and of some other parts of New England, were essentially different from what they had been in the time of the Cottons, and Wilsons, and Nortons, and Mathers, of olden time. They had come to be churches of a mixed character, both in faith and practice; and their pastors, instead of being united in sentiment as formerly, were men of discordant views, differing from each other by every variety of opinion which the records of faith and error can furnish.

The process by which this declension from the faith of 'the fathers' came over these Congregational churches, and the causes which conspired to produce it, I need not attempt to specify. The low state of vital and practical religion through the whole country, with the prevalence of error and infidelity in the community at large, seems, indeed, to have been the immediate and prominent cause of this departure from the primitive Puritan faith in the churches. A pure church could not live and breathe, and maintain its soundness of faith and healthful vigor, in an atmosphere so impure.

Nor need I speak of the more remote causes of declension in the faith and soundness of these churches; those causes which produced this immediate cause, or nearest antecedent, of church corruption. Some of them might be found in the infidel philosophy which led to the French revolution of 1790, and which found its way across the Atlantic in the writings of Voltaire for the learned, and Paine for the illiterate; and, through the medium of political sympathy, obtained a lodgment in the American mind. Some of them might be discovered in the perverting and degrading influence of the sensuous philosophy and gross materialism diffused through the writings of Dr. Priestley, and other speculative writers of that period, who claimed the Christian name, and yet denied the plenary inspiration and infallible authority of the Christian Scriptures. And some of them might, unquestionably, be traced back to the influence of the war of the American revolution on the principles and habits of American society, and, of course, by sympathy and necessary intercourse, on the church itself.

But whatever may have been the causes, immediate or remote, the state of religion at that period was exceedingly low in all the northern portions of our country; and especially in that portion of it, concerning which I am now writing. The Congregational churches in the vicinity of Boston were feeble, and their members few in number. Few came to the solemn feasts of Christianity; and what rendered the case worse was, that those few were of a mixed character, and of various and heterogeneous sentiments; destroying the power of Christian discipline and diminishing the salutary influence of Christian example. In some cases, persons were admitted to church-fellowship without any examination; and in many of the churches there was scarcely any formula of union, or barrier against the intrusion of the thoughtless and impenitent into 'the holy of holies,' in the Christian sanctuary. The consequence was, that men of loose opinions and doubtful characters, whenever they chose, from any worldly consideration, to make the application, could find a ready admittance to some acknowledged Congregational church. Hence persons of all grades of sentiment, from the highest point of ultra-Calvinism to the lowest point of Arminianism,—men who adhered to the Puritan faith and rigid practice of the fathers of New England, and men who scarcely acknowledged the Christian Sabbath as a day of holy rest, or prayer as an essential Christian duty,—men who walked circumspectly in the midst of a perverse generation, and men who mingled with an unbelieving world in all their vain amusements and follies,—men of habitual seriousness, who daily sought the grace of God as their hope of salvation, and men who despised and even ridiculed this seriousness and reliance on the grace of God, were sometimes found in the same church; and notwithstanding their diversity of sentiment and character, meeting together at the same consecrated table of the Lord.

This was the state of the Congregational churches, with few exceptions, at this period, through all the region (and in some cases beyond that region) which embraced the churches connected with the Boston Association of Congregational ministers. And the state of the ministry itself was not much better. The Scripture adage might with great propriety be applied to the case: "Like people, like priests." For, before the separation, which took place soon after the ecclesiastical council in Dorchester, that Association embraced all the ministers who chose to call themselves Congregationalists, in Boston and most of the adjacent towns. Hence this numerous body, like the churches with which they were connected, consisted of men of various theological views, from the most rigid followers of Calvin to the lowest grade of Socinians.

In this state of things, it was difficult to conduct ecclesiastical business, and regulate ministerial exchanges, not only within the limits of the Boston Association, but in all the surrounding region. No ecclesiastical council, called even for the simple purpose of ordination, could act harmoniously and with satisfaction to all parties. The different views of the members frequently caused jealousies, discussions, unpleasant delays, and great dissatisfaction. Some desired no examination of the candidate, as to sentiment and experience, but his own voluntary statement. Some were unwilling to go, or suffer others to go, in their inquiries, beyond certificates of moral character and church-fellowship. It was even contended by some, that when a council was called to introduce a man into the ministry and ordain him as a pastor and teacher, their whole business was to ascertain whether he had been so called to the work, and had so answered the call, as to lay the foundation of an ecclesiastical relation and a legal contract; and then to sanction the relation and confirm the contract. The consequence was, that those ministers who heeded the apostolic direction, "to lay hands suddenly on no man," were sometimes not permitted to make the requisite inquiries to satisfy their minds whether the candidate did or did not possess the required qualifications for a Christian bishop. Hence divisions sometimes ensued; at least, great delay was occasioned, and often great offence given.

But this difficulty, great as it was, did not constitute the greatest trial growing out of the diversity of sentiment which then prevailed in the Congregational churches, and among Congregational ministers. The regulation of ministerial exchanges, consistently with a good conscience, and the preservation of peace in the parishes and good-will among their pastors, was far more difficult. It was, indeed, almost impossible for a minister, who entertained the sentiments of the Puritans, to maintain expected ministerial intercourse, and especially to regulate his exchanges, without either violating the rules of courtesy, or acting inconsistently with the plainest dictates of duty. Under existing circumstances, however, ministers of these sentiments felt themselves obliged to meet this difficulty, and by various devices attempt to overcome it. They professed, or at least were expected, to exchange with all neighboring ministers, promiscuously, without regard to their known sentiments, or manner of preaching. To counteract the evil effects of such exchanges among their own people, they sometimes publicly controverted the doctrines which, as they learned, had been preached in their pulpits ; and in some extreme cases, where their own sentiments had been controverted and even caricatured, they exerted all their ingenuity to avoid another exchange, and thus to prevent a repetition of the injury. But I believe, and indeed had occasion to know, that this was a subject of great trial ; and to feel that it involved an inconsistency of profession and practice, often requiring a refusal to exchange, where the true reason could not be honestly and frankly given, without violating the courtesies of social life, and even seeming to assume dictatorial authority.

By many, therefore, it was thought desirable that an ecclesiastical separation should take place ; so that those who held to the doctrines of the Puritans, and those who had widely departed from their faith, should no longer be included under the same denomination; or, at least, that the custom of interchanging pulpit services by those ministers, whose religious views were irreconcilable with unity of action, and whose preaching, of course, was calculated to counteract each other's labors, should be discontinued. Most of the decidedly evangelical ministers, not only in the region of Boston, but throughout New England, were evidently desirous of the separation, and ready to embrace the first opportunity, which should fairly present itself, of making the attempt and thus getting rid of the oppressive and perplexing custom of promiscuous exchanges.

ORIGIN AND CAUSES OF THE OPPOSITION TO MR. CODMAN, BY A PART OF HIS PARISH.

When Mr. Codman returned from Europe, prepared to enter on the work of the ministry, he found the state of the Congregational churches, and the relation of their ministers, as described above; and he seems early to have formed the resolution of keeping himself free from the entanglement and perplexity of promiscuous exchanges. Accordingly he intimated his intention, in the most delicate manner, to some of his confidential friends. He did not mean, he said, to denounce or condemn others; but feeling his obligation to preach to the people of his charge what seemed to him to be the true gospel, he could not be instrumental of introducing into his pulpit any one who seemed to him to preach what an Apostle had denominated 'another gospel.'

When called, therefore, to settle in Dorchester, he acted consistently with these views, and with reference to this fixed determination. He did not, it is true, publicly and in a formal manner declare his purpose of limiting his circle of exchanges; because he thought such a declaration would be presumptuous and offensive. Nor did he lay down any precise rules for the regulation of exchanges even for himself; because he thought it most safe and convenient to apply the general principle only so far as called for, and as particular practical cases should arise. Any other course, he thought, would be denunciatory. Besides, he viewed the regulation of exchanges as a matter of personal convenience, to be controlled by the judgment of every minister for himself—a right for the exercise of which he alone is responsible to his own Master. But he did adopt means, in the fullest and most explicit manner, to acquaint the church and society in Dorchester with his religious sentiments; and thus gave them an opportunity to reconsider their vote of invitation. So frank was he on this subject, and so desirous of guarding against all misapprehension, as to request them to act again on the subject of the call, with his explicit communication before them. This he did, because it was understood that persons of different religious sentiments belonged to the parish; and this, he thought, was all he could do, to guard against future difficulty.

But notwithstanding this explicit and frank communication, the call was renewed, and the included request, to substitute Watts's Hymns for those of Belknap, complied with. He felt himself, therefore, authorized to accept their invitation; and did accordingly accept it, in the hope that, with the blessing of Heaven, he should be permitted in peace to preach the gospel of peace, and carry out his own principles, in the exercise of his acknowledged right, according to the Congregational Platform. In this, however, he was disappointed. Complaints, in a very few weeks after his ordination, began to be made against him; and within a year an organized opposition was formed, apparently determined to drive him from from his position. Of course, every kind of effort was made, by a few active and influential leaders, to increase the number of the disaffected, till a majority of legal, or apparently legal, voters in the parish was obtained. Then commenced a course of measures of annoyance, which finally ended in the defeat of the plan of the opposition, and the triumph of the cause and principles which Mr. Codman had so boldly espoused and so firmly and perseveringly defended.

The exciting cause of this opposition seems not to have been well understood, especially at a distance from the scene of action. The subject of exchanges was, in my apprehension, merely incidental and subservient to the true cause. It was, however, an incident of great moment in its consequences; and it led to the establishment of a principle of great practical utility in the Congregational churches, throughout the Commonwealth of Massachusetts, and even in other portions of the country, where this form of ecclesiastical organization exists. It was made, at last, by the continual pressure of an influence beyond the limits of the parish, the *ostensible* ground of the whole opposition, and thus led to a discussion and final decision of the question of ministerial rights and duties, in regulating pulpit exchanges—a decision which has relieved the subject from embarrassment, we hope, forever; and produced a line of separation between men of discordant and incongruous views, clearly marked and easily followed. And although some inconvenience has arisen from the separation, in occasionally dividing and weakening small societies, the general effect has been happy; giving peace, where there had been nothing but contention; and leaving those who could not agree to act and worship together, to agree to differ—to separate and act according to their respective views and wishes.

But, as intimated, the cause of the opposition to Mr. Codman was, originally, very far from this subject of exchanges, as those who were near enough to see its rise and observe its progress well knew. To us it was perfectly evident that the pungent preaching, the full and clear exhibition of the humbling doctrines of the gospel, with the practical bearing always given to them, and the application of them to the hearts and consciences of the hearers, was the first great moving cause of the opposition. It was manifest that this was the exciting cause, because the first complaints made against Mr. Codman were confined to this subject. These complaints, whether made directly to him or to others about him, all had reference to his preaching; and especially to its directness and forcible applications. I add this last phrase, because I had opportunity to learn that this was the real ground of offence. Indeed, men will generally bear the abstract truth, if you present it as a mere abstraction, without any direct application of it to them; if you suffer their consciences to remain quiet and undisturbed, while they neglect its requirements. But Mr. Codman's preaching was peculiarly pungent, and his applications generally direct; and what rendered his preaching more offensive, at that time and in that region, was, that his practice was consistent with it, and therefore full of rebuke and admonition.

An incident occurred on the very evening of his ordination, which intimated to him what he might expect from a portion of his parishioners. They planned what they denominated an ordination ball, and towards evening they sent him a formal note, couched indeed in polite terms, inviting him to attend and participate in the 'innocent amusement.' His answer, of course, was prompt and decisive; and though it was intended to be civil and kind, it gave great offence. This little incident, as he stated to me, exceedingly tried his feelings, and filled him with fearful apprehensions of a coming difficulty. For myself, I never entertained a doubt that the invitation was designed to try and perplex him, and that it constituted the first link in the chain of measures which was ultimately thrown around him, involving him in great trials,—a chain which could have been broken only by the hand of a giant.

That portion of his parish who commenced the opposition were a gay people, exceedingly fond of amusements; and there can be no doubt, that they determined to oppose everything which interfered with their favorite indulgences. Hence their opposition to week-day meetings and extra-lectures, of which they early complained, and on account of which they finally presented, to an ecclesiastical council, a formal charge. Hence, too, they began early to complain of his preaching so much on human depravity, the guilt and consequences of sin, the doctrine of the atonement, and the necessity of faith, repentance and regeneration. Indeed, as he stated to me at the time, one of the first visits of expostulation which he received from a complaining parishioner, related to his preaching on the experimental subject of humiliation before God, in view of the entire depravity of the unrenewed heart, and the consequent self-condemnation of the sinner, when his depravity and guilt are discovered by an enlightened understanding, and felt by an awakened conscience. The discourse complained of was founded on these words, ascribed to Job: "But now mine eye seeth thee; wherefore I abhor myself, and repent in dust and ashes." The complaint was heard with patience, and I doubt not answered with meekness. But when the complainant was shown that his objection applied more directly against the text itself, than against anything said in the course of the illustration or application, the explanation gave no satisfaction, but seemed rather to aggravate the spirit of complaint and strengthen the feeling of opposition.

These causes, therefore,—the subjects of his preaching, the manner of his preaching, the frequency and urgent application of his preaching, rather than the fact that he neglected to exchange with some of the Boston ministers,—were most evidently the original causes and lay at the foundation of the opposition. The course which he adopted in regulating his pulpit-exchanges, as a plausible ground of complaint, seems to have been with his opposers an after-thought, probably suggested from without. But however originated, it was subsequently made the principal subject of complaint; and became, as incidentally admitted, in the course of correspondence, by the committee of the opposition, the *ostensible* reason for wishing and vehemently urging a dissolution of his pastoral relation to the people of his charge.

But whatever may have been the cause, or the concurrent causes, which led to the opposition, it was to him an occasion of severe and long-protracted trials; — trials, however, which were sanctified to him, and which resulted in the establishment of the principles for which he contended, and, as he had the satisfaction of believing, in the promotion of the cause to which he had devoted himself and all his energies—the cause of truth, the conversion of sinners, the elevation and purity of the church, the salvation of men and the glory of God.

THE PROGRESS OF THE OPPOSITION AND HISTORY OF THE CONTROVERSY.—THE CALLING OF THE FIRST ECCLESIASTICAL COUNCIL.

The cause or combined causes of the opposition to Mr. Codman, whatever they were, and with whatever motives they moved the actors in this drama, began to operate, as we have seen, and to show their disturbing power, soon after his ordination. The first complaint which was heard in the vicinity of Dorchester, like that first made to him personally, was against his doctrinal preaching, with his earnest manner and directness of personal application. The next was against his *much* preaching and his multiplying religious meetings; though for this complaint there was no other foundation, than the fact that he gave a stated weekly-lecture on Tuesday, and held an occasional family-meeting, or prayer-meeting and conference, in some remote part of the parish. Several other complaints of a similar character,—all, however, springing from the same source and intimately connected with these,—were originated and spread abroad, long before his restricted system of exchanges was made the rallying-point of opposition.

The first step in legal form, for the purpose of attempting to remove Mr. Codman from his ministerial position, which it had become evident the opposition were determined, if possible, to accomplish, was taken on the nineteenth of April, 1810, when a parish meeting was called for this purpose, in accordance with a petition of the leaders. But it appeared that, notwithstanding the unwearied efforts of the malcontents for many months to gain over partisans, they had not yet strength enough to effect their object; for the proposition involved in the first article of the warrant, requiring Mr. Codman to exchange *promiscuously*, was rejected by a negative vote of *fifty-two* to *thirty-four*. Another article, providing for the re-substitution of Belknap's for Watts's Psalms and Hymns, was dismissed. And instead of prohibiting the opening of the meeting-house for lectures, as was proposed by another article, it was voted, "that the meeting-house, in future, as it respects its use for lectures, be under the control of the Rev. Mr. Codman."

But, though thus completely defeated, the opposition did not relax their efforts. They soon rallied, and presented themselves in a new attitude, and commenced a new mode of warfare. In August following, there appeared (with what views and for what purpose none could doubt) an advertisement in the Columbian Centinel of Boston, offering for sale "thirty-eight pews in the Rev. Mr. Codman's meeting-house, and *three horse-sheds*." By means like this, and influences from without and within, the opposition was at length increased, so as to raise, in the minds of the leaders, the hope of obtaining a majority in a parish meeting. And, strange as it may seem to some, the manœuvres practiced had been such as to secure that object. For at a parish meeting called for the purpose, and held on the 8th of October, 1810, it was voted, that "the Rev. Mr. Codman be requested to exchange with the ministers who compose the Boston Association"; and a committee was appointed to communicate this vote to Mr. Codman, and report his answer at an adjourned meeting. At such an adjourned meeting, they did accordingly report his explicit answer: "That he could not pledge himself to exchange with any man or any body of men whatever."

At this meeting, which seems to have been a comparatively small one, a new expedient was adopted, calculated and evidently designed to embarrass and perplex Mr. Codman, and if possible, by increasing his already multiplied labors, to drive him to despair. A committee was chosen to write to the ministers in the several towns, with whom Mr. Codman had been in the habit of exchanging, requesting them not to preach in his pulpit any more, till the difficulties in the parish were removed. Accordingly such letters were written to eight clergymen in the vicinity; not excepting those members of the Boston Association with whom he had exchanged, and with whom, however inconsistent it may seem, he had just been requested by the opposition to exchange.

In this stage of his trials, when it might seem, from the comparatively small number of his friends who attended and voted at the last parish meeting, that they were discouraged or frightened, and that he was about to be forsaken by them and left to be overwhelmed by the growing opposition, he received support and encouragement in a way altogether unexpected. Two addresses were presented to him, about the same time, one signed by seventy-one male members of his parish, the other by one hundred and seventy-nine female members; and what gave peculiar value to these addresses, in his view, was, that these signers included nearly all the members of his church. In these communications his friends, both male and female, entirely approve of his independent course, strongly commend his manner of preaching, bear witness to his fidelity and success in the ministry, urge him not to forsake them in their trials, and pledge their continued support and their united prayers, that he may find protection under the blessing of Heaven.

Though, as I had every reason to believe, he had not entertained a thought of yielding his right to regulate his pulpit exchanges, or of giving up his efforts for the cause of truth and what he esteemed the essential doctrines of the gospel, yet these addresses, coming at such a critical moment, and containing such pledges of affection and assurances of continued support, did unquestionably afford him consolation and encouragement under his heavy trials and pressing cares and labors. Nor was it of small moment to him, that he had the sympathy and prayers of many of his brethren in the ministry. Especially, as he declared to me, did he feel himself encouraged and supported by the firm course pursued by the proscribed ministers in the vicinity. For most of them expressly refused to submit to the dictation of assumed authority; and two of them wrote letters, giving their reasons for the refusal, with an appropriate rebuke.

In the meantime, however, the opposition did not in the least abate their zeal, diminish their efforts, or fail to exert their ingenuity in contriving new expedients of annoyance. Accordingly they took effectual measures to prevent several persons, who attended on the ministry of Mr. Codman, from becoming regular members and legal voters in the incorporated society. In connection with this act of oppression, there appeared another advertisement in two public newspapers in Boston, offering for sale sixty-nine pews, with the following significant and offensive words appended: "Together with all the right, title and interest, the proprietors of the above pews have in the Rev. Mr. Codman."

It would seem that, at this period, there were some apprehensions,—though I believe without foundation,—that Mr. Codman might be induced, by these continued annoyances, to think it consistent with duty to consult his own peace—not to say safety—and ask a dismission from his parish; and being thus "persecuted in one city, to flee to another." For on the 22d of April, 1811, he received another address of his friends, principally male members of his church,—an address signed by Benjamin Hitchborn, Stephen Badlam, James Baker, and fifty-four others,—expressing their sympathy with him in his trials, and declaring "that they saw nothing to justify the origin or continuance of the existing evils." They express their earnest "desire of seeing the unhappy division healed." But they add, "We cannot believe your removal from us would produce this effect; we hope, therefore, that you will not think of taking such a step." To this, they subjoin the following pledge of affection and support: "While we make our fervent supplications to Heaven for your comfort and direction under all your trials, you will rest assured of our esteem and affection, and of our determination to support you as our pastor, so long as you continue to sustain your present character as a minister of the gospel, and give no other occasion of complaint than that which is alleged against you by those who now wish to dissolve the compact, so recently, solemnly and unanimously made between you and the people of your charge."

The opposition, however, nothing daunted by their previous discomfitures, and abating nothing of their zeal in the cause which they had espoused, called another parish meeting, on the 24th of June, 1811. At this meeting, the business seems to have proceeded rapidly and without debate. For Mr. Codman's friends, generally, absented themselves from the meeting, or forbore to take any active part in it; probably having resolved to act by themselves, as they subsequently did, in supporting Mr. Codman in whatever legal and ecclesiastical course he should choose to pursue. A committee, all professed and determined opposers of evangelical sentiment, and several of them acknowledged Universalists, was chosen, "to request that a separation take place between Mr. Codman and the society;" "but should he not comply with the request, to propose to him to join in calling a mutual ecclesiastical council;" and in case of his not acceding to either of the above propositions, "to proceed immediately to the choice of an ex-parte council."

To the committee who communicated these votes of the parish, Mr. Codman promptly replied, that while he lamented the divisions in the parish, he could not hope to see them healed by complying with the first proposition. But he declared his readiness (if the demand should be insisted on) to unite with them in calling a mutual council. He, however, expressed a wish to have the business of making the preparatory arrangements conducted in writing. On this he finally insisted, as the only method of guarding against misapprehension and misrepresentation. He likewise claimed the right of having all the complaints and charges, which they intended to lay before the proposed council, fully and definitely furnished, before the issuing of the letters missive, or the designation of the churches to be invited to constitute said council. The discussion of these points, and especially of the latter, consumed many months; and the correspondence was conducted with much diplomatic skill, and, on Mr. Codman's part, with great courtesy, kindness, and yet firmness of purpose.

The church, as a body, resolved to take no part in calling this proposed council, except so far as to agree to aid their pastor by their sympathies and their prayers; and finally, if necessary, to appoint an advocate to appear before the council, when called, and vindicate *their* rights. They did, indeed, as in duty bound, attend to the complaints made against their pastor by the members of the opposition, — seven in number, — who belonged to their body. These complaints were presented, examined, and finally dismissed, as altogether unfounded or futile, in a church meeting held September 18, 1811. To this meeting,—or rather to a committee of the church, who reported at this meeting,—Mr. Codman presented a full statement of his views and feelings on the whole subject, and most triumphantly vindicated himself against all the charges and complaints of the aggrieved brethren. At least, the committee of the church so considered the subject, and so presented it in their report; and the church, by adopting the report, expressed their full satisfaction with the course which their pastor had pursued, and with the justificatory statement which he had made. Accordingly they declined taking any part in calling a council to examine what they viewed as unfounded charges and unreasonable complaints.

Mr. Codman, however, felt himself compelled, lest an ex-parte council should be called, to unite with the committee of the parish and the complaining members of the church in calling a mutual council, as soon as they should comply with the principal condition named by him, and furnish him with their charges, definitely stated and properly tabled.

At length, this point was so far yielded by the committee, as to furnish all the articles of complaint which they could then make out, or to use their own expression, "as had then transpired." Accordingly, a council was agreed upon, to consist of the usual representatives, a pastor and delegate, from each of twelve churches; six to be nominated by the committee, and six by Mr. Codman.

PROCEEDINGS AND RESULT OF THE FIRST COUNCIL, WITH REMARKS ON THE CHARACTER OF THE MEMBERS.

The representatives of the churches designated, as stated above, met at Dorchester according to invitation by letters missive, on Tuesday, October 30, 1811; consisting of the following pastors and delegates, viz:

From the church in Medfield,	Rev. Thomas Prentiss, D. D. Artemas Woodward, Delegate.
Hatfield, ...	Rev. Joseph Lyman, D. D. Isaac Maltby, Delegate.
Bridgewater, . .	Rev. John Reed, D. D. Simeon Keith, Delegate.
Watertown, . . .	Rev. Richard R. Eliot. Dea. Moses Coolidge, Delegate.
Newton, ...	Rev. William Greenough. Dea. Joseph Adams, Delegate.
Dedham, ...	Rev. Thomas Thacher. Dea. John Richards, Delegate.
Worcester, . . .	Rev. Aaron Bancroft, D. D. Joseph Allen, Delegate.
Weston, ...	Rev. Samuel Kendall, D. D. Nathan Hagar, Delegate.
Worcester, . . .	Rev. Samuel Austin, D. D. Moses N. Child, Delegate.
Charlestown, . .	Rev. Jedidiah Morse, D. D. Jeremiah Evarts, Delegate.
Lancaster, ...	Rev. Nathaniel Thayer. Ebenezer Torry, Delegate.
Salem, ...	Rev. Samuel Worcester, D. D. John Punchard, Delegate.

The council was organized by choosing the Rev. Dr. Prentiss, moderator, and the Rev. Mr. Thayer and the Rev. Dr. Worcester, scribes.

After prayer by the moderator, the parties were admitted by vote to appear before the council and make their communications. By request, the following gentlemen were allowed to appear as advocates, viz: for the complainants, Benjamin Parsons, Esq. and the Hon. Samuel Dexter; for the church, though not directly a party in the contest, yet as having interests at stake in the issue, Daniel Davis, Esq., Solicitor-General of the Commonwealth of Massachusetts; and for Mr. Codman, as his friend and adviser, the Rev. Joshua Bates, of Dedham.

The business before the council was introduced by a speech of Mr. Parsons, the junior advocate for the parish, who presented the following proposition for the decision of the council, with the articles of charge and complaint of the parish committee, as they had been furnished to Mr. Codman, viz:

"Whether, under existing circumstances, it is not expedient that your pastoral relation to this society should be dissolved:

"1st. Because of the great disappointment that a

respectable number of your church and a majority of your society have experienced, at your not exchanging ministerial labors with the Rev. clergy composing the Boston Association, generally; more especially those that were present and performed at the dedication of the meeting-house, and at the organization of the church, and those that were particularly concerned and assisted in your ordination; which the parish had every reason to expect, from your intimations, both antecedent and subsequent to your settlement.

"2d. Because, though we would not deny to a minister all discretion in the choice of those with whom he changes pulpits, yet you have, in our opinion, gone in this respect to such an improper and unwarrantable extreme, as in effect to make us a separate religious society; cutting us off from that intercourse with the greater part of those Christian societies (and of our own denomination) with which we have been on terms of friendship and communion.

"3d. Because we conceive that the lectures and religious meetings which you appoint, or encourage, are so frequent, and held at such times and places, as that they tend rather to disorder and the interruption of domestic union, comfort and duties, than to the promotion of the social virtues and genuine religion.

"4th. Because of your unfeeling and unnatural conduct, to prevent the neighbors and friends of Mr. Thomas Crehore from attending the funeral of his son, by urging several of them personally to attend your lecture, and requesting them to call on your friends to do likewise; also, threatening to forsake them, in case of refusal.

"5th. Because you personally, or by your instigation, circulated cards in Rev. Mr. Harris's parish respecting the Catechism, cautioning them to beware of innovation; undoubtedly meaning for them to guard against their Rev. Pastor, who had previously introduced Dr. Watts's Catechism, agreeably to the printed directions of the school committee, of which you are a member.

"6th. Because of your overbearing conduct, in neglect of the wishes of a majority of the parish, in admitting into the pulpit a number of ministers, whom the parish at a legal meeting had requested not to preach therein until their difficulties had subsided; also your endeavoring to prevent the customary tolling of the bell, for a funeral, as an interference with your lecture.

"7th. Because of your disrespectful observations

towards some of your fathers and brethren in the ministry, whom we believe sustain unimpeachable characters, both as men and Christians.

"8th. Finally, because we conceive, that while your ministerial relation to us shall continue, there will be no prospect of the restoration of that harmony, peace and brotherly love, which have been so unhappily interrupted, and which we ardently wish may soon return."

Mr. Parsons then presented and read the charges of the aggrieved brethren, which had been presented to the church, examined, and dismissed as entirely unfounded. They need not be stated here, however, as they are substantially the same with those of the parish committee, adding only two items of charge; one, the very common charge of "deception," and the other for refusing, as alleged, to attend to the prescribed form of Christian discipline, when some of them intended to take the first and second steps with him.

Mr. Parsons then proceeded to call witnesses and read papers, with the view of supporting these charges and justifying these complaints; but with what success, the sequel will show. When he had presented his proofs and closed his pleadings, Mr.

Codman commenced his defence. He commenced with a few simple and appropriate remarks on the peculiar and trying situation in which he was placed. He had not, he said, intended to call for the assistance of any one to plead his cause; but it had been his purpose to leave the result to the wisdom of the council without pleadings. And though his church had claimed the right to advocate their own interests, he had till the very day before asked no one to plead his cause; and he had only been induced to ask his friend and brother, who now sat by his side, to be present, and assist him if necessary in reading the voluminous papers, which must be presented to the council, and make such remarks as might seem necessary to show their connection and bearing. As to himself, he said, he should do no more than present, and, if able, read those papers. He should introduce no witnesses to rebut the testimony of the many witnesses who had been called upon the stand; nor say anything, by way of recrimination, against his disaffected parishioners. After this brief introduction, he proceeded to read the papers which related to his call and settlement in Dorchester; his declaration of faith before the ordaining council; the complaints of his disaffected parishioners, and the whole correspondence between him and them; together with his letter of defence to the church, answering the complaints of the aggrieved brethren, and the whole correspondence between him and the committee of the parish, till the time of the calling of the council. All this he was able to do without assistance; and having done this, he sat down in perfect calmness, waiting patiently the final issue.

These proceedings, on the part of the complaint and defence, had occupied the attention of the council from Tuesday till Friday afternoon, when, at four o'clock, Mr. Solicitor Davis, as advocate of the church and defender of the legal rights of the minority of the parish, commenced his plea. His argument was able, lucid, and effective. He examined the whole ground; and showed that the course of proceedings against Mr. Codman had been illegal and oppressive; and he argued most conclusively, that an attempt by the malcontents thus to take advantage of their own wrong doings, to induce Mr. Codman to leave his church under oppression, and without any prospect of future peace and harmonious re-settlement of the gospel ministry among them, was an encroachment on the rights of his clients. To this single point he confined his argument; and to me, it seemed, with great propriety and entire success.

Next in course, came the remarks of Mr. Codman's friend, occupying an hour on Friday evening and two hours on Saturday morning. Of these remarks it does not become me to say much. I may say, however, without impropriety, that it seemed an easy task so to exhibit the character of the complaints of the opposition, and so to explain the testimony of the witnesses, as to sweep away all the charges, implying anything wrong, alleged against Mr. Codman; and leave his character, if not perfectly blameless and untarnished, as near the standard of perfection as falls to the lot of man. And, as to the question of dismission for no fault of his own, while he was exercising an acknowledged right, and in the least offensive manner consistent with the claims of conscience, merely because others had created difficulty and division in the parish, and were now seeking occasion to take advantage of their own wrong, to secure their object and deprive the church of the preached gospel, I need only say, that it seemed to me a plain question, easily determined; and I have no doubt that it was made so to appear to all candid and unprejudiced minds.

Mr. Dexter's speech followed, commencing on Saturday at eleven o'clock, and closing at a quarter past two. Of this speech, which closed the public discussion before the council, I could say much; and I most sincerely wish that it had been the practice then, as it is now, by the aid of stenography, to secure to the public and to posterity such splendid productions. It was, indeed, one of the most eloquent speeches of that truly eloquent man; whose language was always pure, chaste, strong and dignified; and, as a cotemporary said of it, "sufficiently correct for the press." He began with great modesty, evidently disappointed in the result of the examination of witnesses, and feeling the weakness of his cause. But according to his professional habits, he proceeded to manifest his faithfulness to his clients, by making the best of a bad cause. In doing this, however, he showed great fairness and candor. He gave up, at once, nearly all the charges against Mr. Codman, as questionable in view of the evidence produced; or, if true, as unimportant to the issue. He suffered himself to make no insinuations against the ministerial and Christian character of Mr. Codman. On the contrary, he admitted all that had been claimed for him by his friends, that he was an exemplary, devoted, able and faithful minister of Jesus Christ. But on the general subject of charity and liberality of sentiment, his eloquence burst forth like a torrent, apparently about to sweep everything before it. It is true, all who heard him did not feel the force of the argument in application to the case in hand; and some may have thought that it was not quite consistent with the admissions which his candor and courtesy had compelled him to make. But it was eloquent and imposing, and seemed to give high satisfaction to his employers. All, indeed, saw and admired the beauty and grandeur of the illustrations of his principal argument in favor of indiscriminate pulpit exchanges and the mingling of all sorts of preaching, drawn from the variety and harmony of nature, — especially from the eccentricity and apparent confusion of the motions of the heavenly bodies, resulting in perfect order, and manifesting unity of design, displaying the beauty of variety and yet producing uniformity and peace and harmony, swelling to a universal chorus the accordant notes of the "music of the spheres." He closed his splendid argument with a most brilliant peroration. And in the midst of this dazzling light the cause was committed to the council.

Thus ended the public hearing and discussion of one of the most exciting and truly interesting causes, which ever agitated the public mind in New England. The council then adjourned, to meet again for private deliberation and decision on the Monday following. They did accordingly meet, and continued their daily sessions and deliberations, till Thursday the 7th of November, when their decision, technically called their result, was published.

From this result I make the following extracts, viz:

"Upon the several articles of charge exhibited against the Rev. Mr. Codman, the council, in the course of their proceedings, passed as follows:

"Voted, 1. That the charge of *intentional deception*, as stated in the first specification of the aggrieved brethren, *has not been supported.*

"2. That the charge of *intentional deception*, as stated in the second specification of the same article, *has not been supported.*

"3. That the charge *of having violated an express rule of Christ, in refusing an aggrieved brother an opportunity to tell his grievances*, as stated in the fourth article of the aggrieved brethren, *has not been supported;* although it appears that the Rev. Mr. Codman and brother Field misunderstood each other in the attempt to take the first step.

"4. That the charge *of unfeeling and unnatural conduct*, as stated in the third article of the parish, *is not supported;*

as it appears that the interference of the Rev. Mr. Codman, in the tender obsequies of a funeral, was made under peculiar circumstances; and that his subsequent explanations ought to be considered as satisfactory.

"5. That *the circulation of a card by the Rev. Mr. Codman, in the town of Dorchester*, alluded to in the fourth article of the charges of the parish, was an indiscreet and improper act, *although it is not proved that there was an evil or unchristian design in the transaction.*

"6. That as the parties who brought forward articles third of the aggrieved brethren, and sixth of the parish, deemed them *unimportant,* this council consider them as virtually withdrawn.

"The following motion was then submitted to the consideration of the council:

"'That in the opinion of this council, the aggrieved brethren, and the majority of this parish, have just cause of complaint against the Rev. Mr. Codman for having neglected to exchange ministerial labors with the ministers of the Boston Association, generally, as presented in the second article of the aggrieved brethren, and in the first article of the committee of the parish.'"

On this motion the council were equally divided; closing their result with the following advice:

"This council, at the conclusion of our result, feel it to be our duty to declare, that we have, as we trust, attended with patience and impartiality to the statements, evidence and pleas, which have been presented to us by the parties in this controversy, and, though unable to decide on the last question which came before us, yet we deeply sympathize with the pastor, church and congregation, under their present unhappy divisions; and unitedly recommend to them 'the things which make for peace, and things wherewith one may edify another.'"

Thus ended the first great Ecclesiastical Council of Dorchester; and it was hoped that the result would put an end to the contention, and that the leading members of the opposition would either become reconciled and give up the contest, under the united and conciliatory advice of the council, or peaceably withdraw from the society, which was a poll-parish, and take measures to connect themselves again with the first parish. This was expected; because their case was seen to be desperate. For the council had acquitted Mr. Codman of every charge brought against him, except one, and that a slight indiscretion; and in mitigation of this charge they add, "though it is not proved that there was an evil or unchristian design in the transaction." Indeed, whoever reads Mr. Codman's explanation of the affair, made to his church, will fully agree with the council, in acquitting him of all moral blame in the case, and doubt the propriety of calling it "an indiscreet and improper act," even with the mitigating and exculpating clause subjoined. What could the opposition expect to obtain, after having been proved in the wrong, at every point, by the decision of the council on the investigation of all their multiplied and reiterated charges against their pastor? It is true that on the question of expediency, in relation to Mr. Codman's dismission, the council were equally divided; and, therefore, no positive decision was made. But here the inability to decide the question positively, operated of necessity precisely as would a negative decision. It left Mr. Codman in full standing in his original position as pastor of the church and minister of the parish, possessing all the rights and under all the obligations which belong to this high relation; and what is more, left him with a character unimpeached and proved to be unimpeachable. Indeed, it is wonderful, and was at the time viewed as an unexampled case, that he came out of the fiery trial so free from injury — that he had been kept for three years so free from imprudent words and acts, amid such high provocations and continual annoyances. He, in his humility, attributed the fact to the restraining grace of God, and to his kind providence in surrounding him with faithful friends; and especially in placing by his side that wise and judicious counsellor, Deacon

Badlam, whom he always consulted in all his emergencies, and whose advice he generally found it safe to follow.

In view of the result of the council, therefore, and in view of all the circumstances in which the result placed Mr. Codman and the disaffected members of his parish, it was hoped that the controversy would cease, and that he might be left to pursue his course of ministerial labors unmolested. But in this, as will appear in the sequel, he and his friends were doomed to be disappointed.

Before I proceed, however, with the history of the opposition to Mr. Codman, it seems desirable that some further account should be given of the character and proceedings of the council. In order to meet this demand, and supply this desideratum, I remark, that the council was constituted by selecting the most prominent ministers of the time. The parties seem to have looked over all the churches in Massachusetts, and to have nominated, each for itself, those whose pastors they deemed among the most influential and most evidently disposed to sympathize with them in their respective views. Probably there was much correspondence and consultation on the subject. Certainly it was one of the most dignified bodies of the kind, which I was ever permitted to behold; and I believe it was so viewed by all who knew the men; and the same remark may be extended generally, to the lay members as well as to their pastors. It was evident, indeed, that the churches which were requested to take part in forming this council, took care to select their respective delegates, to accompany their pastors, from among their most able and experienced members.

It will be seen therefore at once, that the decision of such a council, where the decision was unanimous or nearly so, would have great weight. And this was the fact, as it regarded all the charges which had any bearing on Mr. Codman's character as a Christian minister. The consequence to him was, to give him an elevated standing before the Christian community; and so far to disarm the enemies of what he accounted the truth, and the disaffected members of his parish generally, as to silence the tongue of slander. Henceforth, therefore, he had no charges to meet, nor any slanderous reports to contradict. The opposition were obliged to resort to other means, in their farther attempt to drive him from his post.

But it may be asked, if this council was composed of men of such standing and character, and if they were really so fair and impartial, as to agree in acquitting Mr. Codman of all the charges against him which were calculated to injure his character, how came it to pass that they were divided so equally, and so apparently by party lines, upon the great practical question of dismission? How can this be reconciled with the supposition of fairness, impartiality, or even sincerity and an independent judgment?

I am desirous of explaining this, as far as possible. For I had a high respect for most of the members of that council, and especially those whom I best knew. They were all my seniors; and, though some of them differed from me in religious sentiments, I viewed them as honorable and upright men. I had no apprehension, indeed, that any of them would designedly do Mr. Codman an injury by their decision. And this high opinion of their integrity was fully supported by their agreement in exculpating him from every charge of moral or Christian delinquency. But the question upon which the division took place, was viewed at that period, especially by what was called the liberal party, as a question of expediency, merely;

and the judgment of each man, in this case, seems to have been formed in view of what he considered as expedient, and calculated to produce the best effect; and this, of course, must have depended principally on his religious sentiments and the importance which he attached to the prevalence of those views. This I believe was the true ground of the division; at least, the true cause of the action of those members of the council who were nominated by the committee of the parish, and who were probably known, even before their appointment, to entertain these so-called liberal views, on the general subject. Indeed, we have on record evidence to justify this candid supposition. The arguments used in the secret session of the council, as stated at the time, by one of the most accurate reporters and distinguished members, abundantly proves this. And so important does this statement appear, to complete the history of the case, that I should be glad to see it republished entire, as printed in the 'Panoplist,' a periodical of the times. I can here, however, introduce a short extract only, from the close of the article, which bears honorable testimony to the character of the council, and shows the candor and impartiality of the writer: "Though the council was not so happy as to decide the controversy, the discussions were carried on, in general, with good temper, and apparent good will; and when the council was dissolved, the members separated with many expressions of tenderness and respect."

I add simply, that this testimony corroborates, in my mind, the opinion which I had formed of the fair characters of the members of the council, and seems to me to establish the theory, by which I have attempted to account for their equal division on the great question of expediency before them. They differed in their action on the question, because they differed in their apprehensions of the probable consequences of the result; and this difference depended on their respective religious views and sympathies.

THE EFFECTS OF THE RESULT OF THE FIRST COUNCIL, AND THE CONTINUANCE OF THE CONTROVERSY TILL THE CALLING OF THE SECOND.

When the result of the council was published, as previously stated, there was a prevailing hope that the controversy would cease; that the leading members of the opposition would by agreement withdraw, and either return to the first parish or form a new society, or at least remain quiet under their defeat. But, in this expectation, all who entertained it were doomed to be disappointed. For scarcely had three weeks elapsed before the opposition raised its head again, presenting a bolder front, and a more determined countenance of defiance.* On the 28th of November, at a parish

---

* For myself, however, I had little reason to hope for so happy a result. I had evidence, indeed, from the resentment shown to me personally, for the part which I had been called to take before the council, as Mr. Codman's friend, that the spirit of opposition to Mr. Codman was not subdued. A few days after the session of the council, I received an anonymous letter, purporting (I presume *falsely*) to have been written by female members of the society, in language of unmeasured reproach, and accompanied with a significant token of disrespect.

In this connection, perhaps, I ought to state a fact, which may have been the provoking occasion of the preceding transaction. About the same time I received a substantial present, with a kind note, from a committee of ladies from Dorchester. The present consisted of a silver tea-set, each piece bearing the following inscription:

FROM THE LADIES OF THE REV. MR. CODMAN'S SOCIETY IN DORCHESTER,

TO THE REV. MR. BATES,

AS A TESTIMONY OF THEIR GRATITUDE AND ESTEEM,

NOV. 1811.

meeting called for the purpose, after a long preamble, it was

VOTED, That * * * be a commitee, with full power and authority to appoint and agree with the Rev. Mr. Codman, in choosing a mutual ecclesiastical council; or, in case the Rev. Mr. Codman refuses to join and agree with them in choosing such council, forthwith to appoint an ex-parte ecclesiastical council, to take into consideration the complaints against the Rev. Mr. Codman, on account of his having refused and neglected, contrary to the expectation and wishes of the parish, to exchange ministerial labors with most of the Reverend clergy of the Boston Association of ministers; and to take in view the present unhappy state and situation of the parish, and to give their advice or result, whether it is expedient or necessary that the Rev. Mr. Codman should be dismissed from his ministerial and pastoral office in said parish, or that he should be advised to ask a dismission, and that the parish should be requested to grant the same upon just and honorable terms.

Thus it appeared that the spirit of the opposition, though it had been checked for a moment by the result and advice of the council, had lost nothing in power or zeal. On the contrary, it was evident that, nourished from some secret source, it was actually increasing in both these respects, and gathering strength and courage for a more vigorous and determined onset.

It may perhaps at this day, when the circumstances of the case can be but imperfectly known, be asked, why Mr. Codman did not at once withdraw from the scene of trial, and avoid the gathering storm which seemed ready to burst with overwhelming fury upon his devoted head? He certainly could have done it with apparent advantage to himself, to his personal security and happiness. The council had acquitted him of the faults charged against him, and left him with an untarnished reputation, and even an elevated character; and he could unquestionably have retired and found a place of useful settlement and peaceful labor, in almost any portion of the Christian church. Why, then, it may be inquired, did he not ask a dismission and give up the contest; and thus secure his own peace and happiness? In all ordinary cases, under similar trials, such a course seems to be prudent. But in this case the interests of all the churches were thought to be deeply involved. He seemed, not in his own opinion only, but in the judgment of many of his friends and advisers, to be placed in circumstances of peculiar responsibility, and called to suffer loss and endure persecution for Christ's sake and the cause of evangelical truth and piety. Besides this general consideration of duty, growing out of the peculiar relations which he sustained, and in which the interests of all the churches were involved, there was one which directly appealed to the heart of Christian friendship and covenant-obligation. His own beloved church, with whom he had entered into covenant-engagements, were in danger of being left, if he should flee, as sheep without a shepherd, and of being scattered on the dark mountains. Their pledges of affection and their appeals to his heart had been frequently and urgently made; and now they had become irresistible to a heart of Christian sensibility. If it be asked, then, why he did not seek his own peace and quiet, and at once leave his church and people, when thus perseveringly opposed and persecuted, the answer may be found in these two high considerations of duty and affection. Whoever reads the report of a committee of the church, to whom the reiterated charges of the aggrieved brethren, who acted with the opposition, was referred,— a report presented and unanimously adopted December 12, 1811, as published in the proceedings, page 116, will find an answer to this inquiry, which must afford satisfaction to every candid, intelligent Christian.

In consequence of the decisive action of the church in adopting this report, attempts were again made to purchase the pews belonging to the malcontents in the parish, and induce them to withdraw in peace. But it was all in vain. Accordingly, another diplomatic correspondence ensued, terminating at last in the agreement to call another mutual ecclesiastical council.

THE SECOND COUNCIL.—PROCEEDINGS AND RESULT.—SUBSEQUENT DIFFICULTIES, TILL THE MALCONTENTS WITHDREW FROM THE PARISH.

The second council, by agreement of the parties,—Mr. Codman and the church on the one hand, and the parish committee with the seven aggrieved church members on the other,—met at Dorchester May 12, 1812, and was organized by the choice of Dr. Lathrop, as moderator, and of Dr. Worcester and Mr. Thayer, as scribes. After a session of two days, the following motion was proposed, discussed and acted on by the council, viz:

"In the opinion of this council, under existing circumstances, it is expedient that the ministerial and pastoral relation between the Rev. Mr. Codman and the second parish in Dorchester be dissolved."

What was said in the secret session of the council was, as far as I know, never fully made public. It was reported, however, that the motion embracing the preceding proposition was based on the question of exchanges, in connection with the divided state of the parish. But whatever the arguments were on the one side and the other, the result was what all expected, who knew the sympathies of the members. On taking the question, the ministers and delegates from churches selected by the committee of the parish, all voted in the affirmative; and the ministers and delegates from the churches selected by Mr. Codman and his church, all voted in the negative. Of course it devolved on Dr. Lathrop, the moderator and umpire according to the agreement of the parties, to decide the question. He accordingly gave his vote, which was found to be in the negative. But he added an indefinite recommendation to Mr. Codman to "open a more free and liberal intercourse with his ministerial brethren." Whether the opposition would have submitted to the decision, if this explanation of his vote by the moderator had been withheld, is questionable; indeed, improbable. But the explanation, or rather appended condition, furnished to them the occasion of continued discussion and complaint, and perhaps of hope, that they should ultimately succeed in driving Mr. Codman from his post, and in triumphing over the church.

Mr. Codman, however, declared his acquiescence in the decision of the council, and his determination to follow the advice of the venerable moderator, as far as he conscientiously could; and, as he supposed, according to its true spirit and intended meaning. To his confidential friends he said, that there were several ministers in the vicinity with whom he had never exchanged, with whom, however, he was ready to make the arrangement; and with whom he should have long ago exchanged, if they had made the application, or if he had found it convenient to exchange.

The opposition, however, was not dead, and could not rest. In about two months after the decision of the council, the parish committee opened the controversy again, by directing a letter to Mr. Codman, requiring a categorical answer to the question, whether or not he intended to exchange, and that *indiscriminately*, with twelve ministers of the Boston Association whom they named, and with whom he had never exchanged. To this application Mr. Codman, with his usual promptness, decision and courtesy, returned for answer, "that he should endeavor to comply with the true spirit and meaning of the result of the last council; that the right of regulating his exchanges was admitted to be in him; that the council could not have intended, by admitting the advice of the moderator as a part of their result, that he should bind himself by any pledge, as to exchanging with individuals; that he should endeavor to preach at home, as much as possible; and that, when he did exchange, he should consult the feelings and wishes of his people in general."

This reply seems to have confounded the opposition, and restrained their action, whatever it was intended to be, for several weeks. In the mean time Mr. Codman exchanged with two out of the twelve ministers named by the parish committee. But this act of condescension, so far from allaying the spirit of opposition, seems only to have inflamed it, and driven the restless combination, or rather their leaders, to acts of desperation and self-destruction. For on the 30th of September, about four months from the time of the meeting of the second council, a number of individuals claiming to act for the majority of the parish, addressed a letter to Mr. Codman, repeating their demand for indiscriminate exchanges, and complaining, notwithstanding the fact just stated, "of the infrequency of his exchanges." "Are one or two stars," they strangely ask, in language evidently borrowed from Mr. Dexter's eloquent speech before the first council —"are one or two stars, though of the first magnitude, to content us for the light which might be derived from all the planets of our system, revolving in regular succession?" Still Mr. Codman treated his opposers with kindness and courtesy. In reply to this language of reproach, he refers the writers to his last preceding letter, and states the fact that he had already "opened a more free and liberal intercourse with his ministerial brethren, and should continue to do so, as far as time and circumstances would admit."

The parish difficulties were now rapidly approaching a crisis; and the actors in this comic-tragedy rushing forward to the catastrophe. On the 26th of October, forty-six disaffected members of the parish wrote again to Mr. Codman, declaring that nothing but a separation would restore tranquillity to the church and society, urging him to ask a dismission, and intimating, in the most expressive terms, that it was too late to think of any conciliation by means of exchanges. Mr. Codman replied promptly and explicitly, that he had made up his mind *not to ask a dismission.* His letter, however, which was dated November 12, 1812, breathed a spirit of benevolence in regard to his opposers, and expressed a strong desire still to promote their spiritual good.

But there seems to have been, on their part, no reciprocation of these expressions of kind and benevolent feelings. For on the 24th of the same month a parish meeting was held, in which, by a vote of fifty-five to forty-five, however irregular and illegal, Mr. Codman was declared to be dismissed.

This illegal proceeding was followed by an act of outrage which has no parallel in modern, civilized Christendom. It was known to his opposers, that Mr. Codman had engaged to exchange on the next Sabbath with one of the twelve members of the Boston Association, whom they had named to him, and with all of whom they had endeavored to compel him to exchange. Having induced this gentleman to excuse himself to Mr. Codman for refusing to fulfill his engagement, they procured a dismissed minister from abroad, who was to preach for them as soon as they had succeeded in their determination of excluding Mr. Codman from the pulpit. It was a bold attempt to accomplish, by direct violation of law, what they had failed to do under cover and in accordance with the forms of law.

Mr. Codman heard of the arrangement, and took every prudent measure to prevent the outrage. But he knew what would be the legal effect of allowing them to take and keep peaceable possession of his pulpit; and he was not to be intimidated by threats of violence, nor induced to neglect the duty of meeting his flock in the sanctuary.

Accordingly Mr. Codman went to the house of worship rather earlier than usual on Sabbath morning; and the scene which followed is thus described and left on record by a cotemporary:

"When he entered, he found eight sturdy men posted on the pulpit stairs, four on each side of the pulpit, in such a manner as to obstruct the passage entirely. Mr. Codman was determined to do all in his power to maintain his rights. He advanced, therefore, in his way to the pulpit, till he crowded hard against the bodies of the rioters; and, finding in them no disposition to yield, he turned into the seat under the pulpit, and soon after began public worship. In the mean time, he had expressly demanded admission into the pulpit; and one of his friends, senior deacon of the church, and a magistrate of the county, made a suitable declaration, and ordered the rioters to desist from their unlawful purposes. All this had no effect; and the agitation of the assembly was now considerable. When Mr. Codman began public worship, all became quiet, and the exercises were unusually solemn and affecting. In the midst of the first prayer, the redoubtable preacher for the parish committee made his appearance; and his guard of honor opened and gave him entrance into the pulpit. There he staid during the remainder of the services; and, strange as it may seem, he made no further disturbance till Mr. Codman had pronounced the blessing; unless it be, that he discovered sundry symptoms of uneasiness, and appeared anxious, as the audience shrewdly imagined, to find some gap, or break, into which he might thrust the commencement of *his* services. But no such gap, or break, was he able to find, and he made no noise or other disturbance.

"When Mr. Codman had dismissed the assembly, he stepped forward into the middle of the house, addressed the said preacher by name, expressed surprise at such an intrusion, and forbade his preaching in that place. The magistrate, to whom we have alluded, confirmed the statement of Mr. Codman, and declared such an intrusion to be a violation of all law, order and propriety. Several others urged the same thing.

"The preacher replied, in substance, that he did not wish to do any thing contrary to the peace of the parish, (not he, good peaceable soul, not he,) but he must proceed. The magistrate then made proclamation, that all the friends of law, order and decency, would be expected to retire. They retired accordingly, and the preacher was left to address a comparatively empty house. He went through with his exercises, had a very short intermission, and was nearly through his second sermon, when Mr. Codman and his friends assembled for worship in the afternoon. It seems that the redoubtable preacher was quite a legal character, as he could tell, at the first blush, how the Supreme Court would decide Mr. Codman's controversy; and, being such a legal character, he well knew that possession was a great point in the law. He therefore wisely determined to keep possession of the pulpit during his short intermission. The refreshment, which was afforded him, he took without leaving the house. After the completion of his services, he and his hearers retired, and Mr. Codman ascended the pulpit, and preached as usual. The preacher of the parish committee had forty-eight hearers on the lower floor of the house, at his afternoon service; Mr. Codman had two hundred and twenty. The proportion in the gallery was probably not very different. Mr. Codman preached in the forenoon from these words: *Casting all your care upon him; for he careth for you.* And in the afternoon from—*Father forgive them; for they know not what they do.* Though his sermons had no allusion, not the slightest, to the parish troubles, they were thought to apply admirably.

"Though the preacher of the parish committee was a liberal man, and though Mr. Codman's opposers were all, all liberal men, yet it does not follow that *all other* liberal men were willing to go with them to such a pitch of extravagance. This was very far from being the case. Their proceedings, on this Sabbath, were condemned by men of all parties; and by none more feelingly than by distinguished persons in the liberal party. Some of these persons advised to an immediate prosecution of the intruding preacher for a trespass; and all saw, that these riotous proceedings had removed every plausible covering of the designs and characters of Mr. Codman's principal opposers in the parish. When some of these opposers came into Boston, on Monday morning, they found the current so strong and overwhelming against them, that they were induced to offer terms of compromise, on that very day, which were ultimately accepted, and which secured the meeting-house to Mr. Codman and his friends, and to himself the perfect right of exchanging ministerial labors according to his own sense of duty and propriety."

The terms of the compromise need not be stated here. It is sufficient for our purpose to remark, that they were substantially the same with those which had been twice offered to the disaffected members of the society. Mr. Codman and his friends agreed to purchase, and did purchase, the pews of all who chose to sell them, at the cost, they agreeing to withdraw from the parish, and binding themselves not thereafter to interfere with its proceedings.

Thus ended the mighty struggle; and thus the cause of truth and right obtained a triumph, which gave a check to the prevailing errors of the times, and led to such a disruption of an unnatural alliance between men of antagonistic sentiments, as has given peace generally to the evangelical churches of New England. At least the result was a state of peace in Dorchester, and prosperity to the church of the Redeemer. Within a very short period the second parish in Dorchester was increased, all the pews were occupied, and the congregation became larger than it had ever been. Mr. Codman was blessed with a growing and harmonious church, and enjoyed a long and successful and happy ministry.

In confirmation and illustration of the preceding remark, I adduce the following extracts from an anniversary sermon, preached by Dr. Codman, December 7, 1845,—thirty-seven years from the time of his ordination, and three before his decease:

"Thirty-three years have now passed since our new organization; and we have reason to bless God and be thankful, for the peace and rest and edification we have enjoyed during that period. A gradual increase has been made both to the church and congregation; and, notwithstanding the secession from our society, the loss has been more than supplied. A flourishing church, of the same faith and order with ourselves, now exists in the south part of the town, which owes its origin to the success with which the Lord has been pleased to bless this society." — "The history of the *Second Church in Dorchester* will form an important part of the ecclesiastical history of New England. The views here maintained, of ministerial exchanges, led to the first stand that was taken in the great controversy, that afterwards agitated the churches on the subject of Unitarianism. Had your pastor been driven from his post, it would have been the signal for an attack upon many of his brethren who sympathized with him in his religious opinions. He felt that he was not acting for himself alone, but for others; he felt that he was acting for a cause that was infinitely dearer to him than any personal consideration—*the cause of Christ.* It was this consciousness that supported him under all his trials; that animated him under all the opposition and persecution he had to meet, and enabled him to persevere in the course he had undertaken. I have often looked back with astonishment upon that period."—" Surely, it was God who sustained me. If the Lord had not been on our side, we may now say,—'If it had not been the Lord, who was on our side; when men rose up against us, then they had swallowed us up quick, when their wrath was kindled against us.' "

Thus am I brought to the concluding part of this memorial;—to the notices which, at the beginning, I promised to give of Dr. Codman's prominent traits of character,—traits exhibited, and, in a great measure formed, during his severe trials. And the notices which I am about to give, are the result of my own observation, during the long and intimate intercourse which I was permitted to hold with him.

DR. CODMAN'S NATURAL AND SOCIAL QUALITIES.

I begin with a brief description of him, viewed simply as a man; directing my remarks, under this head, to his personal appearance and to his natural and social qualities. When he was a young man, he was neither remarkably slender, nor the reverse; but rather of a middle size, as well as common stature. His countenance was fair and florid; and his face, though remarkable for nothing as to form or features, except the prominence of his forehead, exhibited much of that indescribable meaning, which in the language of poetry constitutes "the human face divine"—much of strength and dignity, mingled with mildness and benevolence. As he advanced in life, he became somewhat corpulent; not so much so, however, as to prevent his continued activity and vigor, both of body and mind.

His social qualities were of the highest order. He was always cheerful and affable; attractive to the young, communicative and respectful to the aged, and agreeable to all with whom he was called to associate. He was, indeed, of that sanguine temperament which, with a cultivated intellect and a kind heart, never fails to produce the highest style of companionship.

I said he was always cheerful. When I come to speak of him as a Christian, I shall have occasion to remark, that there was another element of character, mingled with this, which produced in him that equanimity and complacency which are the peculiar fruits of sanctified cheerfulness. But I subjoin here, that cheerfulness in him as a natural quality, was of a much higher cast than that which falls to the ordinary lot even of well-ordered minds.

There was an ingredient in his constitutional temperament which gave him a peculiar fondness for social life, and often elevated his cheerfulness to exhilaration of spirits, and set him free from the restraints of dull formality. He was indeed truly courteous, and, in the best sense of the term, polite. He was always happy in his manner of meeting and entertaining his visitors and guests, precise and courtly in giving or receiving introduction to strangers, as well as easy in all his intercourse with his friends; never, in these respects, transgressing the most rigid rules of conventional decorum. Brought up, from childhood, in polished society, improved by foreign travel and intercourse with some of the most refined portions of the most civilized nations in the world, possessing a quick discernment of fitness and propriety, and thus being able to render all these external advantages subservient to an original tact, the want of which no education can supply, he was everywhere accounted a gentleman; and he seldom, if ever, made a mistake in the freest and most unrestrained conversation, or a false movement, even in mixed company, so as to try the feelings of the most delicate and refined, or give offence to the most fastidious. Still he seemed always to be free from restraint in his social intercourse; and his cheerfulness was often relaxed into playfulness, and sometimes into hearty laughter.

He was fond of wit, and even of delicate and well-timed sarcasm. He could enjoy the one and smile at the other, though their shafts were successfully aimed at his own head. I am persuaded, that his buoyancy of spirit and cheerfulness of temper, which he often indulged to a high degree of exhilaration, added very much to his health and personal enjoyment, to his attractiveness as a companion, and to his influence and usefulness in society. John Locke long ago made the remark, that "man is the only *laughing* animal on the earth;" and he seems to have made it not only with a view of distinguishing man from the lower animals, but for the purpose of showing his elevation in the scale of being. Indeed, without a fair proportion of this element in his nature, and a due cultivation and proper exercise of it in social life, no man can be a pleasant companion, or a very attrac ive and useful member of society. A high degree of cheerfulness, such as Dr. Codman possessed, duly regulated and properly indulged, as to time, place and circumstance, always free from gross and vulgar hilarity, is certainly a gift of no ordinary value. Where it exists, it exerts a salutary and elevating influence on every other element of character, which qualifies man for personal enjoyment and pleasant companionship.

Another natural quality or element of Dr. Codman's character, which occurs to my mind, and which was fully developed and eminently prominent, in the time of his severe trials, was the harmonious combination of the two qualities denoted by the terms *fortitude* and *courage.* He was prompt to decide, and bold to execute what he undertook; but there was no rashness in his courage. He was firm and steadfast in purpose, pursuing his prescribed course with untiring perseverance and indomitable patience. Yet there was nothing like obstinacy in his fortitude. This combination of courage and fortitude, viewed as one complex quality of mind, was in him unquestionably modified and controlled by religious principle. But I speak of it here, as a natural quality, which would have given him distinction among men of the world, even if it had not been sanctified by divine grace.

Had he been called to command a ship, and had that ship been brought into collision with another, and ready to sink amid the raging waves and thick darkness of a stormy night, it would have kept him in a state of composure and perfect self-control, with promptitude and energy, devising and employing the fittest means to save the vessel and her crew. If he had been called to fight his country's battles, it would have sustained him in the hour of danger, and led him, undismayed, 'even to the cannon's mouth.' For his was that natural, or, as sometimes denominated, *moral* courage, which, combining with it innate fortitude, never allows the nerves to tremble, or the muscles to be relaxed, or the purpose, once formed, to fail through timid inaction.

Had he not possessed this high quality, sanctified as it was in him by divine grace, he never could have sustained the shock and endured the trials which came upon him in the early part of his ministry; nor would he have dared to take the course which he did, or have been able to pursue it, as he did, to the accomplishment of his purpose, amid the threats and reproaches of enemies on the one hand, and the timid counsels of not a few of his friends, on the other. But while he did not despise the latter, nor disregard the former, his courage and fortitude enabled him to remain steadfast in his deliberately formed purpose, and constant in pursuing the course which he had carefully prescribed for himself. To me, he seemed never to waver in mind or relax his energy of active pursuit, from the beginning to the end of the mighty struggle. And though he did not adopt the precise language of John Foster, because it savors too much of a spirit of boasting, yet his conduct answered to the description which that eminent writer gives of a man of decision and strength of character, where he says: "Without harshness or violence, he will continue every moment to effect some part of his design, coolly replying to each ungracious look and indignant voice, 'I am sorry to oppose you. I am not unfriendly to you, while thus persisting in what excites your di pleasure. It would please me to have your approbation and concurrence; and I think I should have them, if you would seriously consider my reasons. But, meanwhile, I am superior to opinion; I am not to be intimidated by reproaches, nor would your favor and applause be any reward for the sacrifice of my object. It is enough for me, that I stand approved to my own conscience, in the sight of Heaven. It is enough that I can appeal, with confidence, to the highest authority in the universe!'"

Thus am I brought to the notice of another natural quality possessed by Dr. Codman, — a quality which may seem, to some, almost inconsistent with the one last named,—I mean that of *strong sympathy with the afflicted*, and tender compassion for the suffering. Though a stern advocate for justice, always firm to his purpose, and even rigid in self-government, 'he could feel for others' woe;' and he was prompt to act, wherever his arm could reach the distressed, or his voice be heard by the afflicted. This natural quality was indeed in him, like the others already named, a sanctified feeling; and, in most of its manifestations, it was intimately connected and inseparably blended with religious principle, thus constituting Christian charity. Still, however, there was in him a natural and original sensibility of a high order; which, being sanctified by divine grace, gave activity and energy to the principles of Christian benevolence. Indeed, all his benevolent acts were modified and regulated by Christian principle. He never gave alms from impulse, nor from motives of ostentation; but always by rule, and in the best manner to secure the proper end of giving. This trait, however, properly belongs to his Christian character. I shall, therefore, defer the particular remarks which I have to make on it, till I come to the notice of him as a Christian.

But there is one branch of his Christian character, so dependent on original sympathy and high social qualities, as to deserve a passing notice in this connection. I mean *his hospitality*, his abounding hospitality to his brethren in the ministry. His ample patrimony and his favorable position enabled him to exercise this office of a Christian bishop, more frequently and more largely, than probably ever fell to the lot of any other minister in New England. And he did exercise it in the highest and best style of Christian hospitality. Ministers of the gospel from all parts of our own country, clergymen from foreign lands, and missionaries of the cross from the ends of the earth, visited his hospitable mansion; and were always cordially received and generously entertained. Indeed, as has been said in another case, 'Hospitality stood at his door;' and, it may be added, beckoned to the passing pilgrim, and especially to the heralds of salvation, to come in, to sup and lodge; 'to bless and be blessed.'

One other original quality, I may add, he possessed in an eminent degree; a natural *frankness* which, united with Christian principle, forbade all deception and duplicity. And even without that sanctifying influence, it would have been difficult for him to practice the deceiver's art. So open and frank was he, in declaring his religious sentiments before his settlement in Dorchester, that some have supposed this uncalled-for disclosure was one exciting cause of the opposition with which he had to contend; that it awakened a jealousy in the enemies of the truth, and caused them to put the most unfavorable construction on the language of rebuke which subsequently fell from his lips. But however this may have been, it certainly gave him an enviable advantage in the contest. For an appeal to the fact of this frank and full disclosure, enabled him to meet his revilers with boldness, to confound them in the presence of their sympathizing friends, to refute their unfounded charges to the entire satisfaction of all unbiassed minds; and lead a council, divided in religious opinions, to agree in acquitting him of every charge implying duplicity or moral wrong. I remember how his opposers quailed, when the argument in vindication of his course, founded on this fact, was triumphantly placed before the council, and its force admitted by their own principal advocate; when that candid advocate said, in substance, "All these complaints and charges can be disposed of in five minutes, if he will now yield the point with regard to exchanges; if he will agree to exchange henceforth with all the ministers of the Boston Association, indiscriminately." Yes, frankness in him was a natural quality; and, being sanctified by divine grace, it became a brilliant and glorious virtue; a virtue, rendered more brilliant by the trials through which he was called to pass; as a precious stone shines the brighter, the more severe the friction to which it is subjected.

INTELLECTUAL QUALITIES AND LITERARY ATTAINMENTS.

In speaking of Dr. Codman as a scholar, I may without impropriety repeat the remark, made concerning him as an undergraduate, and say that he held, in this respect, among his brethren in the ministry, as among his classmates in college, a highly respectable rank. In mere secular literature, ancient or modern, Dr. Codman never sought distinction. Though he possessed one of the best private libraries in the country, it consisted principally of books on theology. Besides, his multiplied cares and trials, which came upon him soon after his settlement in the ministry, together with his weekly parochial duties and direct preparations for the pulpit, left him very little time for general reading and mere literary and scientific pursuits. Nor had he much more leisure for these purposes, after his parochial trials were over. For these very trials, patiently endured and happily terminated, had given him notoriety, and secured to him a reputation for wisdom and consistency of character, and thus thrown upon him an unusual portion of the care of the surrounding churches. Such, too, was his local situation and domestic establishment, with his ample fortune and kind social disposition, as to bring to his home visitors in great numbers; and thus many of his appropriated hours for study were interrupted. These causes, too, operated to call him often from home, as a member of ecclesiastical councils, or as an active associate in most of the prominent benevolent societies in our country. But, with all these interruptions and hinderances, his acquisitions of knowledge were highly respectable; at least, of that knowledge which had a direct bearing on his profession, or which could be rendered subservient to the great business of a minister's life.

He acquired knowledge with great facility, retained it with great tenacity, and was able to adapt and apply it to useful purposes with great skill and efficiency. All his perceptive powers were strong and active; so that wherever he was, in company or alone, at home or traveling abroad, he found himself at school, learning something for future use, making observations and acquiring useful knowledge. This was true of him, with regard to all practical subjects. But it was peculiarly evident, with reference to practical and experimental religion. He possessed a knowledge of spiritual things, ready, definite and precise, which can be accounted for only on the principle that "spiritual things are spiritually discerned." Of these he seemed, to those who heard him preach, —as a discriminating lady once said to me,—to know more than others who possessed equal means and equally favorable opportunities for acquisition; certainly more than most of his best-instructed brethren. At least, his Christian knowledge, being added to a strong faith, partook largely of the nature of that knowledge which is experimental; which is felt in the heart, as well as seen in the understanding; and thus, when imparted, warming the souls of others into spiritual life, while shedding light upon their path to heaven.

Dr. Codman possessed great versatility of intellectual capacity. He was able to take a general view of all subjects; and gather something, adapted to his purpose, from all sources. His powers of observation, as before stated, were strong and active; and his memory was ready and retentive. But his powers of discrimination and quick discernment were peculiarly noticeable. He seemed to see the conclusion in a logical deduction, without the labor or delay of the ordinary process of ratiocination. Hence he was noted for what has been called common sense—that is, rapid reasoning, or judging correctly with little effort of comparison. He rarely made a mistake in his moral judgment, even where his opinion was necessarily formed without much deliberation. There was something in this rapid action of his mind, like instinct or intuition; and I might, perhaps, ascribe the result to an original and delicate taste. In some modern analyses of mind, this faculty has been denominated æsthetic, or that instinctive power which discovers at once those relations of fitness and adaptation on which the pleasant emotions of beauty depend, without regard to their truth or moral excellence; — by which men discover the beautiful and agreeable in form, color, sound, and motion, without any direct regard to moral qualities—to truth or error, right or wrong. To me, however, the term taste seems to express the whole idea, in the most definite manner. Indeed, there was no quality of his mind more prominent than that of taste, in the largest and best sense of the term. He possessed a good degree of poetic imagination. But his taste for judging the works of imagination far outstripped his genius for their execution. Of the best poets in the English language he was peculiarly fond; and he could point out their faults, as well as their excellences, apparently without the labor of criticism; certainly without the necessity of applying the technical rules of the rhetorician and professional critic.

DR. CODMAN'S CHRISTIAN CHARACTER AND SPIRITUAL ATTAINMENTS.

To exhibit Dr. Codman as a Christian and a man of deep and eminent piety, it is scarcely necessary for me to add anything to what has been made apparent in the records of the preceding reminiscences. His natural qualities,—his intellectual and moral powers, with his distinguished social accomplishments,—were all modified by the grace of God; and, by prayer and meditation, brought under the control of a steady regard to the glory of God.

Of his habits of devotion, as secret and hidden exercises of the soul, I cannot speak. Nor can any one with propriety do it, without recurring to the records of his experience made by his own hand; and such a delicate task belongs only to a confidential biographer. It is no part of the office of one who writes merely from his own memory and personal observations, and records his own reminiscences, his recollections, as they exist in his own mind, and are formed from materials furnished by his own previous observations.

Dr. Codman, I can truly remark, however, as I had occasion to know, was "a man of prayer"— habitual, fervent, persevering prayer. Though of his closet devotion I cannot speak, yet of those of the family and the pulpit I might say much. For I had opportunity, both in my own family and in his, in my own pulpit and in others, to unite with him while he conducted the services of social worship, and to observe their simplicity, directness, humble confidence and fervor of spirit. In these respects, his devotional exercises were always distinguishable from those formal, cold, preaching prayers, which too often, in the place of social worship, fall like lead upon the ear of man; while, as we have reason to fear, they never reach, and were never designed to reach, the ear of the Almighty; — from those prayers, which are evidently studied to please men, and are sometimes spoken of as *eloquent prayers* — which are not offered, even, with the expectation of pleasing God, drawing down the blessing of Heaven, and procuring a spiritual "refreshing from the presence of the Lord." Such as these, were not the social prayers offered by Dr. Codman. He was always serious in his devotional exercises, humble in confession, direct and earnest in petition, devout and full of expressive emotion in strains of adoration and thanksgiving; and thus he carried along with him the pious sympathies and holy aspirations of every pious soul within the sound of his voice.

But in these remarks, I perceive that I am only expressing my own views, according to my own taste; and giving nothing more than my own impressions on the subject of Dr. Codman's personal piety and the character of his devotional performances. Of course, such statements cannot furnish conclusive evidence to those who never had the privilege of uniting with him in acts of social worship, and the opportunity of judging for themselves. There is, however, one view of the subject, as it fell within my observation, which may give strength to the evidence of simple testimony, and enable those, who never saw or heard him, to judge for themselves; provided only, that they have some analogous experience, connected with a delicate taste in spiritual things. I allude to the ease with which he referred all events, as they occurred, to the providence of God, and the readiness with which his mind was brought into a state of elevated devotion. This general fact was so obvious, as to be observed by all who knew him; and to its truth a multitude of witnesses, still living, might be called to testify. He seems to have had the fear of God so constantly before his eyes, and the love of God so largely shed abroad in his heart, as never to have been unprepared to enter into the holy exercises of devotion, with his whole soul. Not with more readiness and certainty does the naturalist trace a newly discovered stream to its source, than he referred every blessing to the Source of all good, and every event to the providence of God.

I recollect an incident, which happily exhibits and beautifully illustrates this tendency of his mind. Or rather, I remember his account of it, soon after its occurrence, with his statement of the feelings which it excited in his bosom, and the train of thought to which it led him. During the height of his parochial trials, when he was beset with difficulties, and oppressed with anxiety for the result of the contest in which he was engaged, and when there was a strong apprehension in the minds of some of his friends that he would be induced to retire and seek repose in some other field of labor,—one afternoon, as he sat in his study, it was announced to him that a large company of little children, in order of procession, were slowly and silently approaching his house. Not knowing what had brought them there, and not suspecting with what intent they had come, he rose and hastily met them at the door, and,—no doubt in his usual kind and happy manner,—saluted them. But, as he stated to me, he was surprised and completely overwhelmed by the declaration of one after another, and finally all, with united voice, that they had come to entreat their dear and beloved pastor not to leave them, the lambs of the flock, and their afflicted parents, as sheep without a shepherd. Said he, as he related the incident, "Though I at once supposed that they had been sent by their parents, I could not help referring the whole to the providence of God." "Nothing," he added, "could have operated more powerfully to cheer my drooping spirits, and animate my hopes of final success, than this simple incident. I thought I saw the hand of God in it, and felt encouraged to buckle on my armor anew for the contest. I remembered," continued he, "that even our blessed Saviour expressed his approbation when little children saluted him, with their hosannas, in the temple; and silenced the objections of unbelief by referring the objectors to the prophetic language of the Psalmist: 'Out of the mouth of babes and sucklings hast thou ordained strength, because of thine enemies.' Yes, I thought, if the blessed Saviour, in his state of humiliation and trials on earth, was pleased with the hosannas of little children, how much more should his humble ministers draw instruction from such favorable indications of Divine Providence as had thus been exhibited to me; — if the Great Shepherd was pleased when little children came to him, and even when in the arms of faith they were brought to him for a blessing, how should his under-shepherds rejoice, when they can secure the affection and confidence of the children and youth of their parish; and how should they take encouragement to labor to bring these lambs of the flock into the fold of the Great Shepherd and Bishop of souls! Yes, I seemed to hear him say unto me, as he said to Simon Peter: 'Lovest thou me?—Feed my sheep!—Feed my lambs!'"

This habit of referring all events and occurrences to the providence of God, led him to look to the Spirit of God for direction and support in all circumstances. It exerted a modifying influence on all his powers and faculties, and gave direction to all his propensities and pursuits.

His religion, as before intimated, modified his natural cheerfulness, and directed his exuberant flow of animal spirits; so that he could be serious, while cheerful; and easily glide from the glee of friendly greetings to the solemn exercises of social worship; and without any forced effort, or apparent constraint, hold sweet converse with Christian friends one moment, and the next be employed in leading the devotional exercises of the pious, in high and holy communion with the Father, and the Son, under the evident influences of the Holy Spirit. Though this remark may, in a measure, be true of all eminently pious men, it was certainly applicable to him, in a high degree and peculiar sense. There was in his social conversation and devotional exercises, a peculiar appropriateness to time, place, and circumstances—a striking fitness and precise adaptation, resulting from natural taste, sanctified by divine grace.

His natural courage and innate fortitude were likewise modified and regulated by the same purifying and controlling influence. His fixed religious principles prevented his courage from running into rashness, and his fortitude from sinking into obstinacy. Thus, where duty called, no obstruction could shake his resolution, or turn him from his determined course. But, where expediency only was involved, "a little child might lead him."

So too his compassion, and all the tender sympathies of his nature, took their cast from his religion, and were sanctified and directed by its principles. His benevolence was truly a Christian benevolence. Though he had the means of doing much in the cause of benevolence, and actually did much, yet he never did it from motives of ostentation, or under the influence of excited feeling. What he gave, was given after due deliberation. He divided his charities among individual objects and benevolent associations, after strict inquiry concerning their comparative merits and importance; and thus, while he gave much and frequently, he always gave according to his own carefully formed and discriminating judgment. His benevolence was far removed from that profuse and indiscriminate liberality, which always sounds a trumpet before it, that it may attract the notice and secure the applause of the world; while it fails to obtain the approbation of God, and often accomplishes but little for the relief and benefit of suffering humanity. Thus he distributed his bounties, especially for the purposes of diffusing the knowledge of salvation and promoting the conversion of the world, with a liberal but judicious hand. For, in the language of the sermon preached by Dr. Storrs at his funeral, we may ask, "What enterprise of benevolence has ever urged a just claim on the advocacy and pecuniary support of the church, that met not with a cordial response from him? What association of unquestionable character enrolls not his name among its benefactors and its elected or honorary officers?" Yes, he gave much, "cheerfully and of a willing mind." While he rejected many imposing claims, and was thought by some, who knew not his motives and principles of action, to be too cautious on the subject, he readily and cheerfully aided, according to his views of their importance, all those objects of benevolence which commended themselves to his deliberate judgment. He once said to me, "that it was one of the most difficult questions of duty which he had to decide, when to give, and when to withhold his hand from giving, — when he should bestow unsolicited, and when he should refuse to grant the requests even of the most importunate applicant for charity." Indeed, I had opportunity to know that he often gave, unasked. More than one instance of this Christian "forwardness" fell within my own observation. One case I may mention, without impropriety. Once, when engaged in soliciting aid for a public and well known cause of benevolence, I met him in the streets of Boston; and before I had presented the claim to him, or made the request, he kindly anticipated the application by proffering a generous donation. To give unasked, I believe, was his general practice; where he had a full knowledge of the case. For he remembered that "the Lord loveth a cheerful giver;" and he loved to act under the influence of this high and holy principle.

Thus all his natural qualities and social sympathies, being sanctified by divine grace, and brought under the control of Christian principle, produced a highly finished moral, social, and Christian character — a character of great symmetry and beauty, exhibiting an example worthy of imitation in all the relations of life.

MINISTERIAL CHARACTER, AS A PREACHER AND A PASTOR.

The various qualities of heart and intellect combined, which I have ascribed to Dr. Codman, constituted him, under the special call and distinguishing grace of God, "a good minister of Jesus Christ."

As a preacher he was solemn, impressive, and, where prejudice had not been awakened, attractive to all classes of people ; and always and everywhere popular with those who concurred with him in theological sentiment. This fact of his general popularity arose, partly from his manner of writing — from the style of his composition and the character of his sermons; and partly from his manner of delivery — his pulpit eloquence.

His style was simple, neat, and perspicuous. There was no affectation about it, and no appearance of labored effort to embellish it, and crowd it with ornament. What he had to say, he said in plain Saxon words, with little transposition and great directness. Yet, even in his most hasty compositions, there was no want of ornament, nor, for purposes of illustration and impression, any deficiency of allusion to the analogies of nature and art. He generally wrote rapidly, for his sermons were usually written at large; and amidst his multiplied cares and pressing calls of duty, he had but a short period allowed him for his direct preparations for the pulpit. Hence simplicity of thought, natural arrangement of words, with an easy and unconstrained introduction of apt illustrations, gave his style much of its beauty and attractiveness. But more of its excellency depended on that instinctive taste, which was so prominent among the natural characteristics of his mind. This enabled him to give a peculiar appropriateness to his discourses, and impart a directness to their applications, always suited to the occasion, and sometimes giving them great force and pungency.

His delivery, too, corresponded perfectly with the character of the style in which his discourses were written. That, likewise, was simple and peculiarly natural. He used much gesture; but it was always easy, and adapted to the subject and the occasion. It never appeared studied or constrained; but always seemed to grow out of his subject, and to be prompted by the emotions of his own soul.

He rarely spoke extemporaneously in the pulpit; and yet his manner very nearly resembled that of the most gifted extemporaneous speakers. When he first returned from Scotland, he preached altogether *memoriter*. But it was perceived by a friend and hinted to him, indeed he soon discovered himself, that the effort of recollection often damped the ardor of his feelings, influenced unfavorably the modulation of his voice, and diminished the animation and impressiveness of his utterance. He accordingly discontinued the practice of committing his discourses to memory; and henceforth depended on spontaneous recollection, with an occasional glance of the eye on his fully-written manuscript.

Thus his style of writing and happy manner of delivering his discourses, rendered his preaching attractive and impressive. There was, however, one quality of his preaching, connected both with the style of his writing and the manner of his speaking, which I hardly know how to describe—a quality, without which all preaching is cold, formal, and comparatively inefficient — a quality, indeed, or rather a gift bestowed, in measure, on all good preachers of the word of God; but on him in an eminent degree. I mean that power which enables the preacher "to hide himself behind his subject," and bring the souls of his hearers into a condition to sympathize with his own soul, and into communion with Him who is the end of the law and the substance of the gospel which he preaches; —that power, exhibited both in writing and speaking on the great themes of Christianity, which compels the hearers to feel that the preacher is "serious in a serious cause"—that he believes what he says, loves what he believes, and feels experimentally and obeys practically, what he thus loves, believes and commends to others; — that power which shows the preacher's inmost thoughts and deepest emotions, and gives him a mysterious control over the thoughts and emotions of his hearers — which brings out his whole soul, absorbed in his holy subject, and absorbing, with it, all kindred souls. This quality, whatever called, this power, however obtained, this "unction from the Holy One," Dr. Codman possessed, as it seemed to me, in an eminent degree; and, added to his other qualities, it made him an attractive and highly acceptable preacher to all who loved the truth that he preached.*

The other branch of Dr. Codman's ministerial character, his character as a pastor, was not, in point of excellence, behind that which he possessed as a teacher of the law of God, and a preacher of the gospel of Christ. Among the people of his charge, — at least among those who reciprocated his kindness, encouraged his familiarity, and finally adhered to his parish,—he was a familiar friend, a kind father, a faithful shepherd. I have sometimes thought, that, if three or four of the leading men of the opposition in his parish had been absent from the place for six months after his ordination; and if the parish itself had been isolated and kept from surrounding influences during the same period, his kind and affectionate manner and his general

---

* It was this quality in his preaching, which was probably the means of building up his society so soon after his opponents withdrew from it. The same thing, unquestionably, served to attract to his house of worship, so constantly, those men of taste and piety, who made Dorchester their place of summer residence. I remember a remark of the late Daniel Webster, which has a delicate bearing on this point, as stated to me by Mr. Codman, soon after: "Sir," said he, "I have become a temporary inhabitant of Dorchester; and while I reside here, I wish to be considered as your parishioner; and in one respect you will find me a good parishioner—always in my place at church every Sabbath—both parts of the day."

deportment, in his pastoral visits, would have won the affections and secured the attachment of many of those, who were finally drawn into the opposition, so that they could never have been led astray by all the arts of intrigue and allurement which might have been subsequently practiced, and brought to bear upon them. But however that might have been, those persons who remained in connection with his church, as well as those who, subsequently to the separation, became members of his parish, manifested peculiar attachment to him, as their pastor and friend. He was, indeed, a faithful and affectionate pastor; visiting all his flock, and watching over them in love. Especially was he noted for his kindness and attention to the poor and afflicted, to whom he diligently ministered, both in things temporal and spiritual.

AN OBJECTION TO THE CONSISTENCY OF DR. CODMAN'S MINISTERIAL INTERCOURSE, ANSWERED.

Thus have I finished the notices, which I proposed to give, of the prominent traits and peculiar characteristics of mind, as observed by me, in

Dr. Codman; and, especially, as displayed by him during the period of my most familiar intercourse with him. I should now close the record with a single reflection on the whole scene of reminiscences as it lies together before my memory; but an apprehended difficulty, in some honest and inquisitive minds, seems to demand of me a passing remark, by way of explanation, and in answer to a plausible objection sometimes made against the consistency of Dr. Codman's ministerial intercourse. It has been asked, "with what propriety he could apply, as he did, to Mr. (afterwards Dr.) Channing to preach his ordination sermon. If he could not conscientiously admit a Unitarian into his pulpit, on exchange, why did he introduce a leader of that denomination, as the preacher to himself and his people, on an occasion so solemn as that of his own public consecration to the work of the ministry?" The question has been often asked, and especially by persons residing at a distance from the scene, and not acquainted with the history of the rise and progress of that denomination in New England.

At the time of Dr. Codman's ordination, there was no known and acknowledged Unitarian minister in Boston, or its vicinity, except Dr. Freeman; and he was not a Congregationalist, but a lay-ordained minister of a society, originally connected with the English Episcopal church, and still at this day retaining the modified forms and liturgy of that church. The Congregational churches and their ministers were none of them publicly known to be Unitarian; certainly none of them claimed the name. Mr. Channing was then a young man, recently settled, as a Congregational minister, over a Congregational society. He was, too, among the most serious and solemn preachers of the day. Whenever he appeared in the pulpit, "he spoke like a dying man to dying men"—he preached as if he felt a deep conviction of sin, and a fearful apprehension of a coming judgment. No one in all that region, as I well remember—for I often heard him at the "Thursday lecture"—preached with more solemnity, or more directness of application, on the guilt of sin, the depravity of human nature, the danger of impenitent sinners, the holiness and spirituality of the divine law, the glories of the divine character, and the riches of redeeming grace. So solemnly and tenderly did he preach on these and kindred subjects, and so forcibly and pungently did he apply them to his hearers, that some of his people, it was said, began to be alarmed under the apprehension that he would come out, as they expressed their fears, "a rigid Hopkinsian." Such, indeed, was his preaching, and such was his conversation, that the most serious portion of the community was attracted for a time to his church and his study. For myself, I can truly say, (for we entered upon the work of the ministry nearly at the same time,) that there was no minister in the vicinity whom I more loved to hear, or with whom I more delighted to hold familiar ministerial intercourse. Such intercourse we held for several years, with confidence and satisfaction on my part, and apparently on his. This intercourse continued, with repeated exchanges of pulpits and friendly discussions in our studies, till, as I had occasion to observe, the general current of his theological views was changed. And with this observed change of his sentiments, there was an evident modification of his feelings, and a marked falling away from the former solemn style and manner of his preaching.

When Mr. Codman invited him to preach at his ordination, Mr. Channing had not passed under the modifying influence of "the new philosophy." Indeed, I have no doubt that whoever is permitted to read his manuscript sermons, written in the early part of his ministry, will find them differing essentially from those discourses which constitute his published works.

As a vindication of Mr. Codman against the charge of inconsistency, let it be remembered, then, that his ordination took place before the public development of American Unitarianism — certainly before Dr. Channing was thought to be inclined to that theory of religion. Indeed, the Dorchester ordination sermon, though not very discriminating in theological sentiment, is full of those solemn appeals and statements, which the author never would have made after he had been trained in the school, had imbibed the spirit and become accustomed to the language, of controversy — after he had exercised all his powers in contending with Stuart and Worcester — certainly not, after he had preached his noted Baltimore and New York sermons.*

---

* I perceive that my recollections on the subject of this change in Dr. Channing's preaching, and the development of American Unitarianism, perfectly harmonizes with those of Samuel Greely, Esq., of Boston, for many years a deacon in the same church, of which Dr. Channing was pastor. In his speech before the Unitarian Convention, recently held in Baltimore, where one of these sermons was preached thirty-three years ago, he says, referring to this discourse: "It was the earliest, open and bold avowal, before clergy and laity, of the distinctive peculiarities of the Unitarian faith."

It has been said that Dr. Channing's mind, towards the close of life, reverted to his early theological sentiments, and that the feelings exhibited in his early preaching were revived. As proof of this, the close of his last published discourse, delivered at Lenox just before his death, has been referred to. But I understand that his most intimate friends deny the alleged fact, and explain away the adduced proof. I have no means of settling the question. Nor would its decision have any direct bearing on the subject under contemplation. I have said, or rather written enough, I trust, to vindicate Mr. Codman from the charge of inconsistency, in selecting the pastor of the church, where his surviving parent, with her family, then attended public worship, to preach his ordination-sermon.

CONCLUSION.

I close these reminiscences with the remark with which I commenced, that the name of John Codman belongs to the ecclesiastical history of New England. For the work which he performed for the Congregational churches of his country has inseparably connected his name with their prosperity, and will carry it down, covered with honor, to future ages. It was indeed a great and good work; difficult of execution, and requiring a peculiar instrumentality. Its magnitude and importance can scarcely be estimated by any, who are ignorant of the state of the Congregational churches, before the separation took place. Nor is it less difficult for such persons to appreciate, or even to perceive the beneficial effects, which have resulted from it. I believe, however, that both parties, both the orthodox and the liberal, as they have been sometimes denominated, admit that the separation has, on the whole, been beneficial; especially in its influence on the cause of peace and social intercourse. I am confident, indeed, that those who constitute the Orthodox portion of the Congregational churches, generally, if not universally, are glad of the change, and fully satisfied that the cause of religion has been promoted by it. They think that the churches with which they are connected, since the change took place, are in a more flourishing condition—much revived in their spiritual character, more harmonious in benevolent action, exerting a higher and better discipline over their respective members, and even increasing in number. They, who can look back to the time of the separation and remember the state of things which then prevailed, see, in the present peace and prosperity of our Zion, much to induce them to rejoice that the separation was made. In Boston and the vicinity; through the Commonwealth of Massachusetts; in all parts of New England; indeed, wherever the Congregational organization of Christian churches exists, they discover more unity, peace, spirituality, and efficient Christian action, than these churches ever exhibited, while they remained in that mixed state, described in a former part of these reminiscences.

They look, for example, at Boston; and instead of seeing, what might be seen fifty years ago, churches nominally Congregational, with a few members, and those of various sentiments, — sentiments so antagonistic as to produce division in feeling, neutralize all benevolent action, and destroy all efficient discipline, — they now behold a large number of Congregational churches, agreeing in sentiment and united in action; built upon the same Apostolical foundation; contending earnestly for "the faith once delivered to the saints"; exercising over their respective members, and over each other, a watchful care and a salutary discipline; laboring together to promote the cause of religion at home, and to send the gospel to the far distant nations of the earth; and thus obeying the last command of the Head of the church, and fulfilling the purpose for which he established a church and directed his followers to act under some well-adapted and efficient organization.

Thus great and good was the work, performed by Dr. Codman for the Congregational churches; and no one, after contemplating the severe trials through which he was compelled to pass, in accomplishing it, can fail to perceive that it was a work of great difficulty. It is doubtful whether there was any other minister, possessing such qualifications, and surrounded by such favorable circumstances of location, wealth and friends, in all the region, as to have been able to accomplish it with success. But God seems to have raised him up for the express purpose, and furnished him with all the means and facilities for the arduous work;—to have given him his birth at the proper time and in the proper place; to have endowed him with the best-adapted talents; and so to have controlled the course of his education, and ordered all the circumstances of his settlement

35

in the ministry, as best to qualify him for the work, and enable him to accomplish it in the best manner.

I do not mean to say that there were not, at the time, other ministers as good and as great as Dr. Codman. But there were none who possessed all the requisite talents and qualifications which were united in him, and who were surrounded with all the favorable circumstances of location, of friendship, and of wealth, which came to his aid. Nor do I intend to intimate, that he labored alone—that he was the only instrument employed by Heaven, to produce this ecclesiastical separation, so important to the peace and prosperity of the Congregational churches of this country. But certainly he took the lead in the work, and was the most prominent instrument in its accomplishment.

Well, therefore, may it be said, that the name of JOHN CODMAN belongs to the ecclesiastical history of New England, and deserves a prominent place among the distinguished ministers of the Congregational churches. Well may all the friends of the peace, purity and order of these churches, rejoice and bless God, that he raised him up at the appropriate time, placed him in the most favorable situation, qualified him for the work, sustained him under his severe trials, aided him him in his arduous labors, and crowned his efforts with success.

SERMONS.

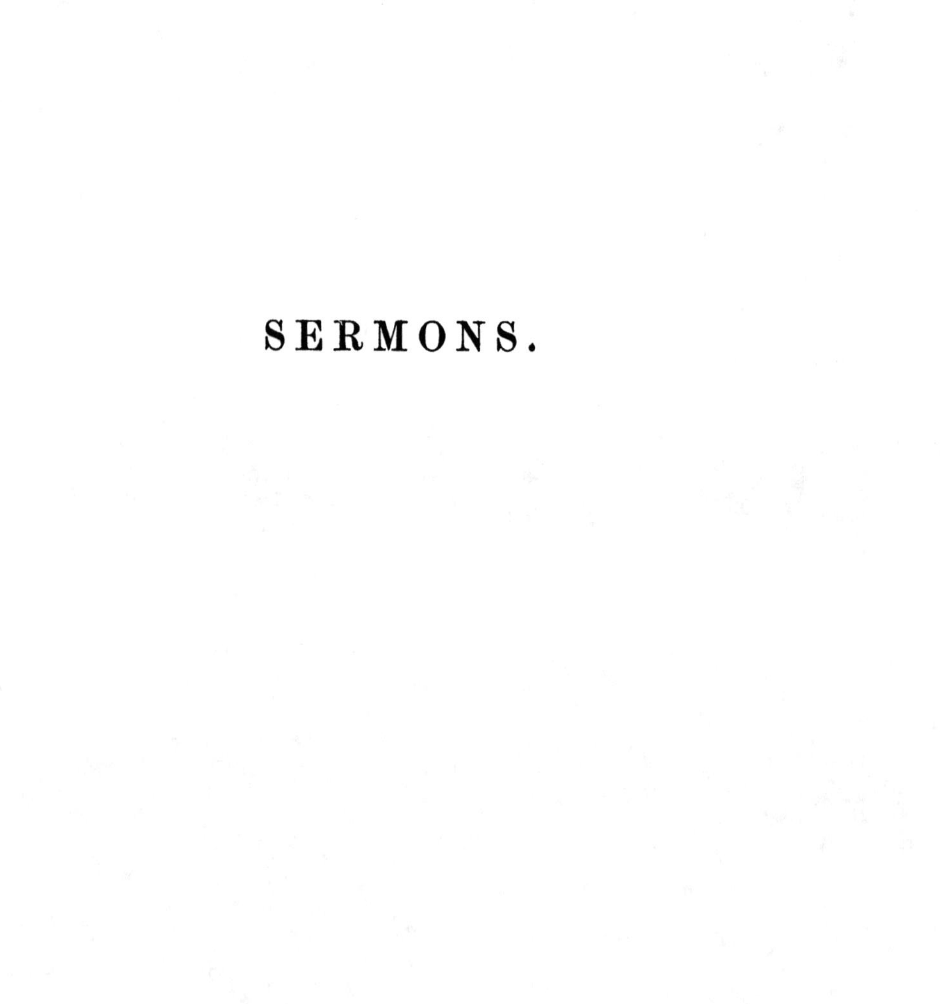

SERMON I.

THE PERSON OF CHRIST.

REVELATION xxii. 16.

I AM THE ROOT AND THE OFFSPRING OF DAVID, AND THE BRIGHT AND MORNING STAR.

To meditate upon Christ, is the delight of the Christian. To select suitable subjects for such meditation is no difficult matter; for the Bible is full of Christ, from Genesis to Revelation. The most ancient of sacred historians, in his account of the creation of the world, directs our attention to the seed of the woman, who was to repair the ruins of the fall. The Prophets loved to prophesy of the Child that was to be born, of the Son that was to be given, and to describe the glories of his kingdom in the latter day. The Angels ushered the new-born Infant into the world with songs of celestial harmony. The Evangelists and Apostles recorded, with inspired faithfulness, the minutest actions of his life, and the precious truths that fell from his lips.

The appearance of the promised Messiah in our world was an event of unspeakable importance to our race, upon which hung our immortal and eternal destiny. It is not surprising that the most intense curiosity should have been excited with regard to the true person and real character of the Messiah. Some entertained one opinion, and some another. Some thought that he was John the Baptist, some Elias, and others Jeremias, or one of the Prophets; and some few, including the Apostle Peter, thought that he was the Christ, the Son of the living God. This last opinion the Saviour himself pronounced correct, and accompanied his decision with a special blessing upon him who expressed it. "And Jesus answered and said unto him, Blessed art thou, Simon Bar-jona, for flesh and blood hath not revealed it unto thee, but my Father which is in heaven. And I say also unto thee, Thou art Peter, and upon this rock I will build my church, and the gates of hell shall not prevail against it."

As in the time of the Saviour, so in our day, different and opposite opinions are entertained of the person of Christ. Some regard him as equal with the Father, and some as inferior to him, possessing only delegated authority. That there are difficulties attending this important subject, will not be denied. Some passages of Scripture, taken separately, seem to teach one doctrine, and some another. But we are not to judge of any doctrine by a few disjointed and separate texts, but by comparing Scripture with Scripture. And especially with regard to the person of Christ, — the subject which has occasioned so much controversy in the Christian world, — we ought to be exceedingly careful not to form hasty and undigested opinions, but prayerfully and humbly to consult the whole of the sacred oracle, in the Old as well as in the New Testament, trusting in the guidance of Him who hath said, "If any man do the will of my Father in heaven, he shall know of the doctrine, whether it be of God."

But principally are we to look for the most satisfactory information on this important subject, to our Lord Jesus Christ himself. Surely he is the very best authority. When he condescends to speak of his own nature and person, every mouth should be stopped, and the most implicit credence given to his declarations. This he has done, very clearly and fully, in several parts of that most interesting and remarkable book, called the Revelation of Saint John. In the commencement of it, he declares himself to be 'the Alpha and Omega, the first and the last, the beginning and the ending, which is, and which was, and which is to come, the Almighty;' and in the close of the same book, he repeats this declaration, and in addition to it affirms, in the words of the text, "I am the Root and the Offspring of David, and the bright and morning Star."

The first part of our subject tends to reconcile many, and some apparently opposite views of the person of Christ. The Messiah is sometimes spoken of as the Mighty God, and sometimes as a new-born infant. He is represented as an object of contempt and abhorrence, and at the same time as universally admired and adored. Sometimes he is said to live forever, and sometimes to die on the cross. He is called the Lord, and yet the Son — the Root and the Offspring of David. Nothing can be conceived more opposite than the characters which were thus represented as combined in the person of the Messiah. But the Pharisees noticed only those passages which flattered their pride, and raised their expectations of temporal grandeur. Our Lord, therefore, often directed their attention to their own prophecies, which described the

Messiah in a more humiliating view. The miracles of Jesus had given abundant evidence of his divine mission. On account of them, therefore, the Jews were bound to believe in him. His humiliation was as clearly foretold as his power and glory; and the accomplishment of it, in his outward state, was an additional reason for their acceptance of him as their Saviour. A due attention to the Scriptures which they professed to understand and explain, would have led them to a discovery of this truth. Hence our Lord, on a particular occasion, solicitous not merely to confound, but to convert and save them, said unto them, "What think ye of Christ, whose son is he?" They said unto him, "The son of David." So far they correctly answered the question. But our Lord proposed a difficulty arising out of this answer, which they could not so readily solve. "He said unto them, How then doth David in spirit call him Lord, saying, The Lord said unto my Lord, Sit thou on my right hand, until I make thine enemies thy footstool. If David then call him Lord, how is he his son?" This question they could not answer, without admitting the claims of Jesus to be the Son of God as well as the son of David, without acknowledging that our Lord united in one person the two natures of God and man.

This hypothesis would have explained at once the difficulty. But this they could not admit, without acknowledging our Lord's divinity. The language of our text explains the difficulty. "I am the Root and the Offspring of David." On the supposition that Christ possesses two natures, the difficulty vanishes. As *man*, he may be called the son of David; and as God, David may, with the strictest propriety, call him Lord. The importance of this distinction in speaking of Christ is very great. It tends to remove many difficulties which, upon any other scheme, would be insuperable. For instance, in one part of the Bible, our Lord informs us that he and his Father are one. In another place, he says, "My Father is greater than I." The Apostle, in speaking of Christ, says, "Who being in the form of God, thought it not robbery to be equal with God;" and our Lord is frequently represented as a man subject to human infirmities—a man of sorrows and acquainted with grief.

Now if we admit not the distinction of the two natures of Jesus Christ, these passages certainly contradict each other; but upon the supposition that two natures are united in the same person, they are immediately reconciled. In his divine nature, Christ and the Father are one. In his human nature and mediatorial character, the Son is *inferior* to the Father. As the second person in the Godhead, it was no robbery for Christ to claim equality with the Father; but in his human nature, it became him to be made in all things like unto his brethren. Indeed, the denial of the two natures of Jesus Christ is the fruitful source of all the errors respecting the person of Christ, which prevail among us. Their advocates produce all those texts which apply to Christ's human nature and mediatorial character, and which *we* acknowledge represent him as inferior to the Father; and they endeavor to explain away those texts which relate to his divine nature and pre-existent state. In this way, they perplex many minds with painful and distressing doubts with regard to one of the most important doctrines of Christianity.

But let it ever be remembered, that the Lord Jesus Christ unites in one person the two natures of God and man. He is both the Root and the Offspring of David. The importance of this doctrine will appear, if we consider that both the glory of Christ and the salvation of men are connected with it. On the union of the divine and human natures, the sufficiency of Christ, as a

Saviour, depends. If he were a mere creature, his obedience could not merit any thing for us. All that he could do would be nothing more than his bounden duty; and after all, he would be only an unprofitable servant, neither would his sufferings have made any atonement for our sins. There is no proportion whatever, between the sufferings of one creature for a time, and the sufferings of myriads of creatures to all eternity. As sin is an infinite evil, and exposes the sinner to an infinite punishment, nothing short of an infinite atonement could save him from destruction. An infinite atonement could not be made by a finite being. Nor is there any such distance between the highest and lowest of creatures, but that they must be equally unable to take away the sins of a ruined world.

Now, were it not for the divine nature of Christ, united with his human nature, he could not have made a sufficient atonement; and consequently the whole race of man must have remained forever miserable. Besides, were it not for the blessed union of the two natures in our Redeemer, his intercession would be utterly unavailing in our behalf. It is the sufficiency of his atonement to satisfy the demands of law and justice, that forms the basis of his intercession. Let that foundation be sapped, by a denial of his Godhead, and the whole superstructure must fall at once. On the other hand, if he be God, as well as man, his obedience, his sufferings, and his intercession, are exactly such as God's honor and man's necessities required.

But the importance of this subject will appear, if we consider, that on a knowledge of this union of the two natures in Jesus Christ, our salvation depends. Without such a view of Christ, we can form no just idea of his character. As we should be wholly ignorant of our own nature, if we supposed we were destitute of souls, so should we be of Christ's nature, if we were unmindful of his divinity; for it is his divinity which gives such a value and efficacy to his sufferings. Were his nature not divine, we should never be encouraged to approach him as our Saviour. Who that felt the burden of sin, — its evil, its bitterness, and its plague,—would ever think of applying to a creature for relief? Our dependence upon a creature must be limited; for, if it were *unlimited*, instead of saving us, it would only subject us to God's heavy displeasure, who will not suffer us to offer to a creature the homage due only to the Creator.

But to obtain salvation, we must love Him, in whom we trust, supremely, and depend upon his merits, entirely. This we could not do, if Jesus Christ were a created being, without incurring the guilt of idolatry and blasphemy. If we think of Christ only as a creature, our knowledge of him, to say the least, would be confused, our gratitude feeble, and our dependence vain. How important then is it, that we should have correct views of the Saviour as the Root and the Offspring of David, as God and man mysteriously united in one person. For want of this scriptural view of the person of the Saviour, how many have defective views of the whole plan of salvation. We speak not now of the heathen who never heard of Christ, for they cannot believe on him of whom they have not heard; but we speak of those who hear of Jesus from Sabbath to Sabbath, but who see no beauty in him that they should desire him; who live under the light of the gospel, but whose eyes are blinded by the god of this world.

It is enough to make a Christian weep, if he has any sensibility, to behold so many immortals, whose souls are as precious as his own, unmindful of the Saviour's excellence and inattentive to his gracious invitation. Shall the Root and the

Offspring of David make an atonement for sin, to raise us to glory, and is it possible, that the very creatures for whom this stupendous sacrifice was made should treat it with indifference, and refuse to be saved by such precious blood! If angels rejoice in the salvation of one single sinner, surely they must weep, if such holy beings can shed a tear, to see so many thousands of precious souls preferring death to life, and hell to heaven. Even among those who do think occasionally of a Saviour, it is painful to reflect on the number who entertain low, mean, unworthy thoughts of his glorious person. How many deny his divinity, and consider him only as a good man, a great prophet, and an inspired teacher. We cannot think too highly of the Son of God. We can never exalt the Saviour too high, nor debase the sinner too low. We need not be afraid of offending Christ by thinking too highly of him; but there is infinite danger of incurring his displeasure by unworthy thoughts of his personal character. He is the Root and the Offspring of David, and the bright and morning Star.

Having dwelt so long on the first part of the text, but little time remains to consider the beautiful metaphor by which our Lord represents himself to the Apostle John — the *bright and morning Star*, the Divine teacher, who hath knowledge and truth in himself; who, like the morning star, dispels the clouds of night, and ushers in the light of day. 'He is the true light, which lighteth every man that cometh into the world. He is the glory of his people Israel, and a light to enlighten the Gentiles.'

Did our time permit, we might dwell upon the beautiful parable in the text. As the morning star is distinguished from other planets and stars, as the harbinger of approaching day, so the Lord Jesus Christ is the harbinger of great joy to all nations. How joyful was the period when the Dayspring from on high first visited our dark and guilty world! 'The people that sat in darkness saw a great light, and to them who sat in the valley of the shadow of death, did light break forth.' The coming of Christ was the fulfilling of God's gracious promise unto the fathers, and the blessed manifestation of God's rich favor and good will to men.

But we must forbear. We can only express our gratitude to God for placing this bright and morning Star in the moral firmament, to be a light to those who sit in darkness, and to guide our feet into the way of peace. What a blessing is it, that in this dark and gloomy world we have a bright and morning Star to illuminate the darkness, and to direct us on the way to happiness and heaven. What encouragement under all the trials and vicissitudes of life, that we can turn our eye upwards, and behold its celestial light, shedding its bright and cheering beams upon our pathway, and animating us with the prospect of a brighter day.

Let us then be exhorted to look unto Jesus, in all times of our trouble, temptation and trial; and when we discern his presence with an eye of faith, we may hail it as the harbinger of peace and comfort. And in that hour, when all earthly consolations fail, when the darkness of the grave seems ready to cover us with its gloomy shroud, how transporting is the glimpse which the dying believer takes of the bright and morning Star, the sure precursor of that glorious, eternal day, which awaits him in the world of spirits. Then, as his dying eye is fixed upon its mild and steady light, he may depart in peace, with the assured hope of a brighter day, a glorious resurrection, and a happy immortality.

Christian friends! We have been meditating upon Christ as the Root and the Offspring of

David — the bright and morning Star. What theme can be more appropriate to the solemnities of a sacramental occasion? With what holy awe, with what fervent love, with what devout adoration should we behold an Incarnate God, as he is evidently set forth crucified before us!

Were it not for the views we entertain of the two natures of the Saviour, were it not that he is God-man, the ordinance we are now to observe would be a cold, unmeaning rite. We are assembled together to commemorate the death, not of a mere martyr, but the vicarious sufferings of the Son of God. In this sacred ordinance, we remember the Root and the Offspring of David — the Son of David, and David's Lord. As the Offspring of David, he died on the cross; as David's Lord, his sufferings received a value which has rendered them efficacious to the salvation of all who believe on his name.

Approach, then, ye humble disciples of Jesus — ye who are not ashamed of your Master—ye who believe in the mystery of his incarnation — ye who desire to imitate his holy example, and to imbibe his blessed spirit. For you this feast was instituted. You will welcome its return with heartfelt joy and gratitude. You will gather around this table, and renewedly pledge your allegiance to the best of Masters; and may the Root and Offspring of David meet you at his table, and arise in each of your hearts as the bright and morning Star. AMEN.

SERMON II.

ON PRAYER.

MATTHEW VI. 5, 6.

AND WHEN THOU PRAYEST, THOU SHALT NOT BE AS THE HYPOCRITES ARE: FOR THEY LOVE TO PRAY STANDING IN THE SYNAGOGUES, AND IN THE CORNERS OF THE STREETS, THAT THEY MAY BE SEEN OF MEN. VERILY, I SAY UNTO YOU, THEY HAVE THEIR REWARD. BUT THOU, WHEN THOU PRAYEST, ENTER INTO THY CLOSET, AND WHEN THOU HAST SHUT THY DOOR, PRAY TO THY FATHER WHICH IS IN SECRET; AND THY FATHER, WHICH SEETH IN SECRET, SHALL REWARD THEE OPENLY.

PRAYER is the very life of religion. It is the thermometer, if I may so express myself, of the soul. In proportion to its lively exercise, its sincere desires and fervent aspirations, may be determined the degree of grace that exists in the soul. Prayer is the Christian's breath. A body, from which the breath has departed, may as well be said to live and move and have a being, as an individual, who is an utter stranger to prayer, can be said to have a spiritual existence. It is prayer that connects the soul, while in this probationary state, with the heavenly world. By prayer, man holds communion with his Maker, rises above this lower world, and has a foretaste of joys yet to be revealed. In answer to prayer, God bows the heavens and comes down and dwells with man. He bends from his lofty throne, and listens to the breathing of a pious soul. His ear, which is forever saluted with the angelic choir, hymning adoration and praise, is open also to the sighing of a broken and contrite heart; and the prayers of his elect, in this lower world, are continually ascending, in one cloud of incense, before his holy seat. Prayer too is the weapon, with which the Christian fights all his battles, and by which he overcomes all his foes of earth and hell. It is a precious instrument in the Christian's armory. The moment it begins to rust, his enemies begin to triumph. Like the best and choicest metals, it brightens with use, and improves by time. Prayer, also, is the bond of Christian union. It binds the disciples of the Lamb together, though separated by seas and mountains. It levels all distinctions, and, at one throne of grace, unites the rich and poor, the high and low, the bond and free.

A duty so important, we may well suppose

would engage the attention of the great Teacher of mankind, who came into the world to atone for sin, and open a way of access to the mercy-seat. It was he alone who could make the sinner's prayer acceptable; for it is the very essence of acceptable prayer, that it should be offered in a Redeemer's name, and be perfumed with the incense of a Saviour's merits. If any one was authorized to instruct the world respecting the duty of prayer, it was the Author of the text; for, in addition to his being divinely appointed to teach mankind, he was a bright example of the duties he taught, and of none more remarkably, than of that enjoined in the text. Jesus Christ, in his human nature, was eminently a man of prayer. He spent whole days and nights in the exercise of this sublime and delightful employment. How often do we read of his retiring, even from his disciples, for secret prayer. When exhausted by wearied nature, they sunk into the arms of sleep, their divine Master was maintaining intercourse with his Father by earnest prayer. Who then so well qualified to discourse on this subject, as he who was the brightest example that ever shone, of earnestness and fervency in prayer?

I will not spend time in proving that prayer is

a duty; because I will not suppose that there is an individual in the congregation who will deny it. But, though all will assent to the necessity and importance of prayer, I fear there are few who realize it so deeply, as to make it their meat and their drink. It may therefore be useful to consider its necessity and importance.

The necessity and importance of prayer may be urged, perhaps sufficiently, from this consideration alone, — that God has been pleased to establish a connection between the request on our part, and the bestowment of his favors. After enumerating a number of blessings which he had in store for ancient Israel, he says, "I will yet for this be *inquired* of by the house of Israel to do it for them." He may, it is true, and he sometimes does bestow his favors unasked; but this is not his usual method of operation. When he sees best to depart from this method, it is with a view to display the sovereignty of his grace. But these instances are so rare, that it would be folly and madness in the extreme, to expect the blessing without first seeking it in prayer. If, then, our blessings, temporal and spiritual, must flow to us through this medium, we cannot but acknowledge the necessity and importance of the duty of prayer.

But to perform this duty merely from this motive, from the expectation of what we are to receive, would be selfishness, altogether inconsistent with the disinterested spirit of the gospel. The child of God does not pray merely with a view to have his petition granted, any more than we breathe merely with a view to live. Prayer is something more than a bare petition for favors desired. It is the holy aspiration of a holy soul in addressing a holy God ; and without this there can be no real, acceptable prayer. We may desire any temporal blessing, and ask it of God ; but unless in so doing our souls are drawn out in holy desires, unless we ask in the name of Christ, and pray in the Spirit, the petition cannot be considered a prayer ; it certainly is not the prayer of faith, and we cannot expect an answer.

But the necessity and importance of prayer may be farther urged, from the consideration that it is absolutely essential to the existence of the divine life. There can be no life of God in the soul without prayer. There can be no communion with God and with Christ, no fellowship with the saints, no intercourse with heaven. Prayer is the key, that opens the door of holy communion. It is the wing, that raises the soul from earth to heaven. It is the carrier between the lower and the upper worlds. To prayer we are indebted for all that holy joy, for all those happy frames, for all those heavenly anticipations which constitute the Christian's song in the house of his pilgrimage, and which form a pleasing contrast, and more than equal balance, to those distressing feelings, those gloomy thoughts, and those anxious forebodings which every Christian has, in a greater or less degree, to encounter in struggling with his corruptions, and in passing through an enemy's country to his heavenly home.

The Saviour cautions his disciples against hypocrisy in the discharge of this solemn and important duty. There is nothing more offensive to God, and more disgusting to every serious mind, than hypocrisy in religion, especially in the duty of prayer, which, of all other duties, seems to require sincerity and truth.

When we consider that the Being whom we profess to address in prayer seeth the heart, and is acquainted with every latent motive, however studiously it may be concealed from men, it seems in the highest degree astonishing, that any should be so presumptuous as to attempt to deceive an omniscient God and to mock the Searcher of hearts. The persons to whom the Saviour alludes by the appellation, *hypocrites*, were the Scribes and Pharisees, whose hypocritical conduct was frequently the subject of his severe reprehension and cutting reproof. They were remarkable for their long prayers and sanctified appearance, while they devoured widows' houses, and indulged in all manner of secret wickedness. Such characters, however, are not peculiar to the Jewish nation, nor to the times in which the gospel was written. They exist now, and will exist, as long as the hearts of men remain unrenewed by divine grace. There are now, no doubt, to be found among us, hypocrites who love to pray standing in the synagogues or places of public worship, that they may be seen of men. 'Verily,' says the Saviour, 'they have their reward.' That is, they have what they desire, the esteem of their fellow-creatures, upon whose credulity they impose; but they have none from Him who seeth not as man seeth, and who will render to every man according to his work. But let no one suppose,—from this caution of the Saviour's not to imitate the hypocrites, who love to pray standing in the synagogues,—that all public prayers and public exercises of religion are to be avoided. This is evidently not the meaning of the Saviour. He was very far from discouraging the *public* worship of God; on the contrary, he recommended it both by precept and example. He himself sacredly observed the public religious institutions of his country, and attended with his countrymen the synagogue on the Sabbath day. "It is of *private* prayer only," says Bishop Porteus, "that our Lord is here speaking; and the hypocrites whom he condemns were those ostentatious Jews who performed their devotions, which ought to have been confined to the closet, in the synagogues, and even in the public streets, that they might be noticed and applauded for their extraordinary piety and sanctity. But this reproof could not possibly mean to extend to public devotions in places of worship. This is evident, from the corners of streets being mentioned; for these are places in which public devotions are never performed." All that the Saviour intended was, to condemn the motive by which hypocrites are actuated—*that they may be seen of men.* And this motive, so far as it prevails in our public assemblies, is certainly to be condemned. Be careful then, my hearers, when you engage in religious exercises in public, that you be influenced by a sense of duty to God, and not by a desire *to be seen and heard of men.*

Especially should ministers of the gospel, whose office it is to appear in public, guard against spiritual pride. They, more than other men, are in danger of splitting on this rock upon which so many have foundered. Let private Christians also, as well as ministers, suffer a word of exhortation. If God has given you gifts, beware lest your gifts prove your ruin. There is reason to fear that many private Christians, who possess remarkable gifts in prayer, have been greatly injured by the ill-judged praise of their brethren, and have insensibly been influenced by the motive of being heard of men. No objection can be raised from our text to meetings for public prayer, provided they are conducted in a proper manner, and provided those who engage in public exercises are not influenced by the motive of being *seen and heard of men.*

Our Lord, however, takes this opportunity of urging upon his disciples the all-important and essential duty of *secret* prayer, without which all *public* prayer will be vain, and worse than in vain. — BUT THOU, WHEN THOU PRAYEST, ENTER INTO THY CLOSET, AND WHEN THOU HAST SHUT THY DOOR, PRAY TO THY FATHER WHICH IS IN SECRET; AND THY FATHER, WHICH SEETH IN SECRET, SHALL REWARD THEE OPENLY.

On the duty of secret prayer, too much cannot be said. It is perhaps the best criterion by which we can judge of our state before God.* Those who habitually and conscientiously practice this duty, and who take delight in its observance, entirely unnoticed, and, as far as possible, unknown to others, have the best evidence that they can have of a state of grace; while those who neglect the duty altogether, and those who but partially perform it, to say the least, have reason to entertain doubts of their spiritual state. The temptations to neglect this duty are so strong, that nothing but a principle of grace can preserve us in its constant and habitual observance. I believe there are few, if any, but have been tempted partially to neglect this all-important duty. Few so habitually realize the divine presence and their own accountability, as not occasionally to dispense with closet duties, or, if they regularly attend to the performance of them, sometimes to engage in them with cold indiffer-

---

* It is the nature of true grace, that however it loves Christian society in its place, yet it, in a peculiar manner, delights in retirement, and secret converse with God. So that if persons appear greatly engaged in social religion, and but little in the religion in the closet, and are often highly affected when with others, and but little moved when they have none but God and Christ to converse with, it looks very darkly upon their religion.—*Edwards on the Affections*, p. 363.

ence and lifeless formality. Alas, the generality of Christians, even of the most sincere and most pious, must mourn their remissness in the discharge of this duty.

As this duty is so infinitely important, and so absolutely essential, we cannot urge it too much. If any have been tempted to forsake their closets, to neglect to pray to their Father which is in secret, let me urge upon them an immediate attention to this neglected duty. A neglect of this duty is the commencement of backsliding, and of all those evils attendant on a state of apostasy. If you value the peace of your own souls, if you value heaven, if you dread hell, go back and visit your neglected closets. There pour out your souls to Him "who seeth in secret." In secret, confess all your sins. Mourn over the hardness of your hearts, your remaining corruptions, and your indwelling sin. In secret, open your whole heart to God. Conceal not its plague. It will be a relief to you thus to unburden your soul, and it will be pleasing to God to hear the groanings of your spirits; for a broken and a contrite heart he will not despise. In secret, acknowledge all the mercies you daily receive from the hand of your great Benefactor. He loves a grateful, as well as a contrite heart. In secret, also, spread all your wants before God. Specify them particularly. However minute, they will be regarded by Him, without whose knowledge not a sparrow falleth to the ground, and by whom the hairs of our head are all numbered. In secret, too, remember all for whom it is your duty to pray. When none are present but a heart-searching God and yourself, you may use particular expressions, which would be improper on more public occasions.

It was said of one of the former ministers of Boston, Dr. Cotton Mather, that he was in the habit, in secret prayer, of praying for his children and the members of his church by name. I do not mention this for universal imitation, but merely to exemplify my idea of the freedom which may be taken in secret prayer, which would be manifestly unsuitable on other occasions. The closet is the place where we may indulge a holy freedom in addressing the throne of grace. Unawed by the presence of critical hearers, and trusting for acceptance in that Being who regards the humble prayer of the illiterate as well as of the learned, the Christian can pour out his soul in holy aspirations before the mercy-seat.

"The absence of every human witness," says

a pious writer,* "emboldens us to throw off all restraint, which would prevent the freedom of our address to God, and invites us to pour out our hearts before him. There, each one can enter into his own particular case; and where is the genuine Christian who has not some important concern to transact with God, which he could not express before any creature, however near and intimate. As deceit lies in generals, the sincerely pious wish to enter minutely into all their sins, infirmities, wants and woes; but whom could we intrust with this unreserved confession, but Him to whose eye our hearts are transparent? In the closet, the numerous class of Christians who complain of being destitute of the gift of prayer, females and young persons, may call upon God, unencumbered with the shackles of a form of prayer. Here, the spontaneous language of an overflowing heart offends no one's ear, however ungrammatical, or even contradictory it might sound. In this hidden sanctuary we may perform that secret, solemn act of personal devotion, the surrender of ourselves to God, and our acceptance of him, in 'an everlasting covenant never to be forgotten.'"

In recommending the subject of secret prayer,

* The Rev. James Bennet, of Romsey, Eng.

the same devotional writer observes, "What though other parts of religion might seem more attractive, have you not observed, that in art and nature, as well as religion, the objects which obtrude themselves upon the sight may be more specious, but the most essentially important retire from notice? The face and hands of the clock catch our eye, while the main-spring, without which all the rest would be an useless picture, is concealed from sight. 'The human face divine,' with its life and expression, excites most notice; but it is the heart, which lies hidden in the breast, visible only to the eye of God, that by its energy and motion circulates the blood, and preserves the whole frame from death. You admire the leaves and flowers of the plant; but the root, which remains concealed and disregarded, supplies the juices and maintains the life and beauty of the whole. We may be more stricken with the glory of public worship; and beholding such an assembly as this, exclaim, 'How goodly are thy tents, O Jacob, and thy tabernacles, O Israel!' But let us never forget that the secret devotion of the closet is so essential to the life and value of our public services, that without it the most specious appearances are but splendid hypocrisy."

But there is a reward attendant upon the discharge of this duty, which claims our attention before we close the subject. 'Thy Father, which seeth in secret, shall reward thee openly.' Although in the discharge of religious duties we should be actuated, not so much by the hope of reward, as from love to God, and a delight in the duty itself, yet certainly it is not improper, that, like Moses, 'we should have respect to the recompense of reward.' We are assured that our heavenly Father will not be an unconcerned spectator of our devotions, nor be inattentive to our supplications. He will reward us openly, by answering our petitions, and granting our requests, so far as his wisdom may see for our good, and for his glory, in ways which will be openly seen and regarded by the world. Indeed, the discharge of this duty carries with it its own reward. What happiness does the Christian enjoy in his closet! He is abundantly rewarded by the hours of sweet communion which he is privileged to spend with his heavenly Father, by that abstractedness from the world, and by that elevation of soul and intercourse with heaven, which are the happy effects of closet devotion. The Christian, who lives by faith and secret prayer, will not only be rewarded in this world, but will be openly rewarded in heaven. The Being whom he has so often adored in his closet, will own his unworthy name before an assembled universe, and will admit him to dwell forever in his presence with this blessed plaudit, "Well done, good and faithful servant!"

Permit me now to close the discourse, by an application to three classes of hearers. First, To those who never pray; Secondly, To those who pray as the hypocrites; and Thirdly, To those who pray in secret, in sincerity and truth.

Are there any, now present, who never pray? Do you believe in a God, and do you think he has no concern in the affairs of men? Do you not know that you are completely in his power, and that he can do with you what seemeth good in his sight? And is it a matter of indifference to you whether you enjoy his favor, or suffer his wrath? Are you not sensible that you have offended this just and holy, gracious and benevolent Being? And will you not ask forgiveness of him? Are you not afraid, that if you treat him with entire neglect and contempt, he will reward you accordingly? Can you 'abide the day of his coming, can you stand when he appeareth; for he is like a refiner's fire, and like fuller's soap.' Are you not afraid to hear language like this addressed unto you: 'Because I have called, and ye have refused, I have stretched out my hands, and no one regarded, but ye have set at nought all my counsel, and would none of my reproof; I also will laugh at your calamity, I will mock when your fear cometh, when your fear cometh as a desolation, and your destruction cometh as a whirlwind, when distress and anguish come upon you. Then shall ye call upon me, but I will not answer; ye shall seek me early, but ye shall not find me; for ye hated knowledge, and did not choose the fear of the Lord. Therefore shall ye eat of your own way, and be filled with your own devices.'

Be persuaded, my friends, if you never prayed before, to begin to-day. When you retire from this house enter into your closets, and when you have shut your door, pray unto your Father which is in secret. Penitently confess all your past transgressions. Conceal no darling sin; but 'cut off the right hand, and pluck out the right eye.' Solemnly promise, that from this time forth you will lead a new and holy life; that wherein you have done iniquity, you will do so no more; and ask of God to grant you his Holy Spirit to enable you to perform all your good resolutions. Remember that of yourselves you can do nothing; that all your sufficiency must be of God. Go to the cross of Christ, and there learn to pray. Look at Him whom you have pierced, and mourn. From his veins flows the fountain, which was opened for sin and all uncleanness, in which you must be washed from all your filthiness, and cleansed from all your idols. In his precious name you must pray, if you expect to be heard: and whatever you ask the Father in his name, believing, you shall receive. And may God grant that many, who never prayed before, may this day lift up holy hands, with a humble and contrite heart, to the seat of mercy, and find acceptance with that Being who heareth and answereth prayer.

My subject now leads me to address a few words to those of my hearers, who pray as the hypocrites. Who you are I know not, nor do I wish to know; for I would avoid personalities, and yet be faithful. But in a few words I will so describe you that you may know yourselves. You come regularly to the sanctuary of God, and stand praying in his house; but your motive is not to seek forgiveness of God, and to inquire the way to heaven, but to be seen of men. You even profess religion and observe the ordinances of Christ, but at the same time you are strangers to your closets; or if you ever visit them, if you ever retire for prayer, it is only to satisfy the remonstrances of conscience which such a discourse as this may excite, but which are soon forgotten when you mix again with the world. My friends, if this is your character,—and you may easily know whether it is,—I beg you to pause and consider the danger of your situation. You are attempting to deceive a Being, with whom the darkness is as the light, and the night as the day. But your attempts are vain. The Most High seeth you and witnesseth all your hypocrisy, and there is nothing he more heartily detests and will more severely punish. If you continue in a state of impenitence, read your doom in the word of God. "The hypocrite's hope shall perish." "The hypocrites in heart heap up wrath." "The Lord of that servant shall come in a day when he looketh not for him, and in an hour that he is not aware of, and shall cut him asunder, and appoint him his portion with the hypocrites."

I must now conclude by addressing a few words of comfort and encouragement to those of my hearers who pray in secret, in sincerity and truth.

However obscure and unknown you may be in the world, you are not unnoticed, my praying friends, by the great Jehovah. He is everywhere present. He witnesses all your retirements. He sees you in the midnight hour, when the eyes of mortals are closed in sleep. He not only sees, but hears. Not a sigh, not a groan escapes his attentive ear. He not only sees and hears, but remembers. He does not forget your wants, though he may not immediately grant an answer to your prayers. He loves to try the faith of his children, and to exercise their patience. But be not discouraged. He will answer prayer, if not in the way which you expect, in a much wiser and better way. Be not weary then of secret prayer, but continually enter your closets and shut your doors about you. A conscientious attention to this duty will fit you for all the scenes and events of life; will support you under all its trials, and strengthen you under all its temptations.

"If I had gone to prayer," said a poor criminal about to be executed for murder, "in the morning of the day I committed the awful deed, I should not have been left to have shed innocent blood." The closet contains the Christian's armor. If he does not put it on in the morning, he cannot expect to overcome the enemies he may have to encounter during the day.

"Finally," my Christian friends, "take unto you the whole armor of God: above all, praying always with all prayer and supplication in the Spirit, and watching thereunto with all perseverance, and supplication for all saints." AMEN.

SERMON III.

THE GOOD AND FAITHFUL SERVANT.

Preached at Milton, October 18, 1836, at the Funeral of the Rev. SAMUEL GILE, D. D., Pastor of the First Congregational Church in that place.

MATTHEW xxv. 21.

WELL DONE, THOU GOOD AND FAITHFUL SERVANT; THOU HAST BEEN FAITHFUL OVER A FEW THINGS, I WILL MAKE THEE RULER OVER MANY THINGS: ENTER THOU INTO THE JOY OF THY LORD.

WE have assembled, my hearers, to pay a tribute of respect to the memory of a much esteemed, much beloved minister of Christ. The circumstances of the occasion are in themselves peculiarly solemn and awful. On the last Sabbath morning, he stood in this desk in his full strength, and apparently in perfect health, and offered public prayer for his beloved people, for the church and the world; and during the short interval of divine service, he resigned his soul into the hands of his Maker, and ascended to the heavenly temple, to spend an eternal Sabbath in the presence of his God.

There is something in the circumstances of his removal from us, which, though tending to inspire our minds with solemn awe, is calculated to impart comfort and support, and even to call forth emotions of praise and thanksgiving. We know that it is appointed unto all men once to die, and that there is no discharge in that war; but there is a great diversity in the manner in which it pleases our heavenly Father to release his creatures from life. Many are removed by lingering sickness and wasting disease, and are called to much bodily pain and suffering; and these circumstances, too, are mercifully ordered, especially where, as in most cases, there is need of time and opportunity to prepare the soul to stand before its God. But where, as in the case of our departed friend, there rests not the shadow of a doubt of personal piety and habitual preparation for death, we cannot but regard the very suddenness of the event as an expression of divine benevolence. It seems to us more like a *translation* than an *ordinary dissolution.* We are reminded of Enoch, who walked with God, and was not, for God took him; and of Elijah, who ascended by a whirlwind in a chariot of fire to heaven. The prayer so beautifully expressed by a Christian poet, seems to have been remarkably granted:

> "O, that without a lingering groan,
> I may the welcome word receive,
> My body with my charge lay down,
> And cease at once to work and live."

In the exercises of this solemn occasion, the duty of directing your attention to the word of God for comfort and support, has devolved upon one who, while he feels inadequate to its fulfillment, from the sudden and awful shock he has sustained, as well as from the shortness of the notice, and the uncommon excellence of the character he is called upon to portray, cannot but acknowledge that there is probably no one else, more intimately acquainted with the private and ministerial character of the departed, and certainly none of his brethren, by whom he was more sincerely esteemed and affectionately beloved. "Alas, my brother! very pleasant hast thou been unto me!"

The words which I have selected as the theme of the present discourse, are a part of the Saviour's memorable parable of the talents. This parable is familiar to you all, and it is unnecessary that I should dwell upon it at the present time, any further than to remark upon its connection with the text.

The words of the text contain the approbation of his Lord, as expressed to that servant to whom he had intrusted five talents, and who went and traded with the same, and made them other five talents. "His Lord said unto him, Well done, thou good and faithful servant; thou hast been faithful over a few things, I will make thee ruler over many things: enter thou into the joy of thy Lord." The natural division of the text will lead us to consider:—

I. The Character, and

II. The Reward, of the good and faithful servant.

I. The Character. In one sense, all the children of men may be said to be the servants of God, for they are all subject to the power and pleasure of God, and are bound by the ties of creation and providence to his service; but especially is the term servant applicable to those of his creatures who have been redeemed from the bondage of sin and Satan, to serve the living and true God; and more especially is it applicable to those who have devoted themselves to the service of God in the gospel of his Son, and who have been solemnly set apart to the high and holy duties of the Christian ministry. It is in this restricted sense, that we propose to consider it in the following discourse.

In attempting to describe the character of the good and faithful servant, (or minister of Christ,) I would notice, among others, the following parts of which it is composed: *Piety—good natural talents and theological learning—practical wisdom and prudence — love for souls — devotedness to his work — ardent desires to promote the glory of God.*

1. The character described in the text implies *piety*, or *personal religion*. Without this, no pretension whatever can be made to that character. It is base hypocrisy for any man to profess to be the servant of God, and especially the messenger of Heaven to his fellow-men, who is destitute of piety. This is the first, and most important and essential qualification in a minister of the gospel, without which he will be only a blind leader of the blind. A man must be converted himself, before he can hope to be instrumental in the conversion of his fellow-men. To constitute a good and faithful servant, or minister of Christ, that change must first be effected in the soul, of which our Lord spake to Nicodemus; and the want of

which, if it disqualifies for admission to the kingdom of heaven, surely disqualifies for the ministry of reconciliation. Deep, and humble, and fervent piety, is an indispensable requisite in the character of the good and faithful servant. It is indeed the basis, or foundation, upon which the character is formed.

Next to piety, *good natural talents and theological learning* are important constituent parts in the character of the good and faithful servant. Without these, however deep and fervent may be his piety, the minister of the gospel cannot be a good and faithful servant; for they are absolutely necessary to enable him to discharge the duties of his office. Especially is a thorough acquaintance with divine truth, as contained in the Scriptures of the Old and New Testament, and sufficient talent wisely to explain and faithfully to apply it, absolutely necessary in a minister of the gospel.

Equally indispensable, in the character of the good and faithful servant, is *practical wisdom and prudence.* By which I mean a sound judgment, wisely to discern the path of duty,—clearly to perceive the difficulties by which this path is sometimes surrounded,—and prudently to avoid, or guard against them. This trait of character is of the first importance in the good and faithful servant; and happy is that servant who possesses it.

Devotedness to his work and love to the souls of men is an essential trait in the character of the good and faithful servant or minister of Christ. He enters the service of God in the ministry of his Son, with entire devotedness and consecration to his work. It is his great desire to spend and be spent for Christ. His soul burns with a longing desire for the salvation of his fellow-men. For this, he is instant in season and out of season. He counts not his life dear unto himself, that he may finish his course with joy, and the ministry which he has received of the Lord Jesus to testify the gospel of the grace of God. He avails himself of every opportunity to promote the salvation of his fellow-men, especially of the flock committed to his pastoral oversight. He will bear them continually on his heart to the throne of grace. He will labor for them both in private and in public, both in the family and in the sanctuary. In all their concerns, he will take the liveliest interest. In one word, his whole soul will be in his work.

An ardent desire for the glory of God must complete this brief and imperfect sketch of the character of the good and faithful servant. His love for the souls of men springs from his desire for the glory of God. It is because he ardently desires that God may be glorified, that he labors for the salvation of souls. It is his great concern, that the Saviour, whom he loves, may see of the travail of his soul and be satisfied. He longs to behold sinners converted to God, — multitudes brought to the knowledge of the truth,—and the church increase and flourish.

II. Let us dwell for a moment on the REWARD promised to such a character. "Well done, thou good and faithful servant; thou hast been faithful over a few things, I will make thee ruler over many things: enter thou into the joy of thy Lord." In this world, the servant of Christ has but a comparatively small sphere of labor assigned him; but, if he is faithful over a few things, he shall be made ruler over many things. It is difficult to conceive exactly of the nature of the reward promised in this remarkable passage of Scripture, because we are, as yet, ignorant of the employments of the saints in glory; but we are led, from the words of the text, to indulge the idea that in the future state, the sphere of usefulness will be greatly enlarged. Heaven is not a state of passive enjoyment, as some seem to imagine. A ruler over many things evidently implies, active employment; and it is delightful thus to contemplate the heavenly world, as a place not of perfect quiescence, but of active service in the employment of the same Saviour for whom we delighted to labor on earth. What new scenes of extended usefulness may open upon the glorified spirit on his admission into the heavenly world! Here, he has been faithful over a few things; there, he shall be made ruler over many things. Here, he has conscientiously and faithfully discharged his duty in the sphere allotted him by the providence of God; there, he shall have other duties assigned him, and be engaged in more sublime, more exalted employments.

"Enter thou into the joy of thy Lord." By this phrase we may understand those joys which God has prepared for those that love him; — those joys which were so feelingly described in this place, on the last Sabbath morning, in the presence of him who has since gone to realize them in heaven; — those joys which eye hath not seen, which ear hath not heard, and which it hath not entered into the heart of man to conceive; — *the joy of thy*

Lord — the joy purchased for his people by his sufferings and death; — *the joy of thy Lord* — the joy of beholding him face to face, without a veil between; the joy of dwelling forever in his presence, where is fullness of joy, and at his right hand, where are pleasures forevermore.

Such is the reward of the good and faithful servant; and such, we doubt not, is the reward that awaited our beloved brother, who has been removed from us in a manner so remarkably solemn and affecting.

It may be expected, on this occasion, that I should give some biographical account of that excellent man, whose lifeless and venerated form lies before us, on its way to the narrow house appointed for all the living.

I have had but little opportunity of knowing his early history previous to my personal acquaintance with him, soon after his settlement in this place. He was born in Plaistow, New Hampshire, July 23, 1780. He was the son of Major Ezekiel Gile, an officer in the revolutionary army, and one of the most respectable inhabitants of the town in which he lived. Both of his parents, it is believed, were pious, and died in the triumphs of that religion which they professed. He entered Dartmouth College in the year 1800; and I have repeatedly learned, from those associated with him in college, as well as from others, that he sustained an unblemished character and a respectable standing as a scholar during his connection with that institution. Upon leaving college, he commenced the study of divinity at Andover, under the superintending care of the Rev. Jonathan French, a divine highly esteemed in those days for his piety and orthodoxy, and for his success in training up young men for the sacred ministry. He was distinguished for his popularity as a preacher. Few young men, at that period, were so acceptable. His commanding presence, his style, which was always rich in imagination, his powerful and mellifluous voice, and especially his holy unction and extraordinary copiousness in addressing the throne of grace, rendered him always a most acceptable and popular preacher. His services were eagerly sought and highly appreciated, and several promising fields of usefulness presented themselves for his acceptance. The ancient and highly respectable church of Christ in this place, being destitute of a pastor, in consequence of the resignation of the Rev. Dr. Joseph McKeen, Mr. Gile was invited to take the pastoral charge of it with great unanimity, and was ordained February 18, 1807.

His religious opinions were at that time well known, and continued the same, without variation, to the close of life. They were what have generally been termed Orthodox, and were conformable to the doctrines contained in the Assembly's Catechism. He was attached to the good old system of faith held by the fathers of New England. He was remote, on the one hand, from a lax system of theology, and on the other, from the extreme of orthodoxy. He was a Calvinist of the old school.* In the belief of these doctrines he lived, and in the the belief of these doctrines he died. Although decided and firm in his religious sentiments, he was liberal and catholic towards those who differed from him. Nothing was further from his bosom, than a spirit of censoriousness and denunciation. He was

* The phrases, *Old and New School*, are variously understood in different parts of the country. It is perhaps proper to state that the distinction, as applied to Dr. Gile, is not intended to be made in reference to the theological controversy that at present agitates some sections of the American church, but rather to the distinction that prevailed in New England when Dr. Gile commenced his ministry. He had no relish for metaphysical speculations and *new* systems of divinity, but harmonized in sentiment with such *old* divines as Flavel, and Henry, and Watts, and Doddridge.

willing that others should enjoy the same right of private judgment he claimed for himself. He was no polemic nor controversialist. His preaching was not so doctrinal as that of many. It was rather experimental and practical.

He was distinguished above most men for his extraordinary gift in prayer. There was a sublimity, a richness, a freedom, a copiousness in his devotional exercises, that partook of the atmosphere of heaven, and raised the souls of those, whose devotions he guided, above this lower world, to sweet and holy communion with God.

But it was not only in the house of God that our departed friend exhibited the character of a good and faithful servant. He was the affectionate and devoted pastor out of the pulpit. In the chamber of sickness, and around the bed of death, and in the house of mourning, he was ever kind, soothing and devoted in his personal attentions. He took the liveliest interest in the temporal as well as in the spiritual concerns of his flock. He was the prudent counsellor, the timely peacemaker, the confiding friend. But I need not dwell on the excellences of his ministerial and pastoral character. You knew him—you appreciated him—you loved him. It was at *home*, in his family and in the midst of his flock, that his character shone in brightest colors. He loved his home. He sought not great things for himself. He shunned, rather than courted, public life. He was not, however, always suffered to remain in the retirement he preferred, but was occasionally drawn out to appear before the public on interesting and important occasions;* and within a short period of his death, he received a flattering notice of respect from a university in a neighboring State.† In the education of indigent pious youth for the gospel ministry, he took the liveliest interest; and was, at the time of his death, the Secretary of the Norfolk Auxiliary Education Society, and a member of the Board of Directors of the Parent Society. Still it was in the retirement of a country parish, and in the midst of his family and friends, that the peculiar traits of his excellent character were developed.

These distinguishing traits were *benevolence*—

---

*He was called to preach before The Foreign Mission Society of Boston and Vicinity,—The Norfolk Education Society,—The Society for Promoting Christian Knowledge,—The Society for Propagating the Gospel,—The Convention of Congregational Ministers,—and on several ordination and other public occasions. His Sermon before the Foreign Mission Society was printed.

† He received the degree of Doctor of Divinity from the University of Vermont, but a few months previous to his decease.

prudence—consistency—patience under trials—and great Christian meekness and forgiveness of injuries.

He was distinguished for *benevolence.* No man felt more tenderly for the poor, and contributed more, according to his ability, for their relief. His heart overflowed with the milk of human kindness. He felt for all in distress, and eloquently pleaded for their relief. He was given to hospitality. His house was ever open to his friends, and often to strangers. He had a large heart; and had his means been as large as his heart, no case of distress would ever have been unrelieved.

He was *eminently* distinguished for *prudence.* In my intimacy with him, for nearly thirty years, I never heard an unguarded expression fall from his lips. His prudence might sometimes, perhaps, have seemed to degenerate into excessive caution; but so rarely is this excellent trait of character to be found, that we may be disposed to pardon the fault into which it sometimes has a tendency to lead. I have known few men more distinguished for practical wisdom, than our departed friend.

He was no less distinguished for *uniformity and consistency of character.* He was endued by nature with a disposition peculiarly amiable; and the grace of God, superadded to it, rendered his temper and conduct singularly uniform and delightfully consistent. The same benignant smile played on his countenance, in the family and in the social circle, and was sometimes seen lingering there, chastened by religious awe, in the house of God. Consistency, that rare virtue, was one of his most striking characteristics.

But the trait in the character of this excellent man, which shone with peculiar lustre, was his *patience under trials, and great Christian meekness and forgiveness of injuries.* He had his trials, and they were painful and severe. His trials, too, were from those sources in which he was most keenly sensitive—his *family* and his *flock.*

The loss of several children in infancy, he bore with Christian submission. For several years, his family consisted, besides the partner of his life, of an only son and an only daughter. The former, after a lingering illness, at a most interesting age, he meekly resigned to the grave, without a murmur; and the latter, a confirmed invalid, has long been the object of his tender care, and still lives to mourn the loss of one of the best, one of the most attentive fathers. I have been with our friend in all these domestic trials, and I can bear testimony to the Christian meekness and exemplary patience with which he has borne them.

His parochial trials, too, he endured with the same meek, and quiet, and gentle spirit. I would fain pass over this portion of his life without particular notice, as it is attended with so many painful associations; but justice to his memory, and the development of his character in an interesting point of light, compels me to notice it.

In all the circumstances attending his exclusion from the other house of worship, and the erection of this building, he exhibited a truly Christian spirit. His trials, in the course of that unhappy controversy, were painful and severe; but he did not murmur nor complain. He continued to manifest towards those who differed from him in religious opinions, and who wished to exclude him from the sanctuary, the same kind, and yielding, and forgiving spirit. He always considered himself as the pastor of the church, and minister of the society, over which he was originally ordained; and was always ready, when called upon, to perform the duties pertaining to that office.* He never indulged in any remarks unfavorable to those who differed from

* He was dismissed from the first parish in Milton, by an *Ex-parte Council*, January 6, 1834. The authority of this Council he never acknowledged, and did not regard himself bound by its result. He

him; but whenever he spoke of them, it was with kindness and affection. The controversy had in a great measure subsided. This convenient and pleasant house had been erected by the *church*, who *unanimously* adhered to their beloved pastor, through all his trials; and there was every prospect, that the evening of his days would be tranquil and happy. But God's ways are not as our ways, nor his thoughts as our thoughts. He had other employment for his good and faithful servant. Having been faithful over a few things, he is made ruler over many things, and entered the joy of his Lord.

And why should we mourn? Why should we wish him to return to share with us in the trials of this sublunary scene? We know that it is all selfishness; but, alas! we are selfish creatures. It is hard to part with those we love. We cling even to their dust.

The bereaved and afflicted widow,* and the only

---

never considered that he unreasonably refused a *Mutual Council*, which unreasonable refusal is necessary, according to the decisions of the Massachusetts Judiciary, to make the result of an Ex-parte Council valid.

* Soon after his settlement in Milton, Mr. Gile was married to Miss Mary Henley White, daughter of the late Isaac White, Esq., of Salem, Mass.

daughter, in her weak and suffering state, claim and receive a large share in our tender sympathy. Their breach is great like the sea, and He alone who hath made the breach can heal it. To God, then—their covenant-keeping God—we commend them. May he sustain them in this hour of their deep affliction! They may also rest assured of the most tender sympathy from the ministerial brethren, with whom the departed was so long and so intimately connected.* They will never forget his widow and his fatherless child; but, in every way in their power, it will be their privilege and duty to console them.

Nor will this beloved church and society cease to remember them, and to provide for their comfort and support. They are a legacy left them by one whom they can never cease to venerate and love. Oh! could he have been permitted to *speak*, when his weeping family and weeping people gathered around his dying couch, he might have addressed them in language somewhat similar to that of his dying Saviour, who, as he agonized on the cross,

* Dr. Gile was a member of the Norfolk Association of Ministers, and was the first (who sustained a pastoral charge) that has died, since the formation of the Association in 1811. His surviving brethren, nineteen in number, have agreed to supply the pulpit, in rotation, for the benefit of his widow.

when he saw his mother and the disciple standing by whom he loved, said unto his mother, 'Woman, behold thy son. Then saith he to the disciple, Behold thy mother. And from that hour that disciple took her unto his own home.' Here are many disciples, whom their pastor loved; and we are persuaded that his bereaved widow and fatherless child will never want a home in their affections and in their sympathies.

My beloved friends of this church and congregation,—to you this solemn dispensation of divine Providence is deeply affecting. Many of you were admitted to the fellowship of the church during the ministry of your late pastor, and you will ever regard him as your spiritual father. You have passed with him through peculiar trials, and they have served to strengthen and cement the ties which have bound you together. You have rejoiced in his growing reputation and increasing usefulness. Perhaps there never was a time when your beloved minister was more engaged in his work, than at the time of his removal from you. His fervent prayers, during the last week, for a revival of religion,—if not by his instrumentality, in any way which might seem good to the great Head of the church, —those who heard them will never forget. Ah!

little did you think that they were to be answered in such a way; that the Lord had no more work for him to do on earth, and that it was reserved for another to *reap* where he has *sown*. O God! how unsearchable are thy judgments, and thy ways past finding out. Even so, Father, for so it seemeth good in thy sight!

And now what remains, my friends, but to imitate the *example* of your beloved pastor,—to be followers of him, as he was of *Christ*. A safer, a more perfect *human* example, it will be difficult to find. All will be constrained to admit the truth of this remark, who had the opportunity of knowing him. Personal enemies, I may say, he had none; and the enemies of the truth which he preached, cannot but acknowledge that he was *sincere*, *conscientious*, and *consistent*. His memory will be held in grateful remembrance, by the inhabitants of this ancient and respectable town, of every political and religious sect. There will be but one opinion respecting his character, and that will be, that he was a good man, and full of the Holy Ghost and of faith; that he was an Israelite indeed, in whom there was no guile.

Being dead, he will long continue to speak by his luminous example. Fathers will delight to hold him up to their children, as a pattern for their imitation. His opinions will be regarded as almost approaching to sacred authority, in times of future excitement; and even those who disregarded and forsook his ministrations when living, shall be convinced that a prophet has been among them. "His work on earth is now done, and his body will go to its repose in the dust; but the memorial of his name and of his good deeds, will be still fresh as the morning breeze, and fragrant as the flower of spring." Even in this world his works shall follow him; and even here he shall receive the plaudits of his fellow-men. But what are these to the plaudit of his Judge?—"Well done, thou good and faithful servant; thou hast been faithful over a few things, I will make thee ruler over many things: enter thou into the joy of thy Lord."

"Servant of God, well done!
Rest from thy loved employ;
The battle fought—the victory won,
Enter thy Master's joy.

Tranquil amidst alarms,
It found him on the field,
A veteran, clad with heavenly arms,
And with his red cross shield.

His sword was in his hand,
  Still warm with recent fight;
Ready that moment, at command,
  Through rock and steel to smite.

At noon-day came the cry,
  'To meet thy God, prepare;'
He heard, and caught his Captain's eye,—
  Then strong in faith and prayer,

His spirit, with a bound,
  Left its encumbering clay;
His tent, at sunset, on the ground
  A darkened ruin lay.

The pains of death are past,
  Labor and sorrow cease;
And life's long warfare closed at last,
  His soul is found in peace.

Soldier of Christ, well done;
  Praise be thy new employ;
And while eternal ages run,
  Rest in thy Saviour's joy."

SERMON IV.

THE SIGNS OF THE TIMES.

Delivered before the Pastoral Association of Massachusetts, in Park-street Church, Boston, May 24, 1836.

MATTHEW XVI. 3.

CAN YE NOT DISCERN THE SIGNS OF THE TIMES.

My respected Fathers and beloved Brethren :

IN addressing you on this occasion, I feel deeply impressed with a sense of the solemn responsibility imposed by the duty I am called upon, in the providence of God, to perform. Under *any* circumstances, to the conscientious minister, *preaching* must always be regarded, with unaffected seriousness and trembling solicitude, as the great ordinance of God in the conversion of the world. To give to every one a portion in due season, to warn the sinner to flee from the wrath to come, and to comfort and establish the people of God, though the ordinary duties of the Christian minister, are not on that account the less solemn and important. Who of my brethren present has not felt a pressure of mind in selecting, on the most common occasion, a subject appropriate to the wants of the flock committed to his pastoral care?—and who does not sympathize with the preacher, when called to address a body of men who sustain, themselves, the pastoral office, and at whose feet he would willingly sit, to receive that instruction which he is expected to give?

Pertinency to the occasion has always appeared to me of the first importance in the selection of a subject. Were I to address a congregation of impenitent sinners, I would urge upon them the duty of immediate repentance and faith in our Lord Jesus Christ. Were I addressing the professed disciples of the Saviour, I would inculcat the necessity of personal holiness and growth in grace. But, called upon as I am at this time to preach to *ministers*, to the pastors of the evangelical Congregational churches of this Commonwealth, I know of no subject more appropriate than a consideration of some of the peculiarities of the times in which we live, and of the appropriate duties which these peculiarities impose upon ministers of the gospel.

I am aware that I have selected a subject of no little delicacy, and no inconsiderable difficulty. A subject to which I feel incompetent, in a single discourse, to do that justice which it demands. But its importance has of late pressed so deeply on my own mind, that I have felt constrained to select it for the consideration of my fathers and brethren, with the hope that it may be in some humble degree useful in discovering that path of duty, which it is desirable for myself, as well as my brethren, to pursue, in these trying and eventful times.

The words of the text, and the connection in which they stand in the chapter from which they are taken, are so familiar to my hearers, that it is unnecessary to enlarge upon them. They are adopted rather as a motto, to lead our thoughts to the subject I have announced, than as containing in themselves any distinct topic for discussion or application. Permit me, then, in the following discourse to call your attention,

I. To SOME OF THE PECULIARITIES OF THE TIMES IN WHICH WE LIVE. And,

II. To THE APPROPRIATE DUTIES, WHICH THESE PECULIARITIES IMPOSE UPON THE PASTORS OF THE CHURCHES IN OUR CONNECTION.

In directing your attention to some of the signs of our times, I shall confine my remarks to those points which more immediately concern the church of God, and the ministry of reconciliation.

I leave to others the consideration of the *political* aspect of the times,—a subject, indeed, of no ordinary interest, but more adapted to the genius of the civilian, than to the taste of the minister of Him 'whose kingdom is not of this world.' It was the preaching of those, who stepped out of their sphere by dwelling upon the *political* character of the times, that Robert Leighton rebuked, when he said: "While so many preach upon the times, one poor brother may be allowed to preach upon eternity." It is because of the bearing of some of the signs of our times upon the *spiritual* and *eternal* interests of men; and, more particularly, upon our own *individual* and *professional* duties, that I am anxious to direct your attention to this subject on the present occasion.

In remarking upon the peculiarities of our times, I shall restrict myself to that view of the subject which has a direct and immediate influence upon the appropriate duties of the pastors of our churches.

That a new and different aspect has been given

to the state of opinion and action in this section of the church, within a few years past, will not, I presume, be questioned by any accurate observer of the signs of the times. Within the memory of the preacher, great changes have taken place on these subjects in this Commonwealth, and throughout our land—changes which most intimately affect the state of religion and the duties of its ministers. Our younger brethren would scarcely credit the facts that might be communicated on this subject by those who have been eye-witnesses of these changes. With this consecrated place, where so many pastors of the churches are now assembled to pay their vows unto the Most High, are many of these changes associated. Comparatively few and feeble were the little band who, in those days, gathered around the cause of evangelical truth, and, in their weakness, but relying on Almighty strength, laid the foundation of this spacious edifice. Those were days which tried men's souls. They were days of controversy, but it was a controversy with those who had departed from 'the faith once delivered to the saints.' They were days of comparative weakness; for God had not then extensively poured out the influences of his Holy Spirit, and blessed our churches with powerful revivals of religion. They were times of limited effort; for the claims of the heathen at home and abroad, the wants of the feeble and destitute of Christ's flock, and the various benevolent objects which constitute the glory of our times, were not then heard in the length and breadth of our land, through the medium of a thousand presses, and from the mouths of innumerable living agents. To those of us who remember the days of former years, the change appears great indeed. We have now fallen upon other times,—in many respects, better times, but not without their peculiar dangers and liabilities to abuse.

The times in which we live, my brethren, appear to me to be distinguished for *excitement.* The spiritual appetite seems to have changed, and, not content with the plain and wholesome food which satisfied our fathers, appears to crave viands more highly seasoned, and more richly varied.

There seems to be an analogy between the improvements of the age in the mechanical arts and in our moral and religious movements. At the present period, distance seems nearly annihilated; and by the wonderful power of art, we pass, almost with the rapidity of the wind, from city to city, through our widely-extended land, and may soon expect to cross oceans and traverse continents with as much ease as our ancestors crossed the rivers and hills of their native State. It is true, now and then, a boiler bursts, and a number of precious lives are lost by the explosion; or in some of our western waters, while the majestic steamer is passing on its high pressure, with almost incredible swiftness, its progress is instantly arrested by some concealed and fatal obstruction, and the souls who had committed themselves to its guidance, are precipitated in a moment into eternity. The accurate observer of our times needs not, I think, to be reminded of the analogy.

Improvements the most valuable, it will be readily admitted, have been introduced into our methods of conducting our moral and religious enterprises. The wonderful power of the press, has been made to bear upon these enterprises with signal success. Knowledge has been extended with astonishing rapidity. The means of religious instruction have been greatly blessed by the Spirit of God; and in many parts of our land, the most powerful revivals of religion have been extensively enjoyed.

But is it not a fact, my brethren, that some unhappy mixture of human depravity and selfish and unsanctified excitement has been blended with that which is spiritual and holy? Under the idea, which at first may have been entertained with sincerity, of being co-workers with the eternal God in the conversion of the world, has not an impulse been sometimes given to our religious movements by the hand of man, other than the Spirit of God would approve? In carrying forward the great operations of the church, has not a system of *high pressure* sometimes been introduced, which has endangered the safety of the church, and by its re-action or explosion, retarded the conversion of the world? 'I speak unto wise men—judge ye what I say.'

Another peculiarity of our times to which I would call your attention, is the success attending the exertions in the cause of *moral* reform.

Every friend of religion and humanity must rejoice in the signal triumph of these efforts. The Temperance reformation, in particular, has constituted an era which will be regarded by after ages as one of the brightest in the history of our country.

Other objects of moral reform have successfully engaged the attention of the friends of philanthropy and the rights of man; but, if the preacher does not much mistake, there is a tendency to extremes in carrying into operation principles of acknowledged and unquestionable importance. There is a certain recklessness of consequences, characteristic of the times in which we live, which seems to set at defiance the cool judgment of thinking men. On this subject it is unnecessary to enlarge. It is introduced merely with a design to prepare the way for the consideration of the appropriate duties which such a state of things imposes upon the pastors of the churches. Connected with this is a *spirit of censoriousness and denunciation*, which unhappily exists to an alarming degree among us. Not content with pursuing a course of measures to a point which others may consider as extreme, there is a disposition, too apparent, to censure and condemn those who, although they may agree in great and fundamental principles, are not prepared to go to the same extent in their application.

Another of the peculiarities of our times, to which I must solicit your attention, is a *spirit of innovation and change, and love of novelty.* I would not plead for a blind attachment to creeds and confessions of faith. They are not, I readily admit, like the Word of God, the infallible standard of our faith; and perhaps we have reason to rejoice that the churches of our connection are not, like those of some of our sister denominations, bound together by any *one* confession of faith, however excellent it may be. But still there is no little danger of abusing our liberty by a departure from the form of sound words, so long and so generally received by the churches of the Reformation, and by an introduction of new doctrines, or rather *new views of old doctrines*, which the Fathers of the Reformation, and the Pilgrim Fathers of New England would have regarded, to say the least, with much jealousy and distrust.

Is there not danger, my respected brethren, of removing the landmarks which our fathers have set—of weakening, in our zeal for philosophical speculations, our confidence in those old-fashioned, but not on that account less important, doctrines of our intimate connection with the progenitors of our race and the Redeemer of our souls,—"the Lord our righteousness?" If not openly denied, are not these precious articles of "the faith once delivered to the saints," explained away by learned criticism, or made too little prominent in our discourses from the pulpit? Are we not in danger, in our zeal for pressing the necessity of the sinner's *immediate* repentance and submission to God, of undervaluing the righteousness of Him who is exalted a Prince and a Saviour, to *give* repentance to Israel and remission of sins? and of losing sight of our dependence on the influence of that Divine Agent, who alone can 'take away the heart of stone and give the heart of flesh,' and make us 'willing in the day of his power?' Are we not in danger of forgetting that 'by the deeds of the law, no flesh shall be justified,' and thus undervaluing that important doctrine of justification by faith alone, which Luther pronounced to be the "*articulus stantis vel cadentis ecclesiæ.*"

Another peculiarity of our times is a spirit of *restlessness and uneasiness*, which seems to pervade alike the ministry and the churches.

Time was, when there was a permanency attached to the pastoral office, which was alike honorable to the ministry and to the people. Many were the pastors, who, like Goldsmith's Vicar, "ne'er had changed, nor wished to change their place." In the quiet and unobtrusive discharge of their ministerial duties, they passed the years of their pilgrimage in one spot, *blessing and blessed*. But, in this active and stirring age, such a happy spectacle is rarely to be found.

Whether the frequent removal of pastors is desirable or not, we will not stop to inquire; or whether the fault, if it is one, is in the ministry, or in the churches, or in both, we will not pretend to decide; but we cannot but deprecate the practice, which is becoming very common in our churches, of settling their pastors for a limited period. It is, in our judgment, calculated to lessen the influence of the pastor, and to restrict his usefulness. When a minister is introduced into the pastoral office, it is desirable that the people should feel that the relation is permanent; and that nothing but circumstances of paramount and imperious necessity should be permitted to sever the tie that has been thus solemnly formed. Nor is this spirit of restlessness and uneasiness confined to the frequent removals and dismissions of ministers. It may be noticed, also, in the members of the churches. There is, in too many instances, a love of novelty and excitement, and a disposition to leave the stated labors of the faithful pastor, for the more stirring and exciting appeals of the itinerant evangelist, or the eloquent declaimer, or the proselyting sectarian.

I hasten to notice, in the last place, as one of the signs of our times, *the spirit of religious controversy and separation* that threatens the peace and unity of some portions of the American church. No accurate and serious observer of the times in which we live can have regarded the present unhappy divisions that exist in a kindred denomination, towards whom we delight to cherish the most respectful and fraternal feelings, without the deepest anxiety and concern. It does not become us, nor would it accord with our feelings, to express any opinion on the merits of that painful controversy, which now agitates that large and respectable body of our fellow Christians; but we may be allowed to learn wisdom from their experience, and to profit by their example. It is a subject of sincere and cordial congratulation, that, notwithstanding the difference of opinion that may perhaps exist on speculative points of theology, there continues among the pastors of the evangelical Congregational churches in this Commonwealth, uninterrupted union and cordiality of feeling. May the Great Head of the church grant that it may be perpetual, and that 'no root of bitterness may be suffered to spring up to trouble us, and thereby many be defiled.' Under the blessing of God, it is evident that much will depend upon the pastors of the churches themselves, whether their present union and prosperity shall continue, or whether they shall be rent with divisions, and become a prey to some of those evils which have passed under review.

My brethren will therefore bear with me a little longer, while I proceed as I proposed, in the SECOND place — To CONSIDER SOME OF THE APPROPRIATE DUTIES, WHICH THE PECULIARITIES OF THE TIMES IMPOSE UPON THE PASTORS OF THE CHURCHES IN OUR CONNECTION.

That the times in which we live are difficult and trying, and call for no ordinary degree of grace and wisdom, will not be doubted. Some of the peculiarities to which we have alluded, may perhaps have a tendency to excite disgust, and produce a spirit of reaction in reflecting and sensitive minds. Against this tendency we cannot too carefully guard. We ought to remember that, while in the present aspect of the times there are some things to be deplored and to be avoided, there are many more things to excite congratulation and encouragement. We live, it is true, in a day of excitement and commotion; but it is a day, also, of hope for the rapid advancement of the Redeemer's kingdom. We must be content to bear with some things that are trying to our sensibilities, for the sake of the greater good that may arise out of others. Let us not, then, my brethren, give way to disgust, and, because everything is not conducted according to our taste and sense of propriety, retire from the scene of action, or seek relief in other connections, or in other pursuits;— but let us stand in our lot, and be stimulated by those very things which try our patience, to increasing fidelity and diligence in the Master's service.

The peculiarities of our times call for great *firmness and steadiness of purpose*, in the pastors of the churches. When a youthful pastor, full of ardor and religious projects, applied for advice to a neighboring clergyman, a little more advanced in years and experience than himself, he received this memorable counsel, contained in one word, thrice repeated: — *Steady, steady, steady.* It is apprehended that there never was a time when this advice was more necessary than at the present period. Much depends upon the *pastors of the churches* to regulate the religious movements of the day. They are the divinely-constituted leaders of the flock. No one more sincerely rejoices than the preacher in the active and zealous and untiring efforts made by the members of the churches, in these times, in promoting revivals of religion, and in advancing the benevolent enterprises of the day. They are the Aarons and Hurs, without whose aid the hands of many a faithful pastor would hang down, and his heart be discouraged. The unwearied labors of our *lay brethren* are the bones and the sinews of our ecclesiastical body. Happy is that pastor who is supported by their influence and animated by their zealous co-operation. But it will not be denied, that in the economy of the church much is expected of the pastor in the *personal oversight* of the flock committed to his charge. He may, and he will delight to avail himself of the assistance and efforts of the brethren in the discharge of some of his pastoral duties; but he ought not to forget that he is *himself* the under-shepherd of the flock, and that there are duties peculiarly and appropriately his *own.*

Independence of mind and action is another duty which the present aspect of the times demands of the pastors of the churches. I am far from wishing to inculcate upon my brethren an *opinionative, dogmatic,* or *unyielding* spirit. The faithful pastor will endeavor, like the great Apostle, "to become all things to all men;" to yield his own opinion and to sacrifice his own feelings in everything in which the vital interests of the church are not concerned, for the sake of peace and union. But there is a point, beyond which he cannot and ought not to go. When he is required to sanction principles and measures which his conscience does not approve by his example and influence, he ought to have independence enough to have an opinion of his own, and to express that opinion on all proper occasions.

I am aware that such a course requires no little degree of independence, and may expose the faithful pastor to many difficulties and embarrassments. The temptation to espouse the popular side, although in his judgment it may not be the correct one, is strong and powerful. We all know that it is much easier to swim with the tide than to stem the current. And perhaps the love of popularity, however we may disguise it, is a besetting sin with ministers of the gospel.

A great, and in itself laudable, desire to please, sometimes blinds the devoted pastor, and prevents him from discerning the path of his duty. But while, like the Apostle, he will endeavor "to please all men in all things, not seeking his own profit, but the profit of many, that they may be saved," there will be occasions when, with the same Apostle, he may be constrained to say, "Do

I now persuade men or God, or do I seek to please men? for if I seek to please men, I should not be the servant of Christ."

The times demand *great circumspection* and *prudence and caution, in those who are invested with the sacred office.* "Be ye wise as serpents," said Jesus to his Apostles, when he sent them forth to preach the gospel. If there ever was a time, since the days of the Apostles, when this direction was necessary, it appears to me it is at the present period. The pastoral office, at any time and under any circumstances, demands great prudence and circumspection in those who are intrusted with its holy functions. Next to piety, *prudence*, or *good common sense*, has always appeared to me the most important qualification for the pastoral office. Good talents and sound learning are desirable, but prudence is indispensable. How many, especially in these difficult times when a man is sometimes made an offender by a word, are the occasions for the exercise of prudence! A hasty or unguarded expression, a rash or ill-concerted measure, will sometimes lead to a train of consequences, which will issue in the removal of a pastor, and in still more injurious influences upon the church of God. In these times, ministers cannot be too cautious in committing themselves to principles or measures of questionable expediency. There are some subjects which, if not immediately connected with pastoral duties, it may be safer for the pastors of the churches to regard with the eye of a spectator than with the warmth and zeal of an enlisted advocate.

But, while the times require great caution and prudence, they also call for the exercise of a *conciliating and affectionate spirit.* The same authority that bade the Apostles be 'as wise as serpents,' enjoined them to be 'as harmless as doves.' A meek and quiet, a gentle and affectionate spirit, is exceedingly desirable in these times of excitement, of controversy, and severe recrimination. Such a spirit, the pastors of the churches ought to cultivate, as the best antidote against the censorious and denunciatiory spirit of the times.

Another of the appropriate duties of the pastors of the churches, imposed by the peculiarities of the times, is *the faithful and discriminate preaching of the doctrines of the gospel.* I know of no better way to counteract the dangerous errors that have been broached among us, than by the faithful exhibition of divine truth. If we have reason to apprehend that there has been a tendency to neglect certain great peculiarities of the Christian faith, let us learn from our mistakes to dwell more upon them in future, to exhibit more clearly to our people *the ruined condition of Adam's race*, and the only way in which sinners can be saved *through the righteousness of Jesus Christ*. While we would call no man master, let us be careful how we depart from that system of faith which was the glory of New England in her brightest day. Let us beware of that spirit of speculation and novelty which, under the garb of critical research, may have a tendency to sap the foundations of our faith in some of the most precious doctrines of the gospel. Above all, let us adhere with uncompromising fidelity to the oracles of truth, unshackled by the commentaries of uninspired and fallible men.

The times require of the pastors of the churches, *particular attention to pastoral duties*. Among the multiplied and diversified objects of religious and benevolent enterprise which characterize the present day, there is no inconsiderable danger of neglecting the ordinary, but highly important duties of the pastoral care. Our religious and benevolent societies have claimed too much of the time and labors of stated pastors. The practice that has so generally prevailed, of calling upon the pastors of the churches to manage the complicated affairs of these institutions, has had a tendency to injure or destroy the influence of some valuable ministers of the gospel in their pastoral relation. While sustaining this relation, the ministers of Christ must devote themselves exclusively to their appropriate work. They must be 'instant in season and out of season,' in the discharge of their pastoral duties. Not only 'in the temple, but in every house, they must not cease to teach and preach Jesus Christ.' In visiting the sick and the dying, in comforting the afflicted and the sorrowful, in directing the inquiring sinner to the way of salvation, in establishing the doubting and desponding, in supporting the aged, and especially in efforts to promote the religious instruction of the young, the faithful pastor will find enough to employ his head and his hands, and have but little time left for the transaction of other business, though it may relate to the concerns of the church at large. Let able and devoted men be selected and consecrated for the special service of directing and managing the great enterprises of the day; but let the pastors of the churches confine themselves to their appropriate sphere, and feed the sheep and the lambs of their flocks.

The peculiarities of the times require of the pastors of the churches, *increasing zeal, activity, and consecration to their great and appropriate work.* The times, we have seen, are distinguished for excitement and for zealous efforts in the great enterprises, religious, moral and benevolent, of the present day. Ministers should not be *behind* the times; but, while they exercise a sound discretion, and maintain a Christian spirit, they should be the most forward in promoting the great objects of benevolence, which are the glory of our age. The Missionary enterprise, foreign and domestic, the Education, Tract and Sabbath School operations, and the circulation of the Scriptures at home and abroad, will receive the entire approbation and cordial support of the pastors of the churches; and I am persuaded, that just in proportion as these benevolent enterprises engage the attention and the affections of ministers and churches, will be the diminution of some of those evils of our times, at which we have glanced in the course of our remarks.

The signs of our times call for *deep, humble and devoted piety* in the pastors of the churches. This is, indeed, a requisition indispensable under any circumstances that may be conceived; but the present times seem to me peculiarly to require a deep-toned piety in the ministers of the gospel. Nothing short of this can secure the pastors of our churches from becoming a prey to some of those evils which have been remarked as characteristic of our times. To the naturally proud heart of the unsanctified pastor, nothing can be more hazardous than the spirit of excitement and proneness to extremes which we have already noticed. It finds a ready admission into his unholy bosom, and kindles there a flame of animal enthusiasm which urges him on to unrestrained irregularities and extravagance. Nor is the love of novelty and innovation, which we have remarked as characteristic of our times, less dangerous to the unsanctified pastor. It finds in him that proneness to 'lean to his own understanding,' and that desire to be 'wise above what is written,' so congenial to the natural heart. When I have trembled at the tendency to philosophical speculation on religious doctrines, I have felt relieved by the conviction that in some minds, that appear to have discovered this inclination, there is at the same time a deep and pervading spirit of piety which may restrain this tendency within its proper bounds. And my conviction is daily strengthened that nothing short of the most humble and fervent piety, will secure us from that spirit of innovation and change which threatens the peace of our churches.

The peculiarities of our times call for *a spirit of humble, fervent and persevering prayer*, from the pastors of the churches. My dear brethren, we frequently address our people upon the necessity of prayer, and urge them to the more frequent and importunate discharge of this duty. Do we not need to be stirred up to it ourselves? What reason does the brief view we have taken of some of the peculiarities of our times present for the deepest humiliation before God, and for earnest supplications to Heaven for the forgiveness of what is past, and for wisdom from above to direct us for the time to come in the way of our duty? If there were more prayer among ministers, there would be less unprofitable speculation, controversy and division.

The peculiarities of our times require of the pastors of our churches *mutual forbearance, confirmed union, and brotherly love*. The associated pastors, whom I have the privilege and satisfaction this day to address, have long known, by their happy experience, how good and how pleasant it is to dwell together in unity. Though differing, in some respects, in their views of theology, they have never been disposed to magnify these differences into points of separation. They have been too much engaged in contending against error in a more dangerous form, and in promoting the religious and benevolent enterprises of the day, to find time to dispute about subjects of minor importance. It is hoped that this spirit of forbearance will be preserved; and that, as a body, we may long continue to know the things that make for our peace. *Union* is *strength* and *power.* Incalculable is the good which may be effected by the combined energies of the pastors of the evangelical Congregational churches of New England. In one broad and united phalanx, let them march forward in the sacramental host.

It is animating to be assured, that in the great articles of their faith and of their discipline, as well as in their religious and benevolent enterprises, they enjoy the sympathies, co-operation and prayers of their brethren in the father-land. The preacher cannot forbear to express the peculiar satisfaction which he feels in having so favorable an opportunity of presenting to his assembled brethren the assurances of the continued interest felt in their welfare and prosperity, by their trans-atlantic friends, with whom it was his privilege so recently to have enjoyed delightful personal communion. Surely, the fraternal and Christian intercourse, which is now so happily established between the friends of truth in the old and new world, is one of the most favorable *signs of the times*, which demands our most grateful and fervent acknowledgments to our common Lord. By the union of British and American Christians, what may not be accomplished in the great work of the world's conversion! Through their united instrumentality, may we not hope that the events predicted in prophecy will soon be accomplished, when "the kingdoms of this world shall become the kingdoms of our Lord and his Christ, and he shall reign forever and ever."

But I must not longer detain you. In all probability, my brethren, we shall not all of us meet again on an occasion like the present. Before this anniversary revolves, some of us will have gone to give an account of our stewardship. Happy shall we be if, warned by the signs of the times, we shall have escaped the dangers they betoken, and availed ourselves of the encouragements they afford. Let us not be too anxious to pry into future events. *The Church is safe*, and He who hath founded it on a rock, will order all the events of his providence for its furtherance and support. "Blessed is he that waiteth. Let us go our way till the end be, for we shall rest and stand in our lot at the end of the days."

SERMON V.

THE IMPORTANCE OF MODERATION IN CIVIL RULERS.

Delivered before His Excellency Edward Everett, Governor, the Honorable Council, and the Legislature of Massachusetts, at the Annual Election, January 1, 1840.

PHILIPPIANS IV. 5.

LET YOUR MODERARION BE KNOWN UNTO ALL MEN: THE LORD IS AT HAND.

The service of this occasion is consecrated, and rendered venerable, by age. Two centuries have marked, with very few exceptions, its annual return. It originated in the piety of our ancestors, and, from a commendable regard to ancient usage, it has been continued by their posterity, from generation to generation. It is grateful to the friends of religion and morality to behold their fellow-citizens, high in office and authority, repairing to the house of God to seek wisdom and guidance from on high, before they commence the important and responsible duties of legislation. This public acknowledgment of their dependence upon the uncreated Source of wisdom and intelligence, is well becoming the descendants of an ancestry, distinguished for their piety and their regard to religious institutions. The Fathers of this ancient Commonwealth were men of faith and prayer. They laid broad the foundations of government in religious principle and sacred conformity to God's everlasting law. No people, since the dispersion of ancient Israel, were so remarkable for their religious character, as the first settlers of Massachusetts. Exiled from the land of their fathers on account of their attachment to the purity of God's word and worship, they incorporated their religious principles with their civil institutions. They undertook no important measure, they engaged in no hazardous enterprise, they proceeded to no responsible duty, without invoking the presence and blessing of that all-wise Being, by whom kings reign, and princes decree justice. To his word, also, as the great statute-book of first and last resort, they unhesitatingly applied for counsel and direction in all cases of doubt and difficulty and important bearing. This deep veneration for the institutions of religion, which so clearly stamped the character of our Pilgrim Fathers, has been cherished by their posterity, and I trust that our civil rulers will never cease to pay their annual homage, in the house of prayer, to the Creator and Governor of the Universe.

The present occasion naturally invites our attention to such subjects, as may be pertinent to the situation and correspondent duties of an assembled legislature. In reflecting upon the peculiarities of the times in which we live, upon the tendency to excitement, and extremes, and party spirit, by which they are confessedly distinguished, I have thought that I might perform a service, not altogether unprofitable nor unacceptable, by inculcating upon the respected auditory I am called to address, a spirit of moderation in the discharge of those important duties, upon which they are about to enter in their legislative and executive capacity.

The words of the text form part of the Apostle Paul's exhortation to the church at Philippi; and may, with propriety, be applied to any class or description of men. And it surely will not be foreign from the design of the author of the text, who hath directed that supplications, prayers, intercession, and giving of thanks be made for all that are in authority, that those sustaining important offices of power and trust, should be exhorted to *let their moderation be known unto all men,* and should be reminded of their responsibility, by the solemn and impressive consideration, that *the Lord is at hand.*

Confining myself, therefore, to the occasion upon which we have assembled, I shall consider the text, in its application to the character and duties of political men.

The subject which I have selected, is one of no ordinary delicacy. But I trust it may not be thought presumptuous, nor stepping aside from his vocation, for a minister of the gospel to attempt to moderate the zeal of party, to allay the excitement of the public mind with regard to agitating topics, and to endeavor to recommend that firm, yet moderate course of legislation which, while it shrinks not from duty in the enactment and support of wholesome laws, avoids all unnecessary occasions of irritation towards those who may honestly differ in opinion, on questions of expediency.

It is desirable to have correct and definite views of the nature of that moderation, which they who are clothed with authority, and appointed to rule over their fellow-men, should possess, and to distinguish between a time-serving and timid policy, and a calm, dispassionate, fearless and independent course of conduct. The moderation, which I would commend, is widely different from that extreme caution, which avoids committal for fear of giving offence. Such a course, although too often adopted by candidates for popular favor, will be regarded with decided disapprobation by every honest and ingenuous mind. The most perfect decision of opinion, and the utmost frankness in the avowal of it, are not at all inconsistent with the spirit and temper enjoined in the text.

Equally remote from this spirit, is that cold indifference and political apathy, which can regard without emotion the changes and revolutions that are continually taking place in the public mind. It cannot be expected that such subjects will be viewed with indifference, especially by those who, from their official stations, are more particularly affected by them. But the judicious statesman and wise legislator, while he carefully watches these fluctuations of opinion, and gives to each agitating topic, as it presents itself, that attention which it deserves, will guard against that exclusive and immoderate devotedness to any one measure, or course of measures, that shall blind his vision to everything that is excellent in those who may differ from him in opinion, or that shall tinge, with his own peculiar views, the medium through which he regards every other subject. There is such a thing as political, as well as religious fanaticism, which consists in a zeal that is not tempered with knowledge—in a reckless pursuit of an object, without regard to consequences—in an attachment to party, rather than to principle. I need not observe, that party spirit, even in a good cause, is dangerous. When influenced by this spirit, men are apt to pursue the most desirable and praiseworthy ends by questionable, if not unjustifiable means. That the end justifies the means, is a maxim as unsound in politics as it is in morals. Especially when morals and politics are so blended together, as they are in some of the questions which are now agitated, we cannot be too careful in watching the motives which actuate our conduct, in guarding the frame of our spirits from an undue and dangerous excitement, and in exercising that moderation which is never more necessary, than when strong and confirmed prejudices are to be overcome, great and serious difficulties to be removed, and important and benevolent objects to be gained.

Of the necessity of complying with the exhortation in the text, we shall be convinced, if we consider that we live in an age of excitement. In no part of the world are the effects of excitement more sensibly experienced than in our own country. There is in the American character, if I mistake not, a tendency to extremes. This tendency may be traced to the nature of our republican institutions, which, by removing many of those restraints by which older and less liberal governments are encumbered, present greater facilities for carrying into operation enterprises of a political or moral nature. While we sacredly cherish these institutions, we may not be insensible to the dangers arising from their abuse. It cannot be denied, that under a republican government, there is reason to apprehend that liberty may degenerate into licentiousness, and that objects, in themselves praiseworthy and benevolent, may fail of their design, by being pressed to a hazardous extreme. This tendency of our institutions evidently demands a different policy from that which might be necessary under an older and more restricted form of government, where long abuses and confirmed evils imperiously call for reformation. What would be justifiable and commendable under one form of government, might be injurious and ruinous under another. A government and a country like ours, which are as yet but in their infancy, call not for the same radical reform, which the corruptions of centuries may have rendered necessary in the governments of the old world. We need, rather, a *conservative influence*, to restrain that proneness to innovation and change, which is the tendency of our times and our country, and to keep pure and inviolate those great principles of civil liberty and constitutional law, which form the basis of our political institutions.

The evils, to which we are exposed under our peculiar form of government, arise not from arbitrary oppression, nor aristocratic influence. The rich have not the power, if they had the inclination, to oppress the poor. No one class of society enjoys exclusive privileges. The road to emolument and fame is alike open to all. We have no established hierarchy to monopolize the offices of the church, and to trample upon the rights of conscience, no other nobility than the nobility of industry and perseverance, no royal blood but such as flows in every honest heart. The elective franchise is enjoyed by us in its widest extent. We have no rotten boroughs to be reformed, no disqualifying acts of parliament to be repealed, no restrictions on the freedom of the press to be removed, no difficulties in the way of universal education to be overcome. Our free and happy constitution guarantees to us as much liberty as is good for man. It secures to us the inestimable blessings of civil and religious freedom. It protects us in the enjoyment of our personal rights, and permits every man to sit under his own vine and fig tree, having none to molest or make him afraid. And what more can we desire? Under what government, even the most Utopian that ever entered into the conception of political enthusiasm, are to be found greater securities for personal freedom, for individual happiness, for social comfort and for public improvement, than are the portion of our favored Republic?

We will not boast of our happy lot, for boasting is as unbecoming in a people as in individuals; but we will be grateful to that Being who hath appointed the bounds of our habitation, by whose merciful providence the lines have fallen unto us in such pleasant places, and who hath given us such a goodly heritage. It is obvious, then, that the same reasons do not exist, among us, for that spirit of *radicalism*, which has sometimes manifested itself in other countries and under other forms of government. Happy shall we be, as a people, if we realize the value of our privileges, and remain contented with that degree of liberty which is secured to us by the constitution. Our danger lies in imitating that restless and unquiet spirit which, however necessary and justifiable under other circumstances, is out of place under a government of equal rights and privileges.

While we suitably appreciate the value of our free institutions, let us not forget that they are liable to abuse. Let us carefully guard against a spirit of reckless agitation, which, for its own private and party purposes, would destroy the foundations of order and government, and mutilate, if not demolish, that beautiful fabric which was framed by the wisdom and piety of our venerated ancestors, cemented by the blood of the heroes of the Revolution, and brought to its present state of unrivaled excellence by the sage counsels and deliberate judgment of some of the wisest and most enlightened statesmen the world ever knew. Nothing is more necessary and desirable, in sustaining our invaluable institutions, than the exercise of the same spirit of moderation which actuated the fathers of the Republic. They were men eminently distinguished for this trait of character. While they betrayed no want of courage and daring, in those times which tried men's souls; while, in the battle-field, they fought with noble intrepidity for the liberties and independence of their country, they manifested, in all their discussions and deliberations in the council-chamber, and in the national congress, a remarkable degree of wisdom and moderation. May the spirit which animated their fathers, descend upon their children!

But I would not be understood to imply, that our institutions are so perfect as to need no improvement, or that there are no alarming evils in our community that need correction. The institutions of our beloved Commonwealth are, I believe, as perfect as those of any government on the earth; and no people have richer sources of happiness, and more abundant causes of gratitude, than they who live under the shadow of its constitution and laws. I do not say that the constitution should never be amended, nor that all the laws in the statute-book are wise and salutary, and should never be repealed. Doubtless, such amendments and such modifications and repeals may sometimes be necessary. But a wise and judicious legislature will not attempt any essential or important changes, without great caution and deliberation.

That there are alarming evils in our Commonwealth, that need to be corrected, no one can doubt; and that the Legislature, as guardians of the public weal, may do much to restrain the practice of iniquity, and to support and encourage the friends of good morals, few, if any, will be disposed to question. The cause of *Temperance* is one in which all the friends of humanity are deeply concerned. It is a cause vitally connected with the best interests of the Commonwealth. It is a cause which, in its advocacy, embraces men of all parties and denominations in politics and religion. The interest which this cause has awakened in every part of the Commonwealth, has been unusually great and powerful. All classes of the community have, in a greater or less degree, partaken of the excitement. It will not be supposed that the ministers of religion, whose duty it is to reason of righteousness, *temperance*, and a judgment to come, can have been unconcerned spectators of the progress of a reformation, so intimately connected with religion and morality. As a body, they have ever cheerfully given their warm and unwavering support to this philanthropic cause. From their official stations they have seen, perhaps, more than most of their fellow-citizens, the misery produced in families and neighborhoods, by the practice that was once so prevalent, of retailing, in small quantities, the means of intoxication. The tears of the broken-hearted wife, and the wretchedness of neglected children, have affected their hearts, and have led them to rejoice in any measures that may be constitutionally and lawfully employed to lessen the sources of temptation, and to check a traffic so disastrous in its consequences to the peace and happiness of society. Whether the course pursued by recent acts of legislation, is the best calculated to effect the desired object, is a question that remains to be decided. On this subject, it cannot be denied, there is a great difference of opinion in the community—a difference of opinion that is certainly entitled to respectful consideration from a wise and prudent legislature. Whatever measures may be adopted by those to whom the direction of our civil affairs is now to be intrusted, it is earnestly to be desired that they may be distinguished by a spirit of candor, forbearance and moderation.

I have said that we live in an age of excitement. Exciting topics, rapidly and extensively, pervade the community. But in no condition of society is their influence more obvious, than in our halls of legislation. The representatives of a people among whom an excitement prevails, will not only partake of it in common with their constituents, but, as in many cases they are selected for the express purpose of advocating or opposing a particular course of measures, they may be supposed to be more affected by it than their fellow-citizens in general. And when we consider their relative situation, and juxtaposition for a considerable period of time, it will not be surprising that the tendency to excitement should be greatly increased. Difference of sentiment will often lead to a warmth of debate, which may sometimes become personal, and be attended with the most unhappy consequences. Instances of this kind have not been wanting in the highest councils of our land, where this excitement has terminated in the effusion of human blood. I blush for my country, when I reflect on the instances of *dueling* that have occurred among our public men. They who are selected by their fellow-citizens for the express purpose of making their laws, and preserving their liberties, should be the last to trample on the one, and abuse the other. And yet it cannot be denied, mortifying as is the acknowledgment, that there is no class of men more frequently guilty of this sin, than they who fill the highest places of power and trust, who legislate for others, and whose example ought to give additional weight to their legislation.

But it is not merely the fact, that we live in an age of excitement, which calls for the discharge of the duty under consideration. Its importance will appear, if we consider the influence of legislation upon the great public interests of the Commonwealth. To the legislature the people look for the encouragement of those various objects and enterprises which so intimately affect their prosperity. Plans of improvement by which the resources and wealth of the State may be rendered available and increased, the promotion of education and the diffusion of useful knowledge among all classes of the community, the facilities needed by the merchant, the farmer, the manufacturer, the mechanic and the various professions, for effecting their respective purposes and designs, will all receive, in their turn, the attention of an enlightened legislature. With so many interests depending upon them, it will be readily acknowledged, that in no class of men is a spirit of wise and careful deliberation more necessary, than in a legislative assembly. Such an assembly, especially a numerous one, is in peculiar danger of precipitancy in legislation. It has not the advantage of the cool, dispassionate reflection of retirement, but is frequently called upon to act, with very little notice of the subject to be acted upon, and sometimes under the strong current of an excited public opinion.

The public good, rather than public opinion, ought to influence the views and control the actions of political men. Whatever may be for the good of the people, whose interests they represent, they should steadily pursue; although the course they adopt may not, at the time, be universally popular. It is not unfrequently the case, that the doings of a legislature may not at once commend themselves to popular regard, while at the same time they may be beneficial in their tendency, and in their issue have a salutary and most important influence in promoting the best interests of the people. The wise and cautious will look beyond the mere immediate effects of legislation to its more permanent results, and remember that in the discharge of duty they ought to be governed more by a respect to the best interests of the community and the welfare and happiness of posterity, than by a regard to their own immediate influence and standing with the public. Popularity is often temporary and evanescent; but what is done with a sincere regard to the good of the people, will survive the contending opinions of the public, and remain a standing monument of wise and judicious legislation.

But it is not merely in the suppression of the evils that exist in the community, that the legislature will exercise a wholesome authority. They will not be slow to encourage all good designs and laudable efforts for the promotion of the public good, for the increase of useful knowledge, for the advancement of the cause of benevolence and philanthropy, and for the general happiness and welfare of their constituents. Under their fostering care, the ancient University in this vicinity, which has long been the child of their adoption, will continue to flourish; and the other literary institutions of the State, although of more recent origin, I trust will not be forgotten.

The ministers of religion have been accustomed, on these occasions, to commend to the legislature the interests of education. They ask no endowments for themselves or their churches; but the cause of good learning is one which was dear to their fathers, and should be dear to their children. For this our honored ancestors made suitable provision in the early settlement of the country. And as the country has increased, and the wants of the community multiplied, may it not be expected that adequate provision will be made by a wise and considerate legislature for the encouragement of seminaries of learning, within the bounds of the Commonwealth, without distinction of sect or party?

It has been a source of great satisfaction to the friends of humanity, to witness the attention of the legislature directed to the state of our prisons and penitentiaries, and the condition of their misguided and unhappy inmates. The improvements that have been made in prison discipline, within a few years, are alike honorable to private benevolence and legislative encouragement. While rulers are a terror to evil doers, they may, with consistency, so far soften the rigor of the law as to provide for the outward condition, and especially the moral, intellectual and religious improvement of the unhappy convict. The means that have been used for these purposes have been so signally successful, as to create a new era in the annals of punitive legislation.

In the discharge of the important and responsible duties of their official station, my respected hearers, I doubt not, will feel the force of the injunction of the Apostle, and *let their moderation be known unto all men.* They will realize the importance of permanent, rather than temporary and occasional legislation; and will be satisfied that a few laws, well digested, and adopted with suitable deliberation, are better than a larger number of statutes, crudely framed and hastily passed, under the exciting influence of party spirit.

While I would urge the importance of wise and deliberate legislation, in view of its influence upon the great public interests of the State, as well as in reference to the times of excitement in which we live, may I be permitted to say one word in favor of the cultivation of a spirit of forbearance and moderation between the two great political parties, into which the inhabitants of the Commonwealth are, apparently, so equally divided? I rejoice to believe that political party now, is widely different from what it was in former days,—that it has lost much of the asperity for which it was once distinguished. Whether it is that other subjects have absorbed a portion of that rancor and bitterness which were once so manifest in political discussions, or whether the points of difference between the two great parties, that have so long divided our country, are deemed of less magnitude than formerly, or whether each party has learned to feel more kindly, and to act with more urbanity, than in seasons of great political excitement, I will not pretend to say. But times appear to be changed in this respect, for the better; and instead of the high-seasoned political sermons which I well remember to have heard on these occasions, in former years, a minister of Jesus may now find his more appropriate, and certainly more welcome sphere, in inculcating upon his hearers the messages of that gospel which breathes peace on earth and good will to men. As an ambassador, then, of the Prince of peace, I may be allowed to express the hope, that whatever differences of opinion may exist in the Commonwealth, a spirit of mutual condescension and forbearance will infuse itself into all the deliberations, and pervade all the doings of its legislature.

The solemn and powerful motive to the right discharge of the duties recommended in this discourse, remains to be considered and enforced. *The Lord is at hand.*

An impression seems to have existed, in the minds of some of the primitive Christians, that the end of the world was approaching, and that the Lord Jesus Christ would soon appear, the second time, in the clouds of heaven, with power and great glory, when all who were in their graves, together with those who were alive at his coming, should stand before his judgment-seat, and receive, according to the deeds done in the body, whether they be good, or whether they be evil. Hence the sacred writers, in enforcing the various duties they urge upon mankind, frequently draw their motives from an approaching judgment, and the unseen realities of the eternal world. These motives, however, ought not to lose any of their force; because the Apostles might not have been made acquainted, by inspiration, with the precise time of Christ's coming to judgment. It is of little consequence, so far as the practical effect is concerned, whether, in the order of time, the day of judgment is near or remote. If we believe the Scriptures, we know that God has appointed a day, in the which he will judge the world by Jesus Christ, and however scoffers may say, Where is the promise of his coming? we are assured that the day of the Lord will come as a thief in the night, in the which the heavens shall pass away with a great noise, and the elements shall melt with fervent heat; the earth also, and the works that are therein, shall be burnt up. Well, then, does the Apostle argue from this assured fact—*seeing that all these things must be dissolved, what manner of persons ought we to be, in all holy conversation and godliness?*

Without perplexing our minds with calculations as to the exact period of the duration of the world, and the time of the general judgment, which are among the secret things which belong to God, and which he has not thought proper to reveal to us, it is sufficient to know, that nothing is more uncertain than human life, and that to every accountable being, when he quits this mortal scene, *the Lord is at hand* to bestow upon him the riches of his grace, or to visit him with the reward of his iniquity.

I am aware that it is difficult to impress upon the minds of those, who are associated together like the members of a legislature, a sense of personal accountability. They are exceedingly apt to forget, in the heat of debate, in the bustle of business, in the strife of party, that there is a God who rules in the earth, and who will require of his intelligent creatures an account of their conduct, not only in the more retired and private walks of life, but in those active scenes, and more public duties, to which they are called by the suffrages of their fellow-men. In a numerous legislative assembly there is a sort of feeling of divided responsibleness, which tends to weaken, if not destroy, the paramount sense of personal accountability. But it is the duty of the faithful preacher of God's word, to hold up to civil rulers the solemn and awful realities of a future judgment and retribution; to remind them, that although they are like gods, they shall die as men; that, in the grave, there is no distinction of rank or office, and that, at the judgment-seat, the doings of every individual of our race, in all the various relations which he sustained, private, social and public, shall be impartially reviewed; that, to whom much is given, of them much will be required; and that those who, on earth, were elevated above their fellow-men, who were appointed to frame and execute their laws, will have to give an account to the great Lawgiver of the universe, of the manner in which they have discharged their official duties, and fulfilled their public trusts.

May you, my respected hearers, enter upon the business of legislation under an impressive sense of your responsibleness; and so discharge the important duties of your high and conspicuous station, as best to secure the testimony of your own consciences, the welfare and happiness of your constituents, and the favor and approbation of God.

While this discourse has been particularly addressed to the Members of the Legislature, it is capable of a more general application. I need not say, that if a spirit of forbearance and moderation is necessary in civil rulers, it is no less so in the people whom they represent. A legislature will, of course, take its complexion from the character of the people. How important then is it, that the people should be influenced by correct principles; that they should cultivate a spirit of moderation, and not allow the excitement of party to warp their judgment, nor the desire to further any cause, however good in itself, to betray them into measures of questionable propriety, or of hazardous adoption. In conducting the different objects of reformation which have, of late, taken such deep hold of the public mind, it is of the greatest importance to avoid those extremes which, by disgusting the sober and more rational part of the community, tend to retard rather than to advance the cause of true philanthropy. The desired object is far more likely to be gained by a calm, discreet and moderate course of conduct, than by hasty, violent and fitful measures which, in many cases, by their reaction, only injure the cause they were designed to promote. It is to be hoped that the spirit of moderation, recommended in this discourse, will commend itself to the people of this Commonwealth; and that they will sustain thei r legislature in whatever measures they in their wisdom may adopt for the public good. It is impossible that the wisest legislature, with the best intentions, should give universal satisfaction. If the laws which they make are unjust, or unequal, or inexpedient, they can be repealed by the same authority by which they were enacted. But while they continue in force, it is the duty of all good citizens to give them their support, to frown on every attempt at their evasion, and to sustain those who execute them, in the discharge of their duty. This is incumbent on them, not only as men, acting under a sense of moral obligation, but as republicans, who profess to acknowledge and to submit to the will of the majority. The supremacy of the law is one of the first and most important principles in every well-regulated commonwealth; and under a democratic form of government, where the power of legislation resides in the people, there can be no excuse for the violation of the laws.

But the people of Massachusetts, while they are reminded of their privileges and their duty, will, I trust, suitably appreciate the one, and faithfully discharge the other. May the rich blessings they enjoy, long be continued to them by a beneficent Providence. Long may they behold, as they do this day, their Nobles from themselves, and their Governor from the midst of them. May our beloved Commonwealth ever be the object of the divine favor! And may the last words of an Italian patriot be the prayer of each of her sons—*Esto perpetua!*

It has been customary, on these occasions, to offer respectful salutations to the different branches of the Legislature. And it is a usage, of which the preacher is most happy to avail himself, as it affords him the opportunity of enforcing the sentiments he has endeavored to inculcate, by referring to the distinguished example of moderation exhibited by the honored individual who has, for several successive years, sustained the high and responsible office of Chief Magistrate of the Commonwealth.

The meekness of wisdom, with which your Excellency has borne the honors of your exalted station, the calm and dispassionate, and at the same time firm and dignified course of conduct, amidst agitating topics and conflicting interests, which has distinguished your administration, the desire you have uniformly manifested for the intellectual and moral improvement of the community, and the patriotic zeal you have evinced for the prosperity of our common country, will never be forgotten by a grateful people. The wise and good, of all parties, will duly appreciate your untiring labors for the public weal; and their best wishes and fervent prayers for your personal happiness will attend you, whether you continue to discharge the duties of your official station, or retire to the more quiet occupations of private life.

His Honor the Lieutenant Governor, the Executive Council, with the Senate and House of Representatives, will accept the congratulations of the occasion, and the assurance that, whatever changes may take place in the political character of the Commonwealth, as long as they are actuated by a spirit of forbearance and moderation, they will continue to receive and enjoy the respect and confidence of all the friends of order and good government.

Changes are continually taking place, not only in the political, but in the natural world. Times and seasons change. The earth has performed another of its annual revolutions; and, with the return of this anniversary, we are brought to the commencement of a *new year*. What changes may take place during the year upon which we have this day entered, are known only to Him, who seeth the end from the beginning. It is the dictate of wisdom to prepare for the changes of life. We shall never all of us meet again, in like circumstances, in this house of prayer. In all probability, before this year shall close, some of us will have closed our career on earth, and have entered upon the untried scenes of eternity.

In view of the solemnities of a dying hour, and an approaching judgment, let us be careful to maintain a conscience void of offence towards God and towards man; and, whether in a private or public station, let us endeavor faithfully to discharge our duty, and to *let our moderation be known unto all men. The Lord is at hand.*

SERMON VI.

THE DOCTRINE OF JESUS.

MATTHEW VII. 28, 29.

AND IT CAME TO PASS, WHEN JESUS HAD ENDED THESE SAYINGS, THE PEOPLE WERE ASTONISHED AT HIS DOCTRINE; FOR HE TAUGHT THEM AS ONE HAVING AUTHORITY, AND NOT AS THE SCRIBES.

OUR blessed Lord, having concluded his admirable Sermon on the Mount, the faithful historian informs us of the effect it produced upon the minds of his hearers. "The people were astonished at his doctrine; for he taught them as one having authority, and not as the Scribes."

These remarks of the Evangelist, upon the reception of the Saviour's preaching by the people, afford us an interesting subject of discourse, and will lead us, in the first place, to consider the *doctrine of Jesus;* Secondly, *his manner of teaching;* and, Thirdly, *its effect upon his hearers.*

Let us, in the first place, consider the doctrine of Jesus. It may be said of the Saviour, with the utmost propriety, that his doctrine dropped as the rain, and his speech distilled as the dew.

The doctrine of Jesus is the doctrine of God, for in his human and mediatorial character he says, "My doctrine is not mine, but his that sent me." It claims the Supreme Intelligence for its author.

It must therefore, in the first place, be *true*. There is a great, an almost infinite variety of doctrines in the world, some of which are utterly false, and many of which contain much error mixed with truth. But the doctrine of Jesus alone can lay claim to infallibility, for it cometh immediately from God, the God of truth and the Source of all wisdom, with whom is no variableness neither shadow of turning.

The word *doctrine*, as used in the text and in parallel passages of Scripture, is to be understood in the most extensive sense, as signifying the whole system of doctrines as taught by Christ, particularly those contained in the Sermon on the Mount, to which the word more immediately refers.

The Christian system then is true, when compared with all the other systems of religion that have ever been taught among men. The systems of doctrine inculcated by heathen philosophers, though containing some truth, abound with many false sentiments and erroneous principles. For all the truth they contain, they are indebted to the dim light of nature, and to traditionary hints from Revelation; for probably there never was a time when the world was wholly destitute of a revelation. But the faint light of truth which they emit bears but a small proportion to the dark cloud of error with which they are overshadowed.

The doctrine of the false prophet, which has a large number of disciples, has borrowed some truth from the Christian system, but contains much error and delusion peculiar to itself. The sanguinary means by which it is propagated, are very foreign from the spirit of the religion of the Prince of peace, the weapons of which are not carnal but spiritual; and the sensual gratifications, both here and hereafter, to which its followers are invited, are widely different from the pure pleasures and holy joys which are the present, and will be the everlasting portion of the disciples of the Lamb. This leads us to observe,

Secondly, The doctrine of Jesus is *pure*. Purity is one of its distinguishing characteristics. It enjoins purity of heart as essential to salvation. One of those beatitudes, with which the Saviour's Sermon on the Mount is introduced, is, "Blessed are the pure in heart, for they shall see God." And without holiness, we are assured, no man shall see the Lord. All other systems of doctrine, while they attempt to restrain the outward conduct, make little pretensions to the regulation of the heart and the government of the temper; but it is this which constitutes the essence of the doctrine of Jesus.

He taught that all outward acts of religion were but a solemn mockery, if the heart was not right with God. He insisted on purity of heart as an indispensable requisite to admission into his kingdom. He taught the absolute necessity of being born again, of being renewed in the spirit of our minds, as a qualification for heaven. From his doctrine we learn, that nothing will be admitted into the heavenly state that worketh abomination, or that maketh a lie, but they only who are washed in the laver of regeneration, and are sanctified by the Holy Ghost. It is one important part of his doctrine, that God is a spirit; and they that worship him, must worship him in spirit and in truth. The religion of the cross is spiritual; and it is spirituality that distinguishes the disciple of Christ from the man of the world.

Again. The doctrine of Jesus is distinguished for its *sublimity*. It opens to our view the mysteries of another world. It gives us some idea of the glories of the heavenly state, and it draws aside the curtain that conceals the horrors of the world of darkness and despair. It treats of the creation of all things out of nothing. How sublime is the description given in the Book of God, of the work of Creation! 'Let there be light,' said God, 'and there was light.' This single passage is often quoted as one of the most remarkable instances of the truly sublime, contained either in ancient or modern, sacred or profane writing.

But especially is the subject to which the doctrine of Jesus particularly relates, remarkable for its sublimity. The redemption of a lost world by the Son of God, is the most exalted subject that ever engaged the attention of human beings. It is probably the most grand and wonderful event that ever took place in the Universe of God. When we consider that He who thought it no robbery to be equal with God, took upon himself the form of a servant, and humbled himself to live in this world of sin and sorrow, and to suffer on the cross as a sacrifice for the sins of men, we are overwhelmed with astonishment. We look in vain for such an instance of exalted virtue in the history of the world. It stands unrivaled and unparalleled, and is, and will for ever be the subject of wonder and admiration, not only of men but of angels.

The doctrine of Jesus is alarming to sinners. To the impenitent, while they remain such, it offers no comfort; but denounces against them, as the just punishment of their impenitence and unbelief, indignation and wrath, tribulation and anguish. It is a doctrine full of alarm to the careless and secure. To the hypocrite it speaks in language of terror. To the unrenewed and unholy it declares the wrath of God, and the curse of his violated law. It gives no encouragement but to those who sincerely repent, and unfeignedly believe the gospel.

But while the doctrine of Jesus is alarming to sinners, it is full of comfort and satisfaction to the children of God. Its language is, 'There is no condemnation to them that are in Christ Jesus, who walk not after the flesh but after the Spirit.'

To the saints, all its precious promises are addressed. They are the heirs of God, and joint heirs with Jesus Christ. 'All things are theirs, whether Paul, or Apollos, or Cephas, or things present, or things to come.'

In affliction, the doctrine of Jesus is full of comfort and support. It makes our bed in our sickness, and smooths for us the pillow of death. It addresses language like this to all the children of God, when they are bowed down with sorrow, and sinking under the weight of trials: 'Fear not, for I am with thee; be not dismayed, for I am thy God.' 'When thou passest through the waters I will be with thee, and through the rivers they shall not overflow thee; when thou walkest through the fire thou shalt not be burnt, neither shall the flame kindle upon thee. Yea, when thou walkest through the valley of the shadow of death thou shalt fear no evil'—for God will be with you, his rod and staff they will comfort you.

Such, my hearers, is the doctrine of Jesus—a doctrine remarkable for its truth, its purity, its sublimity, its terror to the wicked, and its comfort to the righteous.

Let us now, as we proposed, Secondly, notice Christ's manner of teaching. 'He taught them,' says the Evangelist, 'as one having authority, and not as the Scribes.' 'Never man spake like this man,' was the testimony borne by his enemies to his manner of teaching. There was something very peculiar in the Saviour's manner, which attracted general attention; something which plainly indicated that the speaker was more than human, that he was divine. His manner was dignified, solemn, bold and impressive; affectionate, tender, mild, conciliating and persuasive. It was so dignified and impressive, that frequently, when his enemies endeavored to entangle him in his talk, they were awed into silence, and constrained to admire the gracious words that fell from his lips. How admirable was his reply to the captious Scribes, who interrogated him respecting the tribute: "Render therefore unto Cæsar the things which are Cæsar's, and unto God the things that are God's." Sometimes he would reply to their impertinent questions, by proposing other questions, which they could not, or dared not answer. The boldness of his manner is strikingly illustrated in his address to his hypocritical countrymen: "Ye serpents, ye generation of vipers, how can ye escape the damnation of hell?"

But though the Saviour was remarkable for his dignified, solemn and impressive mode of address, he was still more distinguished for the affectionate, mild and persuasive manner in which he taught his disciples the great truths of religion. How tender is his expostulation with his own countrymen: 'O Jerusalem, Jerusalem! thou that killest the prophets, and stonest them which are sent unto thee! how often would I have gathered you together as a hen gathereth her chickens under her wings, but ye would not.' With what affection and tenderness did he collect little children around him, and assure them that 'of such is the kingdom of heaven.' With the proud and self-righteous, he was bold and even severe; but with the broken-hearted, and those of a contrite spirit, he was all tenderness and compassion. He never broke the bruised reed, nor quenched the smoking flax. His language to such is, "Come unto me, all ye that labor and are heavy laden, and I will give you rest." "If any man thirst, let him come unto me and drink. Whosoever cometh unto me, I will in no wise cast out." Jesus excelled all the other teachers, in the mild, gracious and winning manner of his address. He lays before sinners the awful consequences of impenitence, to awaken in them a sense of their danger; but he dwells with peculiar pleasure on the mercy and grace which he came to display. He preached the terrors of the future world to the obstinate and impenitent sinner; but to the penitent and humble he ministered the sweet encouragements of infinite grace. In the synagogue of Capernaum he read and applied to himself the words of the Prophet: 'The Spirit of the Lord God is upon me, because he hath anointed me to preach the gospel to the poor; he hath sent me to heal the broken-hearted, to preach deliverance to the captives, and the opening of the prison to them that are bound.' And the people who heard him, bare him witness, and wondered at the gracious words which proceeded out of his mouth.

With great propriety then might the Evangelist say, that he taught them as one having authority, and not as the Scribes. His manner of teaching must have been a striking contrast to that of those teachers whom the Jews were accustomed to hear expound the Law and the Prophets. Inflated with a sense of their own importance, the Scribes taught the people in a haughty, supercilious manner, totally unlike that of the great Teacher of righteousness. The Scribes were ostentatious in their appearance. They loved greetings in the market-places, and to be called of men Rabbi! Rabbi! whereas nothing could be more unassuming than the appearance of the meek and lowly Jesus. The Scribes insisted on mere external forms and ceremonies as essential to salvation; while the doctrine of Jesus and his Apostles was, "that circumcision availeth nothing, nor uncircumcision, but a new creature." The Scribes garnished the outside of the sepulchre, while nothing remained within but dead men's bones; but Christ insisted upon inward purity and sanctification. The Scribes were narrow and bigoted in their views, confining salvation to their own people, and excluding all the Gentiles from the kingdom of heaven; whereas Jesus hath shown the rich extent of God's mercy to a guilty race, and the way in which pardon and salvation can be obtained by all who receive the gospel, of whatever nation, of whatever age, and of whatever character. To us may be applied the words which Christ spake to his disciples: "Blessed are your eyes, for they see; and your ears, for they hear. For verily I say unto you, that many prophets and righteous men have desired to see those things which ye see, and have not seen them; and to hear those things which ye hear, and have not heard them."

We now proceed, as we proposed in the last place, to consider the effect of the doctrine of Jesus upon his hearers.

They were astonished at his doctrine. Something more than mere astonishment, as the word is generally understood, is implied in the use of it in this connection; for we read in the commencement of the next chapter, that "when he came down from the mountain great multitudes followed him." The doctrine of Jesus must have made a powerful impression on their minds; and there is reason to hope, that to many it was blessed by the Spirit of God as the instrument of their conversion. Some were astonished to hear such gracious words fall from his lips. Some believed the things that were spoken, and some believed not. The same effect is produced by the doctrine of Jesus in every age and part of the world. It could not be heard with indifference and unconcern, for "it is quick and powerful, sharper than any two-edged sword, and is a discerner of the thoughts and intents of the heart."

It carries conviction home to the conscience, and searches into the secret recesses of the soul. When this doctrine is preached in its purity, its searching effects are always more or less visible. It draws out the different feelings of the human heart. In some, it excites the warmest opposition; in others, the greatest delight and satisfaction. To oppose this doctrine, the strongest and most violent passions are often brought into exercise; while to favor and enjoy it, the most indefatigable pains are often taken, and the greatest sacrifices are often made. Indeed, it is a doctrine to which no one, who hears it preached with faithfulness, can listen with indifference. It either delights or offends. To some, it is like water to a thirsty soul; while to others, nothing can be more unpalatable. To some, it is a savor of life unto life; while to others, it is a savor of death unto death. To some, the preaching of the cross is foolishness; while to others, it is the wisdom of God and the power of God unto salvation.

In closing this discourse, suffer me, my friends, to inquire, What effect has the doctrine of Jesus had upon you? Have you received with meekness the engrafted Word which is able to save your souls? or have you been ready to exclaim, in view of the purity and spirituality of the Saviour's doctrine, 'These are hard sayings; who can hear them?' Let me assure you they are true sayings, and that except your righteousness exceed the righteousnes of the Scribes and Pharisees, you shall in no case enter the kingdom of heaven. The morality of the Saviour's doctrine, particularly his Sermon on the Mount, is a different thing from what many have supposed. It is something more than a collection of moral sayings to regulate the outward conduct. It contains, in the strongest expressions, the doctrine of regeneration, and the absolute necessity of self-denial. It inculcates secret duties as essential to true religion. It expressly asserts, that strait is the gate, and narrow is the way that leadeth unto life, and few there be that find it. It cautions us against worldly-mindedness, and urges us to lay up our treasures in heaven, where neither moth nor rust doth corrupt, and where thieves do not break through and steal.

Let me entreat you, then, to ponder these sayings of Jesus in your minds. They contain rules for practical piety in almost every situation in life. If we reduce these rules to daily practice, do to others as we would that others should do to us, and let our light shine before men, we shall more adorn the doctrine of God our Saviour, and induce others to glorify our Father in heaven.

> 'Thus would our lips and lives express
> The holy gospel we profess;
> Thus would our works and virtues shine,
> To prove the doctrine all divine.'

www.ingramcontent.com/pod-product-compliance
Lightning Source LLC
LaVergne TN
LVHW020109110826
845151LV00001B/105

* 9 7 8 1 4 2 5 5 4 4 1 4 0 *